Word and Music Studies

Essays on Word/Music Adaptation and on Surveying the Field

WORD AND MUSIC STUDIES
9

Series Editors

Walter Bernhart
Michael Halliwell
Lawrence Kramer
Suzanne M. Lodato
Werner Wolf

The book series WORD AND MUSIC STUDIES (WMS) is the central organ of the International Association for Word and Music Studies (WMA), an association founded in 1997 to promote transdisciplinary scholarly inquiry devoted to the relations between literature/verbal texts/language and music. WMA aims to provide an international forum for musicologists and literary scholars with an interest in interart/intermedial studies and in crossing cultural as well as disciplinary boundaries.

WORD AND MUSIC STUDIES will publish, generally on an annual basis, theme-oriented volumes, documenting and critically assessing the scope, theory, methodology, and the disciplinary and institutional dimensions and prospects of the field on an international scale: conference proceedings, collections of scholarly essays, and, occasionally, monographs on pertinent individual topics as well as research reports and bibliographical and lexicographical work.

Word and Music Studies

Essays on Word/Music Adaptation and on Surveying the Field

Edited by
David Francis Urrows

Rodopi

Amsterdam - New York, NY 2008

Cover design: Pier Post

The paper on which this book is printed meets the requirements of "ISO 9706: 1994, Information and documentation - Paper for documents - Requirements for permanence".

ISBN-13: 978-90-420-2430-4
©Editions Rodopi B.V., Amsterdam - New York, NY 2008
Printed in The Netherlands

Contents

Preface vii

Introduction ix

Word/Music Adaptation

Simon Williams
Berlioz's *Roméo et Juliette* Symphony and the European
Reception of Shakespeare 1

Walter Bernhart
From Novel to Song via Myth: *Wuthering Heights* as a Case of
Popular Intermedial Adaptation 13

Michael Halliwell
From Novel into Film into Opera: Multiple Transformations of
Emily Brontë's *Wuthering Heights* 29

Ulla-Britta Lagerroth
Adaptations of *Othello*: Shakespeare – Verdi – Zeffirelli 59

Bernhard Kuhn
The Spoken Opera-Film *Fedora* (1942): Intermedial
Transposition and Implicit Operatic References in Film 75

Frédérique Arroyas
Literary Mediations of Baroque Music:
Biber, Bach, and Nancy Huston 93

Peter Dayan
Interart Contraband: What Passed between García, Liszt
and Sand in "Le Contrebandier" 115

David Francis Urrows
Conscientious Translation: Liszt, Robert Franz,
and the Phenomenology of Lied Transcription 135

William P. Dougherty
Longing for Longing: Song as Transmutation 161

Suzanne M. Lodato
Strauss, *Idomeneo* and Postmodernism 177

Surveying the Field

Werner Wolf
Description: A Common Potential of Words and Music? 197

Lawrence Kramer
Whose Classical Music? Reflections on Film Adaptation 227

Notes on Contributors 243

Preface

Anyone with the slightest acquaintance with publishing and academic writing will know that it is something of a truism to say, 'Everybody needs an editor – including the editor'. This was without doubt true for the present volume. I would like to thank in particular Prof. Walter Bernhart, the founder and president of the Word and Music Association, for all his help, advice, and patience in assembling and editing the manuscript of this book. With authors spread across the globe, this was truly a global undertaking made possible by both technology (the internet) and that old-fashioned engine of progress, human effort. For his role in this project I offer Prof. Bernhart unstinting thanks. Likewise, Katharina Bantleon found time in her busy academic life at the University of Graz to bring precision and accuracy to the articles printed here, and has been both encouraging and endlessly helpful. I would also like to thank my assistant at Hong Kong Baptist University, Joyce Lo Yuet Wing, for her efforts in getting the papers into a format in which I could work. And of course, I thank the authors themselves for contributing their highly original – and in some cases quite personal – research, thoughts, conclusions, and challenges to this volume. *Vivat academia, vivant professores ... semper sint in flore!*

D. F. U.
Hong Kong, March 2008

Introduction

The Fifth International Conference of the International Association for Word and Music Studies, held on the balmy campus of the University of California at Santa Barbara, was the source of the papers in the present volume. As in the case of previous WMA conferences, a particular theme was chosen for the August 2005 meeting: "Word/Music Adaptation". This was meant to be understood in a broad sense, including – to follow the conference call for papers – "the many processes by which one work frames itself as a version of another: an extended paraphrase, re-enactment, parallel, recounting, transposition, condensation, expansion, travesty, meta-commentary". As an alternative to specific papers on word/music adaptation, the scholarly community was also invited to speak on general theoretical and methodological aspects of word and music studies, in a section called "Surveying the Field".

So central to the business (for lack of a more elegant term) of word and music studies is the sub-field of adaptation studies, that most of the papers heard presented research, findings, questionings, speculation, and opinions on this theme. Ten of the twelve papers selected for this volume are all adaptation studies of one kind or another. The exceptions to this are, in the "Surveying the Field" section, first, Werner Wolf's scrupulously argued, theoretically oriented media-comparative essay on description; and second, Lawrence Kramer's persuasive article on the use and reception of classical music in films. The editorial aim in the "Word/Music Adaptation" section is in a very general way to proceed from the word side of the word/music slash to the musical side. Thus the adaptation articles move from those which have a stronger emphasis on literature, literary originals, linguistics, and semiotics, towards those with a more music-theoretic or musicologically-based methodology and focus. In between, two papers deal with the unusual adaptation (in these cases perhaps more specifically, absorption) of music into literary narrative (Arroyas and Dayan), and several with the intersections of literature, music, and film (Kuhn and Lagerroth). Opera – needless to say – is also a prominent topic (Williams, Halliwell, Lagerroth, Kuhn, Lodato). If there are exceptions to this long-range arc, then these reflect an editorial desire to link papers with similar topics or figures. Readers will make many more connections for themselves.

In the conference several similar issues were brought forward, quite independently, by many of the participants: and at least one of these topics of spontaneous similarity is worth commenting upon. The point to which I refer is, that in a number of the now-published articles, what might to some extent be called a 'fidelity discourse' occupies a position of concern and criticism. Adaptations of any kind – a novel into a play, a play into an opera, and opera into a film, a film into a comic book, or a novelization, or a pop song – have been often viewed with grave critical distrust, particularly during the twentieth century. Walter Bernhart rightly avers that in the post-World War II era (and long after) they were usually 'cultural anathemas' (cf. below 26). (For an example see Suzanne Lodato's article on Richard Strauss's reworking of Mozart's *Idomeneo*, an adaptation once condemned as a "gross act of mutilation"; below 178.) A discourse, and attendant system of valuation, has pervaded many discussions of almost any kind of adaptation, which can be summarized as follows: the possible merit of an adaptation is gauged in direct, if arbitrary, relationship to its perceived 'fidelity' to its model, or original. The 'virtue' of fidelity has in turn tended to lend a moral dimension to discussion here: this is a faithful adaptation of that play; that is (merely) a bastardization of this novel. And so forth. Adaptation has also been interpreted – usually quite negatively – as an act of disruption, necessitating a power struggle for dominance by one medium over another. (The philosopher Susanne Langer, commenting on this "primary apparition" of a given work of art, supported as much as she subverted the 'fidelity discourse' in her famously caustic remark that "[t]here are no happy marriages in art – only successful rape"; 86.)

That the whole argument entailed by the notions of 'virtue' and 'fidelity' appears now to be called into question, is reflected in many of the papers published here. For example, Ulla-Britta Lagerroth maintains that in film studies, at least, "the fidelity discourse seems to have been abandoned" (below 59), and she speaks for many authors when she says this anyway. Michael Halliwell, quoting Linda Hutcheon, takes the view that "[t]emporal precedence does not mean anything more than temporal priority" (below 55), and thus challenges the idea that adaptations (and the adaptors themselves) are under some sort of *a priori* obligation to their sources. In my own contribution, I have discussed the sea-change which has affected perceptions and appreciation of the music of Franz Liszt, and the revaluing of the once-reviled genre of piano transcriptions and arrangements, in the past several decades. And Walter Bernhart has noted both that he agrees with James Naremore in his assertion that "adaptation study is moving from the margins to the centre of contemporary intermedia studies" (below 26), and also calls for what might be called the free love approach with his rallying-cry, 'Fertility, not Fidelity!'.

Prof. Bernhart's tongue is probably protruding into his cheek in the making of such a statement (almost rising to the status, nevertheless, of a conference slogan). And yet there is everything scholarly about his challenging discussion of literary adaptation in the popular music sphere, and his exposition of aspects of structural criticism to help analyze Kate Bush's song, "Wuthering Heights". But behind this and other papers lies a palpable frustration with the devaluing of adaptation, arrangement, transcription, palimpsest, fantasy – a devaluation which was typical of the twentieth century's obsession with textual purity, with historical accuracy, with, in short, that difficult-to-define quality, **authenticity**. Today, at the end of the first decade of the twenty-first century, it is something more of a challenge to speak of 'authenticity' without a lot of qualification and explanation than it was over a decade ago, when Richard Taruskin challenged us to see 'authenticity' as a quintessentially modern obsession. In some ways it has become more difficult to speak with assurance about an authorial 'text' (and this notion has provided seemingly endless fodder for debate in literature, the arts, and semiotics in the past three decades). This does not mean, of course, that fidelity is, *ipso facto*, **not** a virtue, or not relevant to the process by which adaptations are qualified. Every paper here wrestles with this issue to some extent, with a range of stimulating and varying conclusions.

A second point which merits a comment is both the wide range of creative personalities illustrating the subjects and objects of word/music adaptation found here; and at the same time the recurrence of a few major figures (in two cases, figures of some controversy): Shakespeare (Williams and Lagerroth), Emily Brontë (Bernhart and Halliwell), Liszt (Dayan and Urrows), and Richard Strauss (Lodato and Wolf). Canonical authors such as Shakespeare and Brontë need, I would venture, neither explanation nor defence. Liszt, on the other hand, was hardly taken seriously as a composer by much of the musical establishment for most of the twentieth century. And as for Richard Strauss, it might bear mentioning that so problematic has

Strauss's legacy been seen since his death in 1949 (for political as well as aesthetic reasons) that the very first article on Strauss ever to be published in the august *Journal of the American Musicological Society* appeared only in 2004. Berlioz – significantly, a great literary and critical, as well as musical, mind – and Verdi appear in connection with operatic and symphonic adaptations of Shakespeare (Williams and Lagerroth). On the literary side, analysis of the writings of George Sand (Dayan) and Nancy Huston (Arroyas) suggest a growing Francophone interest in word and music studies, also adumbrated in Simon Williams's paper on Berlioz and Shakespeare. A host of less-well-known (even obscure) figures from all periods of Western music history further enliven these pages: Heinrich Ignaz Franz Biber (Arroyas), Manuel García (Dayan), Robert Franz (Urrows), Umberto Giordano (Kuhn), Bernard Herrmann and Carlisle Floyd (Halliwell), the pop singer-songwriter Kate Bush (Bernhart), and the many nineteenth-century lied composers recovered in William Dougherty's perceptive and highly-detailed essay on musical settings and interpretations of Goethe's poem, "Nur wer die Sehnsucht kennt". And in the world of the cinema, we cover the opera-film of the 1940s (Kuhn), the film-opera of the 1980s (Lagerroth), as well as a glimpse into contemporary cinema as an entity mediating music and meaning (Kramer).

John Henry Newman once observed that "to live is to change, and to be perfect is to have changed often" (41). To me, this suggests that Cardinal Newman knew a thing or two about adapting and adaptation. For him, it was of the essence of life as we know it. If it is true, then, that adaptation studies are now central to intermedia studies, as well as to field- and genre-specific studies in music, literature, and film, then these essays are not appearing a moment too soon.

David Francis Urrows

Hong Kong, February 2008

References

Langer, Susanne K. (1957). *Problems of Art: Ten Philosophical Lectures*. New York, NY: Scribner's.

Newman, John Henry Cardinal (1878). *An Essay on the Development of Christian Doctrine*. London: Pickering.

Taruskin, Richard (1995). "What – or Where – Is the Original?" In: *Text and Act: Essays on Music and Performance*. Oxford: Oxford University Press. 90-154.

Word/Music Adaptation

Berlioz's *Roméo et Juliette* Symphony and the European Reception of Shakespeare

Simon Williams, Santa Barbara, CA

Berlioz's *Roméo et Juliette* symphony has been infrequently performed complete as it is generically an indeterminate piece, half oratorio, half opera. Although Berlioz may have considered writing *Romeo and Juliet* as an opera, conditions were against this and the symphonic form seemed more suitable to what he wished to express. The symphony is not so much a representation of the story of the drama as a work that records the impact of Shakespeare's plays upon the imagination of Berlioz and, more broadly, of the entire romantic generation. This accounts for the stirring ending, which eschews the tragedy entirely and presents the unification of the Montagues and Capulets. The ending is, in essence, a hymn of praise to Shakespeare as a figure who can unite disparate people and classes and therefore serve as a means of bringing about social cohesion.

The most persistent theme in critical discussions of Berlioz's *Roméo et Juliette* has been the generic nature of the 'symphonie dramatique'. Berlioz was little concerned with producing generically pure works, which was one reason why he was constantly in conflict with the French musical establishment. But *Roméo et Juliette* is, perhaps, the most individual, even idiosyncratic work he wrote. "Ce sera une chose vraiment unique", Emile Deschamps, the poet who provided the words for his music, wrote to him, "un *libretto* pour une symphonie! – un orchestre qui représente un opera! Et tout alors grace à votre talent deviendra charmant en restant fort original"[1] (Berlioz 2001: II, 562). Certainly the symphony's first audiences found it both original and enchanting; in fact, the first run of three performances at the end of 1839 was, perhaps, the highest and happiest point of Berlioz's troubled relationship with the Parisian musical establishment and public. It was, Julian Rushton claims, "a triumph, perhaps the greatest of Berlioz's chequered career" (14). But, as David Cairns points out, *Roméo et Juliette* still "remains one of Berlioz's least performed

---

[1] 'This will be something truly unique [...] a *libretto* for a symphony! – an orchestra that represents an opera!'

works" (II, 205). It was rarely given complete in Berlioz's lifetime and, in order for any of the music to be heard at all, Berlioz himself initiated the practice that was followed until fairly recently of including only extracts – usually one or all of the three central orchestral movements – in concert programs. The main problem that troubles audiences is that Berlioz's work, as commentators have observed, is "a rather awkward compromise between symphony and opera or oratorio" (ibid. 202).

The relationship between the play and the symphony is also uncertain. Ian Kemp, in an intricately argued essay, sees the symphony as an attempt by Berlioz to articulate Shakespeare's play "in his own terms" (46). But does the symphony recreate the play in a linear fashion? And does it capture the full range of Shakespeare's tragedy that sustains two major themes: the powerlessness of the private world, embodied in romantic love, to resist the insistent authority of the family and the ingrained violence of society; and the incapacity of romantic love to sustain itself as a vital and vitalizing force?

To determine these questions – and in doing so to place the symphony within the larger context of the reception of Shakespeare in Europe during the romantic age – we should briefly revisit the events through which the symphony originated. Berlioz considered his first encounter with Shakespeare to be the "plus grand drame de [sa] vie"[2] (1870: 65). The fateful date was September 11, 1827, when he saw the Drury Lane Company perform *Hamlet* at the Odéon. Although Berlioz had virtually no English, he was transformed by the experience. "Shakespeare", he wrote in his *Mémoires*, "en tombant ainsi sur moi à l'improviste, me foudroya. Son éclair, en m'ouvrant le ciel de l'art avec un fracas sublime, m'en illumine les plus lointaines profondeurs. Je reconnus la vrai grandeur, la vraie beauté, la vraie vérité dramatique."[3] (Ibid.) But this first contact with Shakespeare did not lead to a sudden rush of energy in the enthusiastic young composer. On the contrary, he felt as if he had been devastated by the experience and, after he had also seen *Romeo and Juliet*, nothing

---

[2] '[…] grandest drama of [his] life'.

[3] "Shakespeare, coming upon me unawares, struck me like a thunderbolt. The lightning flash of that sublime discovery opened before me at a stroke the whole heaven of art, illuminating it to its remotest depths. I recognized the meaning of dramatic grandeur, beauty, truth." (Berlioz 2002: 70f.)

would persuade him to go close to the English players again – "de nouvelles éprouves m'eussent terrassé; je les craignais comme on craint les grandes douleurs physiques; l'idée seule de m'y exposer me faisait frémir"[4] (ibid. 68).

Any reader familiar with the *Mémoires* will know that Berlioz's reminiscences of his youth should be taken with a pinch of salt; in fact, few of the romantics, not even Byron, viewed their lives quite as dramatically as Berlioz did. Nevertheless, his experience of Shakespeare as a power that transformed his entire being was far from being peculiar to him; in fact, conversion to Shakespeare had become quite an established rite of passage among the romantics. About sixty years before, in the heyday of the German *Sturm und Drang*, Goethe had described his first reading of Shakespeare as if it were a moment of conversion that transformed his entire life. "Die erste Seite, die ich in ihm las", he wrote in his youthful speech "Zum Shakespeares-Tag",

> machte mich auf zeitlebens ihm eigen, und wie ich mit dem ersten Stücke fertig war, stund ich wie ein Blindgeborner, dem eine Wunderhand das Gesicht in einem Augenblicke schenkt. Ich erkannte, ich fühlte aufs lebhafteste meine Existenz um eine Unendlichkeit erweitert, alles war mir neu, unbekannt und das ungewohnte Licht machte mir Augenschmerzen.[5] (Goethe XII, 224-225)

Goethe's conversion to Shakespeare became paradigmatic for the romantics; it was always felt as a profoundly personal experience. Shakespeare spoke initially to the individual's imagination, primarily because he was invariably first encountered in print rather than performance. Reading his plays nourished the emotions and expanded readers' understanding of their inner world. When, in *Wilhelm Meisters Lehrjahre,* Goethe introduces his hero to Shakespeare, it is not in the public glare of the theatre, but in an obscure room far removed from the bustle of the stage. Here Wilhelm reads the entire works and experiences Shakespeare as a magician who expands and transforms

---

[4] "Another such ordeal would have felled me. I dreaded it as one dreads acute physical pain. The mere thought of laying myself open to it made me shudder." (Berlioz 2002: 74)

[5] 'The first page I read of him made me his own for the rest of my life, and as I finished the first play I stood like one who has been blind from birth being given the gift of sight by a miraculous hand. I understood, I felt in the liveliest way, how my existence extended to infinity, everything was new to me, unknown, and the unaccustomed light hurt my eyes.'

his mind (cf. Goethe VII, 191-192). Even though Wilhelm is utterly devoted to the theatre, Shakespeare the dramatist, who wrote plays that were designed for performance, is a distinctly secondary concern.

Wilhelm's reaction is characteristic for his time. Shakespeare's plays in their 'original' form were commonly considered to be unsuited for the stage. Goethe and Herder, two of the most persuasive German advocates for Shakespeare in the late 18th century, insisted that staging his plays was likely to destroy rather than enhance their unique power to speak to the imagination. To put Shakespeare on stage, Herder argued, would be to place before an audience "Trümmer von Kolossus, von Pyramide […], die jeder anstaunet und keiner begreift"[6] (Herder I, 895), while Goethe could never even contemplate a performance of a Shakespeare play unless it had been rigorously adapted (see Goethe, "Shakespeare und keine Ende", XII, 295-298). When he and other practitioners, such as Friedrich Ludwig Schröder, did put Shakespeare on the stage, it was invariably in versions that had been tailored to the neoclassical and sentimentalist principles then prevalent in the German theatre. Shakespeare the poet preceded Shakespeare the playwright in the romantic imagination. It was only in the early decades of the 19th century that relatively complete versions of Shakespeare found their way to the German stage, in the Schlegel/Tieck translations.

France proved even more resistant to unadapted Shakespeare. Victor Hugo, Alexandre Dumas *père* and Alfred de Vigny, who led the romantic revolt against what they conceived to be the stultifying dominance of neoclassicism in serious drama, took Shakespeare to be their guiding light. He was the spirit behind Hugo's inflammatory "Préface de *Cromwell*" that advocated the admixture in art of the grotesque and the beautiful as an expression of the duality of the human condition. Not only did the French romantics value the aesthetic ambivalence of Shakespeare's work, they shared, with their German counterparts, an enthusiasm for its egalitarian implications. In contrast to the aristocratic leanings of neoclassical drama, Shakespeare revealed a humanity that gave his kings affinity with the people and patrician politicians common interest with laborers. However, while Shakespeare's democratic spirit was compatible with both the

---

[6] ' […] the ruins of a colossus, of pyramids, which each person gazes at in wonder and none understand'.

popular melodrama of the Parisian boulevards and the flamboyant romantic verse tragedies that enjoyed quite a vogue in the 1830s, his plays with their multiple plots, their flouting of the unities, and their mixture of the comic with the tragic and the farcical with the pathetic, were virtually never seen on the Parisian stage[7]. In France even more than Germany, the neoclassical aesthetic provided the theatrical norm, and though Hugo's theory and dramatic practice challenged it, it retained its hold over French theatre for several decades after the romantic era.

Berlioz's ardor for Shakespeare was even more intense and personal than that of his literary contemporaries, partly because of Harriet Smithson's presence in the Drury Lane company. Harriet played Ophelia in the performance of *Hamlet* that had so transported Berlioz and the following night she played Juliet. Berlioz, frantic to see her in this latter role, booked two tickets to make doubly sure he could get in. "Aussi, dès le troisième acte, respirant à peine [...] je me di avec une entiè conviction: Ah! je suis perdu."[8] (1870: 67) Harriet and Shakespeare between them had engulfed him. "The two passions", as Cairns observes, "are inextricably linked; the 'flame of Shakespeare's genius' which brands him is held against his heart by the priestess-goddess" (Cairns I, 252). Although Berlioz later insisted that he did not decide to marry Harriet the evening he first saw her, the die had been cast. A few years later they did marry, but the consequence was a sadly deteriorating relationship marked by Harriet's alcoholic withdrawal from the world due to her failed career and the relentless decline of Berlioz's once passionate feelings for her. His passion for Shakespeare, however, survived.

By the time he set to work on the *Roméo et Juliette* symphony in 1838, the personal and professional trajectories of his life were becoming clear. His marriage to Harriet was already in trouble – they were to separate in 1844 – and, after the failure of *Benvenuto Cellini* at the Opéra in September 1838, it was becoming increasingly apparent that for both artistic and political reasons he could not rely upon

---

[7] John Pemble provides a stimulating account of Shakespeare's advent in France in *Shakespeare Goes to Paris: How the Bard Conquered France* (see especially 93-117).

[8] "By the third act, scarcely able to breather [...] I knew that I was lost." (Berlioz, *The Memoirs of Hector Berlioz* 73)

Paris's most prestigious musical institution to make his mark. This may have precipitated his decision not to write his *Roméo et Juliette* as an opera, as the chances of it being performed were minimal. But ever since he had first conceived of setting the work to music, back in 1827, he had been uncertain about its suitability for the stage. He had no reason to doubt the theatrical effectiveness of the story's action. In Florence in 1831, he had seen Bellini's *I Capuleti e i Montecchi*, a work he mistakenly believed to be based on *Romeo and Juliet*, and he was deeply disappointed by the composer's and librettist's failure to rise to the dramatic opportunities offered by the vibrantly contrasting scenes of the play. "Where was the musical drama, the dramatic music, that such poetry should give birth to?" (Cairns I, 447). No doubt, he had speculated, probably with considerable frequency, as to his capacity to provide the very music that Bellini he felt had failed to compose, but when, early in 1839, he set to work *Roméo et Juliette*, it was clear that he had interests other than those of dramatic representation in mind. Given the gradual and painful dissolution of his marriage, the play no doubt came to stand in his imagination as symbolic for a youthful love that had past its prime and had now become the cause of present misery. The symphony would therefore incorporate personal themes. Furthermore, one of the most notable and initially puzzling features of Deschamps' text, which had been written in very close collaboration with Berlioz, is the absence of any attempt to recapture Shakespeare's dialogue in French. This suggests that the symphony is as much, perhaps more *about* Shakespeare and his impact on the imagination, than it is an attempt to recreate the drama, which would necessarily involve sustained focus on the specifics of dramatic action.

The order of Shakespeare's action is not entirely ignored. The fugue that opens the symphony unambiguously represents violent fighting, the posturing of the warring families, and the absolute authority of the Prince who attempts to quell it. But from then until the seventh and final movement of the symphony, Berlioz abandons virtually all interest in the turbulent life of the streets and turns instead primarily to matters of the heart and of Shakespeare himself. As soon as the sound of the fighting has died away, the Prologue begins with a semi-chorus launching into a solemn chant that has a distinctly religious aura about it. Although this might strike one initially as akin to a Greek chorus, in fact it is not, as the chorus and a contralto solo simply relate the opening events of the play; they are not represented. The semi-chorus and contralto sing of the violence, which has already been represented in the opening fugue, and then tell of Romeo wandering distractedly through the streets, already in love with Juliet (Rosalind being quite absent), and the ball, into which he wanders as if by chance. The events of the play are distanced; the chorus and the contralto soloist meditate on them rather than recreate them; in fact, the entire prologue has a markedly soporific effect after the excitement of the opening fugue. Only at the conclusion does the chorus breaks from its somnolence and springs to life, as it tells of Romeo leaping to the balcony and gathering Juliet in his arms in a sweeping melody that has all the immediacy of an operatic declaration of love. This is followed by the Strophes in which the contralto solo does not, as one might expect, draw upon the poetry of the balcony scene; instead she meditates on how the ecstasy of first love, as experienced by Romeo and Juliet, is equivalent to the poetry of Shakespeare.

> Quel art dans sa langue choisie
> Rendrait vos célestes appas?
> Premier amour, n'êtes vous pas
> Plus haut que toute poésie?
> Ou ne seriez-vous point dans notre exil mortel
> Cette poésie elle-même
> Dont Shakespeare, lui seul, eut le secret suprême
> Et qu'il remporta dans le ciel?[9]

The love of Romeo and Juliet is treated as equivalent to the power of Shakespeare's imagination, which indicates that the symphony is in part at least about the transformative power of Shakespeare's poetry, a power that had been fused in Berlioz's imagination with his love for Harriet when he had seen her perform the role in 1827. The association of love and creative imagination is made even more specific by the recitative and scherzetto that follows, which is a quicksilver rendering by the solo tenor of words that approximate Shakespeare's Queen Mab speech, a passage that centers on the workings of the imagination from which poetry springs. The flickering melody of Queen

---

[9] "What art, in his chosen tongue, could describe your heavenly delights? First love? Are you not above all poetry? Or rather are you not, in this vale of tears, that poetry itself of which Shakespeare alone had the secret, and which he took with him to heaven?" (Emile Duchamps, Paroles: *Roméo et Juliette,* tr. David Cairns in booklet accompanying Philips recording 442 134-2: 1996. 10-11.)

Mab does not recall the love music that has immediately preceded it, but echoes the themes of the fugue with which the symphony opened, which described the Capulets and Montagues brawling in the street, suggesting that Berlioz may be drawing parallels between violence and the unfettered workings of the imagination, as if they come from the same sources of energy.

If Berlioz's theme is the source and power of Shakespeare's imagination, then the sequence of the three central, orchestral movements becomes clearer. In the first, "Roméo seul", Romeo himself might serve as an exemplum of the way in which poetry transforms and casts magic on the world, as expounded on by the contralto solo in the Strophes. While Shakespeare's Romeo is consistently presented with the objectivity that is intrinsic to drama, with Berlioz's romantic hero we hear and feel the world through his subjective experience. Hence, there is nothing hostile in the music of the ball when Romeo first hears it because it is painted with and expresses his feelings for Juliet; that it emanates from a world that is hostile to him is of no significance. Ultimately the ball erupts and a vigorous dance rhythm dominates to the end of the movement and briefly the violence represented by the opening fugue returns; the insistent cheerfulness is set off by some few darker moments, especially in the brass, where one glimpses the threat offered by Tybalt. These are momentary and while they seem to goad the dance rhythms to a peak of virtually apocalyptic energy, the ball does nothing to dispel the languorous atmosphere that characterized the first part of the movement.

The languor of the world as it is heard through the ears of Romeo returns to prevail over the central movement of the symphony, "Nuit sereine" followed by the celebrated "Scène d'amour". The chorus of revelers, like the sounds of the ball in "Roméo seul", reflects or even composes the continuation of Romeo's reverie after the ball; the nostalgic, gently lilting fragments of their song provide a transition into to the "Scène d'amour" that follows. Some commentators have argued that this passage follows quite literally the dialogue of Shakespeare's balcony scene[10], though listeners who are not armed with a copy of Shakespeare's text will probably agree with Daniel Albright that it represents less the balcony scene of Shakespeare 2:2, as it does the

---

[10] Kemp finds close and literal parallels between the progression of Shakespeare's scene and the development of Berlioz's movement (cf. 65-67).

entire love of Romeo and Juliet, compressed into a fifteen-minute movement – "it is not any single love duet, but all the love duets in Shakespeare's text rolled into one" (64). Based principally on the ecstatic theme first sung by the chorus as Romeo and Juliet fell into each other's arms, the movement does not only depict wooing, but consummation. As has often been observed, it precedes the '*Liebesnacht*' of Wagner's *Tristan und Isolde*, but in doing so it distances itself from Shakespeare's play. The ardor of sexual passion not only grips Berlioz's two lovers but, as in the later *Tristan,* is felt as a powerful force of reconciliation and compassion, through which, we sense, the conflicts that rend the wider public world might be resolved. To Shakespeare, however, the ameliorative powers of romantic love were of little concern. He never suggests that the love of Romeo and Juliet *per se* can heal the wounds that society inflicts upon itself, only that society might shame itself into some form of permanent truce by seeing in Romeo and Juliet's deaths the damage its inborn drive toward violence has done. Berlioz, in contrast, like many of his fellow romantics, saw romantic love as a power that can heal and prevent social division and diffuse violence. The influence of this love is similar in nature to the transformative effect that the romantic work of art ideally has upon those who encounter it. This is not an issue upon which Berlioz insists, but much of the "Scène d'amour" is built upon fragments of the passionate melody sung by the chorus when describing Romeo sweeping up Juliet in his arms, followed by the contralto solo that identifies first love with Shakespeare's poetry. This suggests a possible reading of the "Scène" as a hymn to Shakespeare. Its climactic moment comprises a complete and very insistent re-capitulation of this melody. This link between the workings of the creative imagination and love is possibly confirmed by Berlioz's placement of the purely orchestral Queen Mab movement immediately after the "Scène".

Although Berlioz never loses sight of Shakespeare's play, the central sections of the symphony are devoted less toward expounding the tragic pattern of Shakespeare's play, but more upon meditating on how the play both accesses emotional realms that were of compelling interest to the romantics, and on the kinship between the experience of first love and the process of artistic creation as embodied in Shakespeare's plays. Grand opera with its consequential dramatic action and distinctly unromantic propensity, in Parisian opera especially, to favor impersonal public interests above individual ones, was a quite inappropriate genre for Berlioz's theme. At the same time, the theatre is not entirely forgotten, nor should it be as Berlioz's enthusiasm for Shakespeare was, unlike that of many romantics, first set aflame in the theatre. Hence, the closing section of the symphony is introduced by the fifth movement that comprises the theatrical "Convoi funèbre de Juliette" – Juliet's funeral march – an episode that was inserted into the play by Garrick, whose version the Drury Lane company was using[11]. The funeral march, in which the chorus repeats persistently the phrase "Jetez des fleurs", extends the contemplative mood of most of the second section, but with a distinct note of despair, uncomprehending sorrow being its dominant mood. It provides a fitting introduction to the sixth movement, "Roméo au tombeau", which sustains the subjective mode that has predominated for much of the symphony, though with the magic gone. The broken phrases, jagged rhythms, and impetuous outbursts follow the events of the Garrick version of the tomb scene, in which Juliet awakes before Romeo dies and they engage in a desperate bout of hope that they will live, before this is exposed as a delusion by Romeo's death. For most of the movement, Romeo once again provides the prism by which we understand the action, though in the brief passage where he is united with Juliet there is an operatic objectivity and energy in the music that quickly fades to nothingness as both lovers die.

By common agreement, the final movement is the least Shakespearean in the entire symphony, even though Berlioz claimed it was actually a scene from the play, though, he added rather enigmatically, one that had never been played in any theatre. Indeed it had not, nor could it have been as Shakespeare could never have written it. His understanding of tragedy was radically different from that of the romantics. For him, tragedy was grim and not subject to any mitigating vision of harmony being ultimately achieved, either within life or somewhere beyond it. As we have already seen, although Shakespeare invested great value in Romeo and Juliet's love, he does not allow it to circumscribe the entire action, nor does he consider it to extend into any form of afterlife. He ends his play with a sudden, uncompro-

---

[11] In fact, the funeral was not performed in Paris as the censors would not allow the representation of a religious rite on the stage.

mising brutality, as articulated in the words of the Prince close to the end of the play:

> See what a scourge is laid upon your hate,
> That heaven finds means to kill your joys with love!
> And I for winking at your discords too
> Have lost a brace of kinsmen. All are punished. [V:3]

In contrast, Berlioz's final movement denies Shakespeare's sense of tragedy entirely, and, on first hearing at least, it also seems to fly in the face of the previous movements. Music reminiscent of church, military parade grounds, and the grandiosity of French classical culture, seems an inappropriate way to end a work that has explored the deepest recesses of love and the imagination. Nevertheless, it complements and even expands the romantic gravitation of the symphony. Berlioz's Friar Laurence, who is a pillar of strength in contrast to Shakespeare's timid and morally questionable friar, forges peace between the warring families, through appealing to their compassion that arises from the sight of their children's corpses. The symphony ends with a chorus of reconciliation as mighty as the ending of Beethoven's Ninth Symphony on which it is clearly based. Berlioz is being consistent with his romantic tastes and affiliations. However much the romantics prized Shakespeare, they did not believe in tragedy as something irreconcilable and irresolvable. The punishment that the Prince claims has been brought upon the warring families is not a recourse to which the romantics would ultimately admit. They believed in reconciliation, not tragedy, in the possibility of utopia, not persistent alienation. This is something they had even discovered from Shakespeare, as they prized him for his universalism. Through his plays different people could be reconciled. It is this romantic reading of Shakespeare that Berlioz recalls at the end of his symphony. Friar Laurence's call for peace and the chorus of the united families at the end of the opera can be read not only as a rewriting of Shakespeare's story, but as a hymn of praise to Shakespeare himself.

Berlioz's *Roméo et Juliette* symphony is both a lyrical and a dramatic work. It is part reminiscence, as in it he was recalling the passions of his youth and his first encounter with Shakespeare, part meditation, as he speculates on the nature of Shakespeare's poetic imagination, which is clearly aligned with the love that is the central theme of the symphony. Stage representation alone would not have allowed for this sustained association between the creative imagination and love.

But Berlioz's symphony can also be placed in the larger context of the romantic reception of Shakespeare's work. It was as a poet more than a dramatist that Shakespeare first spoke to the romantics. The lyrical aspects of his work were uppermost in the German reception because technically and conceptually that theatre was unable to accommodate his unadapted texts. This was no less the case in France, where the neoclassical perspective was the only one in which tragedy could be performed. It would still be some decades before Shakespeare's plays would be seen on French stages in anything approaching complete versions. For the romantic age, however, Berlioz's *Roméo et Juliette* symphony offered one of the most complex expressions of the potential richness of his work.

References

Albright, Daniel (2001). *Berlioz's Semi-Operas:* Roméo et Juliette *and* La damnation de Faust. Rochester, NY: University of Rochester Press.

Berlioz, Hector (2002). *The Memoirs of Hector Berlioz*. David Cairns, tr. and ed. New York/Toronto: Knopf.

— (1972-2001). *Correspondance Générale*. Pierre Citron, ed. 7 vols. Paris: Flammarion.

— (1870). *Mémoires de Hector Berlioz*. Paris: Michel Levy.

Cairns, David (2000). *Berlioz*. 2 vols. Berkeley/Los Angeles, CA: University of California Press.

Goethe, Johann Wolfgang von (1973). *Goethes Werke*. Erich Trunz, ed. 14 vols. Munich: Beck.

Herder, Johann Gottfried (1953). *Werke*. Karl-Gustav Gerold, ed. 2 vols. Munich: Hanser.

Kemp, Ian (1992). "*Romeo and Juliet* and *Roméo et Juliette*". Peter Bloom, ed. *Berlioz Studies*. Cambridge: Cambridge University Press. 37-79.

Pemble, John (2005). *Shakespeare Goes to Paris: How the Bard Conquered France*. London: Hambledon and London.

Rushton, Julian (1994). *Berlioz:* Roméo et Juliette. Cambridge Music Handbooks. Cambridge: Cambridge University Press.

From Novel to Song via Myth
Wuthering Heights as a Case of Popular Intermedial Adaptation

Walter Bernhart, Graz

This paper argues that adaptations of literary works into later, frequently popular, versions of them in other media are rarely cases of direct intermedial transposition but generally pass through a more abstract, essentially media-indifferent stage, which is based on the *Stoff*, or 'subject matter', of the literary source rather than on its more essentially 'literary' elements. Successful *Stoffe* for intermedial adaptation prove to be fertile towards generating myths or icons, which in turn stimulate further creative responses in various cultural contexts. Yet this successful myth-generating quality of a literary source very well ultimately rests in a highly literary quality of the source itself, namely in its ability to create a vivid 'storyworld' and to guarantee the reader's 'immersion' in this storyworld. Thus, concerning source/target text relationships, critical attention is directed not so much towards the issue of the target text's 'fidelity' to the source, but more so towards the source text's 'fertility' relating to its 'immersive', 'storyworld-building' and 'myth-generating' power. The case is argued by analysing the adaptive process from Emily Brontë's famous novel *Wuthering Heights* to Kate Bush's highly successful eponymous popular song of the 1970s.

In 2005 we proudly celebrated four hundred years of Cervantes's *Don Quixote*, which has given critics worldwide ample opportunity to contemplate the reception history of this extraordinary book. In a perceptive *Times Literary Supplement* review, Jeremy Lawrance observed that "the book's recognition as a world classic goes back to the eighteenth century and its status as world myth to the nineteenth". He added that various "forms of repackaging" of the novel (such as various "curios" from comic strips to "Quixotic cookery") have "spared [us] the trouble of reading a thousand-page Spanish Baroque novel" (Lawrance).

I take the cue for my discussion of Emily Brontë's novel *Wuthering Heights* and its afterlife in adaptation from this comment, and from another one made by a clever journalist who described a classic novel as "a timeless read that I never have time to read" (online 1). As we are concerned with Word and Music Studies, the example and case of adaptation by which I have chosen to demonstrate my views is a musical one, namely Kate Bush's extremely successful song of 1978, called "Wuthering Heights". What I plan to develop, however, is a more general reflection on adaptive processes from literary texts into popular media and – to indicate one of my main points right at the start – to demonstrate that such intermedial transpositions are often processes which do not involve a direct transformation from one medium into another, but rather tend to pass through a stage of a far more abstract, essentially extra-medial condition.

Kate Bush, "Wuthering Heights"

Out on the wiley and windy moors
We'd roll and fall in green.
You had a temper like my jealousy:
Too hot, too greedy.
How could you leave me, 5
When I needed to possess you?
I hated you. I loved you, too.

Bad dreams in the night.
You told me I was going to lose the fight,
Leave behind my wuthering, wuthering 10
Wuthering Heights.

Heathcliff, it's me, your Cathy, I've come home. I'm so cold,
Let me in at your window.

Ooh, it gets dark! It gets lonely,
On the other side from you. 15

I pine a lot. I find a lot
Falls through without you.
I'm coming back, love.
Cruel Heathcliff, my one dream,
My only master. 20

Too long I roam in the night.
I'm coming back to his side, to put it right.
I'm coming home to wuthering, wuthering,
Wuthering Heights.

Heathcliff, it's me, your Cathy, I've come home. I'm so cold, 25
Let me in at your window.

> Ooh! Let me have it.
> Let me grab your soul away.
> Ooh! Let me have it.
> Let me grab your soul away.   30
> You know it's me – Cathy!
>
> Heathcliff, it's me, your Cathy, I've come home. I'm so cold,
> Let me in at your window.
>
> AHHHHHHH YAAAAA YAAAA OHHHH YAAAAAAA
> (Online 2)

In this song, Catherine Bush (which is Kate's official name) obviously sings in the role of the older Catherine from Emily Brontë's novel. The sound of this song has been called 'exotic' and "idiosyncratic", with its "repertoire of unearthly shrieks and guttural whispers" creating "a surreal world of affect" (Kruse 453-455). Patsy Stoneman, the authority on *Brontë Transformations*, tellingly talks about "the shriek of a banshee" (212), i. e., of an Irish death fairy. (Kate Bush is of Irish descent.) We sense in this song the identification of the singer with the dead Cathy returning to Wuthering Heights at night to haunt Heathcliff in her frustrated hope of becoming finally re-united with her star-crossed lover. Cathy remembers their harmonious early childhood out on the moors and wants to recover it, but there is also aggressiveness involved in the song, in the form of jealousy, greed, possessiveness – see the final statement of the song: "Let me grab your soul away." (l. 30), and there is an obsessive mixture of love and hate: "I hated you. I loved you, too." (l. 7) This is basically in the spirit of Brontë's novel, but it is strange that the song talks about Cathy's jealousy. In the book it is of course Heathcliff who is jealous of Cathy marrying Edgar Linton; Cathy, in fact, has no reason to be jealous. The first stanza of the song would come far more convincingly from Heathcliff: "How could you leave me, / When I needed to possess you?" (ll. 5-6)

This inaccuracy does not come as much of a surprise when one reads what Kate Bush has to say about the genesis of her song: "I remember my brother John talking about the story, but I couldn't relate to it enough. So I borrowed the book and read a few pages, picking out a few lines. So I actually wrote the song before I had read the book right through." (Online 3) Of course, early on in the book we find the episode when Lockwood meets Cathy's ghost at the window, wishing to be let in[1]. Yet in the book it is Heathcliff who is anguished by this, not Cathy, and it is he who cries out for her as she has vanished into the dark. It is not unexpected – as Kate Bush reports in true honesty – that the Brontë Society thinks her song "a disgrace" (ibid.), but, as far as the present argument is concerned, I am certainly not blaming Kate's 'reading' – or 'non-reading' – of the story. For Kate Bush goes on in her report: "The name Cathy helped, and made it easier to project my own feelings of want for someone so much that you hate them. I could understand how Cathy felt." (Ibid.)

This, it seems to me, is a legitimate position to take as it answers an individual demand in a creative person, and what needs to interest us in our context – i. e., in a discussion of intermedial adaptations – is the following: what has happened to the story of Heathcliff and Cathy since its early formulation in 1847 that would encourage a creative person like Kate Bush to want to 'project her own feelings' into it and make her 'understand' the heroine? Thus, what should interest us in this context is not so much the 'fidelity' of the adaptation to its source, but the 'fertility' of the source for later adaptations. That could become a slogan: **'fertility'**, **not 'fidelity'**.

The 'fertility' of Emily Brontë's novel – and that of her sister Charlotte's *Jane Eyre* – shows itself most clearly in the fact that a veritable Brontë industry has developed over the one-and-a-half centuries since these works of genius came out of the remote Yorkshire moors. Thanks to Lucasta Miller's very recent monograph on *The Brontë Myth*, we now have detailed knowledge of the stages of the Brontë reception and their transformation into cultural icons. Miller concentrates on the mythification and mystification of Charlotte's and Emily's own lives, and carefully traces how Emily, in particular, became the "famous sphinx of English Literature" (259), "The Mystic of the Moors" (251), who – ridiculously so – "was recently voted twentieth most erotic person of the millennium […] in a poll among readers of the *Erotic Review*" (269). I am mentioning this as it shows very clearly how the heroine of the novel *Wuthering Heights* and its author merge in the popular imagination, all this being deeply ironical in view of the maidenly life led by the sisters at the Haworth Parsonage and of the overt (if not covert) sexlessness of the

---

[1] This scene has been called "the most memorable ghost scene in literature" (Miller 258).

novel. Miller observes that Emily was quite neglected in the high-Victorian decades after her death in 1848 (cf. 223), but that she started to fascinate people during what Miller calls the "Brontë epidemic" of the 1890s (111). She quotes D. H. Lawrence as being thrilled by the "dangerousness" of the novel *Wuthering Heights* and finding there "human passion as a mythic force" (262). Initiated by Charlotte's "imaginative rewritings of Emily" (279) after her sister's untimely and mysterious death, Emily began to be transformed "into something larger, and more abstract, than life: an embodiment of Romantic visionary poetics"; and later poetic appropriations "remodeled her along archetypal lines", testifying to the author's "magnetism". To mention one famous instance, in Ted Hughes's imagination, Emily's (purported) death wish merged with the vision of the ghostly Catherine from the novel, and the Heathcliff-Cathy myth served the poet as a model for explaining to himself his own situation with his suicidal wife, Sylvia Plath (cf. 279-283).

Thus, it is obvious that *Wuthering Heights* has by now become canonized as a great tragic love story: it has turned into "an archetype of (R)romantic [sic] love" (Stoneman 221), in which the landscape, 'wild nature', represented by the Yorkshire moors, plays an important role, giving the tragic lovers a cosmic, elemental dimension far beyond our everyday social world. In this context, Heathcliff, as a popular icon, reflects the Byronic hero type, the mysterious, homeless wanderer, of strong masculine fascination, but a guilty, anguished, "fierce, pitiless, wolfish man", as Cathy describes him in the novel to Isabella, Heathcliff's wife (Brontë 102). The special feature of Cathy's and Heathcliff's tragic love – as in contrast to that other pair of great nineteenth-century romantic lovers, Tristan and Isolde – is what Stoneman calls the "twin soul theme", is what she identifies as the "fascinating core of the novel", namely the feeling that there is "an existence of yours beyond you" (online 4). This notion finds its most famous expression in Cathy's confession to Nelly when she says "I *am* Heathcliff", and in the description of her love for Heathcliff: "My love for Heathcliff resembles the external rocks beneath – a source of little visible delight, but necessary." (Brontë 82) The fact that the two people experience an existence 'beyond themselves' contributes to a central notion of the novel, which is the notion of 'transgression'. According to Miller, this is "the main thematic idea which holds the novel together" and implies "the dissolving of normative boundaries" such as the boundary between dream and reality, or that between the natural and the supernatural worlds (211).

These two 'transgressive', elementally identical people, having a single 'twin soul', however, experience their identity only as children out on the stormy moors, but these 'children of storm' have hopelessly lost their primeval union in adulthood and find themselves tragically separated and in constant frustrated search for its recovery. Stoneman observes that this pair of lovers has become an "icon of loss", which "suggests that *Wuthering Heights* occupies a place in the popular imagination of the present comparable to that of *Jane Eyre* in the melodramatic imagination of the nineteenth century. *Jane Eyre* was reproduced predominantly as a social drama, the story of the orphan denied her place in family and class. *Wuthering Heights*", Stoneman continues, "seems [to have] come to represent the more existential loss of the twentieth century, the fantasy of those orphaned by a non-existent God and alienated from a society which pretends to belong to us all." (213) This is a far-reaching observation that goes a long way towards accounting for the extraordinary impact of the *Wuthering Heights* myth on our present-day cultural climate.

Yet it is an interesting facet of the Brontë reception during the last century that the most effective appropriation of Emily's novel was William Wyler's notorious film version of 1939, in which Laurence Olivier appeared as Heathcliff and Merle Oberon as Catherine. It was the same year when *Gone with the Wind* came out, and both were truly American, Hollywood products, which, in the case of *Wuthering Heights*, implied a drastic re-reading of the novel. Heathcliff, in this film, is more amiable (after all, he is played by Laurence Olivier), Catherine is more of a typically American capricious girl, the story has a decisive social twist and becomes the story of 'the lady and the stable boy' where it is the social barriers that prevent a happy union of the two[2]. This is a far cry from the novel's original spirit, and Stoneman asserts that Catherine and Heathcliff in this film "miss out on the unique quality of the novel" (online 4). Yet the two lovers "on the hilltop" out on the moors – a famous image from the film – have "become a visual emblem of what the novel 'means'" to a mass audience (Stoneman 127).

---

[2] This reading by Wyler's film was first identified by Bluestone, cf. 99 (ch. 3: "*Wuthering Heights*" 91-114).

This 1939 Hollywood version of *Wuthering Heights*, with its "'lovers on the hill' mythology" (155) may truly form "a watershed in popular perception" of the story, as Stoneman asserts (6), and created the now most popular image of the novel. Yet, it is interesting to observe how Kate Bush fits into this picture. In fact, one can find little of this sentimental, "'weepy'" (213) Hollywood version of *Wuthering Heights* in the song, which shows far more of the Byronic hero spirit and the feeling of existential loss. As already observed, 'dark' emotions prevail in the song, indicated by its key-words: "jealousy", "greedy", "possess", "cold", "lonely", "bad dreams", "hate", "grab", "master" – "on the wiley, windy moors" (online 2). Bush's text very well represents the 'icon of loss' and, at the same time, the profound unwillingness to accept that loss, an existential anguish much in keeping with modernist sensibilities, as already observed.

What persuasively matches with this condition, as expressed in the lyrics, is the extraordinary, very strange music of the song. Kate Bush's unusual subjects – as she says herself, she is interested in "human beings in extreme religious or spiritual states" (online 5) – find their equivalent in extreme sound constellations, her shrill high voice, and the obsessive repetitiveness of the music. Kate's own description of how she came to write the song is significant in this respect: it perfectly fulfils the cliché of visionary romantic inspiration. She says: "Well, I wrote ["Wuthering Heights"] in my flat, sitting at the upright piano one night in March at about midnight. There was a full moon and the curtains were open, and every time I looked up for ideas, I looked at the moon. Actually, it came quite easily. I couldn't seem to get out of the chorus – it had a really circular feel to it, which is why it repeats." (Online 3) This situation, of course, is totally stereotyped but, strangely enough, the music very well captures the hypnotic mood described, and it all seems a perfect equivalent to the 'icon of loss' as it appears in the lyrics. It is also telling that Kate Bush, when asked what comes first when writing her songs, the words or the music, said: "[...] the music seems to be sparked off by an idea before the lyrics, and the lyrics usually fit in just behind the music." (Online 6) It is significant that an 'idea' comes first, stimulating the music, to which the lyrics are fitted afterwards. It seems clear that the 'idea' which triggered the whole process in Kate Bush's song was the Heathcliff icon and the *Wuthering Heights* myth, as they appeared to the singer and as they were suggested to her – however vaguely – by her superficial perusal of the novel. This 'idea' is basically a mixture of the Byronic hero myth and the 'icon of loss', as described.

But one additional feature may further account for the tremendous popularity of the song. (It was number one for weeks in the UK and several other countries, it went into gold after four months, and was top ten in many European and South American countries, also in South Africa – but interestingly not so in the United States; cf. online 7.) I have already mentioned that Emily Brontë was, very ironically, voted one of the most erotic women of the millennium (although, it would appear, her life and novel are sexless). Yet it is clear that much of the tragedy of the Catherine-Heathcliff relationship lies in the fact that it is a case of unconsummated love. This is an essential element of the myth, which distinguishes Catherine and Heathcliff clearly from other Great Lovers, such as Romeo and Juliet, Abelard and Eloise, or Tristan and Isolde. The author Mary Evans very perceptively observes that *Wuthering Heights*, the novel, is "so erotically charged" precisely because this love is unconsummated and "knowledge of the other person as a physical being" is missing and the person remains "an object of fantasy" (online 4). (In this respect, all those transformations of *Wuthering Heights* that feature sexual intimacy between the two protagonists seriously undermine the myth[3].) Thus, the tremendous success of the *Wuthering Heights* myth seems to be essentially rooted in the motive of unconsummated love between two people who, as 'transgressive' creatures, are elementally linked (the 'twin soul motive') but have lost each other (the 'icon of loss'). Jane Allen, a successful TV scriptwriter and -editor, has made a pertinent point by saying that an indispensable ingredient of any successful TV story now is what she refers to by a four-letter acronym, *urst*, which stands for 'Unresolved Sexual Tension'. This is "absolutely the backbone of an ongoing series", she says, and it is "usually internal obstacles", such as lack of courage or imagination, which cause *urst*, rather than external ones (online 4). Is this an (ultimate) explanation why *Wuthering Heights* has been such a success?

* * *

---

[3] A significant case is Robert Fuest's film version of 1970 with Timothy Dalton and Anna Calder-Marshall.

Having investigated a particular case of intermedial adaptation from a famous novel into a popular song, I will now look at some methodological and theoretical implications of the adaptive process described. There has as yet been little reflection on the issue of adaptation in Word and Music Studies, in contrast to Film Studies where adaptation has been a central concern for quite some time now. A very useful, up-to-date collection of essays on the 'state of the art' of adaptation has been edited by James Naremore (2000). It is impressive that even the earliest essay in that collection, a famous text by André Bazin from 1948, observes that "[w]ith time, we do see the ghosts of famous characters rise far above the great novels from which they emanate. [...] Novels, as we all know, are mythmakers." (23) Similarly, Dudley Andrew, another authority on adaptation theory, observes that a successful novel exists "as a continuing form or archetype in culture", and that what he calls the "adaptive material [...] claims the status of myth" (30). This "myth" or "archetype" exists "outside texts altogether", as Andrew, additionally, observes (ibid.), and Robert Ray in the same collection asserts that popular narratives "rely [...] heavily on codes that are never medium-specific", yet the strength of those cultural codes "depends on a signifier's connotation remaining consistent as it migrates from form to form" (40). Thus, in such cases, in the process of transformation from one medium to another, a stage is passed where no form of media-specificity exists any longer but where a 'connotative' element of the source text remains active that proves to be powerful and 'fertile' enough to form the inspiration for further actualizations in other media.

If one wants to identify this media-independent connotative element that remains, it is usually referred to as an 'idea' – so does Kate Bush, as quoted before, or Alfred Hitchcock, who said, "[I] read a **story** only once, and if I like the basic **idea**, I just forget about the book and start to create cinema" (qtd. Naremore 7; my emphases). The vagueness of the terms used for the particular media-independent element referred to becomes obvious when others call it the 'story' (quite in contrast to what, e. g., Hitchcock says in the quotation just given): a film director will probably say that what he needs as the basis for a film is 'a good story', in many cases drawn from a novel. In narrative theory the well-known distinction has been made between 'story' (or *fabula*) and 'discourse' (or *sjuzhet*, in Russian Formalist terminology), and it is generally seen as the distinction between the 'subject matter', the 'what' of a text, and its 'treatment', the 'how' of a text, or, in short, between 'matter' and 'manner'. The recently published *Routledge Encyclopedia of Narrative Theory* (2005) identifies the 'story' as something that "can be taken as a non-textual given, as independent of the presentation in discourse" (Shen 567). What 'story' implies, however, – according to Rimmon-Kenan – is that it forms a "reconstructed", "synthetic" version of the 'plot' (3); in other words, it puts the specific structure of the 'plot' into a chronological, more abstract sequence of events. Yet – and this is the point to be made in the present context – the 'story' is event-oriented. But much of the 'connotative' element investigated here is situated on a more abstract level than 'reconstructed events'. It is interesting that the English language seems to be lacking a definite term equivalent to the German word *Stoff*, which is precisely the element that concerns us here. Typical *Stoffe* are Oedipus, Everyman, Don Juan, Don Quixote, Faust, or Tristan and Isolde. (Only rarely there is talk in English of 'the stuff of myth' or – as in one definition of the Russian Formalists' *fabula* – of "the basic story stuff"; Shen 566. The closest English equivalent to German *Stoff* seems to be '**subject matter**', which, however, is too general and also too abstract; see below.)

German structuralist criticism was interested in the notion of *Stoff*, and one can quote the authoritative definition given by Wolfgang Kayser in *Das sprachliche Kunstwerk*, which first came out in 1948 and was the 'bible' of German literary criticism of its day: 'Anything that lives outside a literary work in its own history and now has an effect on the literary work, is called *STOFF*. It is always tied to particular figures, involves activities, and is more or less fixed temporally and spatially.'[4] This is a very cautious definition and makes sure that, although 'activities' ('*Vorgänge*') are part of a *Stoff*, they need not amount to a string of 'events' as in a 'story' and, similarly, time and space are necessary elements of a *Stoff* but, as the definition says, need no final fixation ('more or less fixed'). This is what distinguishes the *Stoff* from the *Thema* ('theme'), 'problem', or 'idea' of a work,

---

[4] "Was außerhalb eines literarischen Werkes in eigener Überlieferung lebt und nun auf seinen Inhalt gewirkt hat, heißt STOFF. Der Stoff ist immer an bestimmte Figuren gebunden, ist vorgangsmäßig und zeitlich und räumlich mehr oder weniger fixiert" (Kayser 56).

which always refer to the 'cognitive content'[5] only, without any element of concretization. To further complicate matters, 'theme' needs to be additionally distinguished from 'motive'. ('Motives' are, e. g., 'mysterious origin', 'enemy brothers', 'love conflict through different backgrounds' – all these, incidentally, to be found in *Wuthering Heights*.) A 'motive' – according to Gero von Wilpert, another earlier German authority in literary criticism – is 'a structural unit as a typical, significant situation, which contains general thematic conceptions'[6]. So there are, in fact, at least five levels on the 'what' side of a work, in rising order of abstraction: 'plot' – 'story' – '*Stoff*' – 'motive' – 'theme'. What concerns us in the present context is *Stoff* as the one element which seems to live on most powerfully in the process of popular intermedial transformations.

Why does all this matter in a contemporary discussion of adaptations? Although I have quoted definitions of *Stoff*, motive, theme, etc. as given by structuralist critics, it is well known that for this generation of critics *Stoff* was only of a subordinate significance in literature (cf. Wilpert, s. v. "Stoff") and that what was considered to be shaping and 'really' constituting literary works were the 'value-creating forces of form'[7]. This was the familiar formalist position in German criticism, and it found its American equivalent in Clement Greenberg's view, inaugurated in his famous essay "Avant-Garde and Kitsch" of 1939, a central manifesto of modernism. There Greenberg asserts that "subject matter or content becomes something to be avoided like a plague" and that "[c]ontent is to be dissolved so completely into form that the work of art or literature cannot be reduced in whole or in part to anything not itself" (online 8). Yet, what we experience in all the successful adaptations of literary works into popular media is, in fact, exactly the opposite of what is here asserted, namely that the texts are radically reduced – as we have seen with Kate Bush, for example, or in the Hitchcock quotation given above – and that they survive only as a *Stoff* in the form of cultural codes, quite independent of the verbal shape they have found in the literary source. It seems unavoidable to draw the conclusion that in

---

[5] "[...] geistigen Gehalt" (Wilpert, s. v. "Stoff").

[6] "[...] strukturelle Einheit als typische, bedeutungsvolle Situation, die allgemeine thematische Vorstellungen umfaßt" (ibid., s. v. "Motiv").

[7] "[...] wertschaffende Formkräfte" (ibid., s. v. "Quelle").

the process of intermedial transformation from a literary source into a popular medium the literary qualities of the source are essentially lost and become irrelevant. What survives – if it *does* survive – is a *Stoff* in the form of a 'myth' or an 'icon' quite independent of its earlier literary manifestation, and frequently users of myths are quite unaware of their literary origins.

However, there remains the fact asserted by Dudley Andrew that "[w]ell over half of all commercial films have come from literary originals" (29), which implies the assumption that, after all, there must be qualities in literary texts that encourage the development of a powerful *Stoff* that might even become a 'myth' and catch the general popular imagination. Literature always carries an element of prestige and, thus, may encourage artists to use literary sources for adaptations, and there are certainly strong market mechanisms which – as literary texts are usually readily available – make literary texts attractive to prospective adaptors. Yet the question of specific literary qualities which make such texts favoured sources for intermedial adaptations was already a concern for Bazin, which is evident when, at one point, he said that "[i]nsofar as the style of the original has managed to create a character and impose him on the public consciousness, that character acquires a greater autonomy, which might in certain cases lead as far as quasi-transcendence of the work" (23). This is not far from asserting – as 'modernists' would do – that, after all, it is the formal artistry of the literary text, its "style", which does the job. The difference in perspective to the 'postmodernist' Bazin, however, is that Bazin does not claim that formal artistry creates a complex, autonomous **work of art**, but a great – work-transcending – autonomous **character**.

More recent narrative theory has increasingly been concentrating on the 'story' side of the story-discourse dichotomy, and one newly developed notion of interest in our context is that of the '**storyworld**', as defined by David Herman: "[...] storyworlds are mentally and emotionally projected environments" established by a text. Readers "do not merely reconstruct a sequence of events and a set of existents [i. e., a 'story'], but imaginatively (emotionally, viscerally) inhabit a world in which things matter" (569). The point here is that verbal narratives are capable of creating a world which is cognitively and, above all, emotionally engaging; and Herman continues: "[...] the grounding of stories in storyworlds goes a long way towards explaining narratives' 'immersiveness'", which introduces another more recent narrative key term, namely **'immersion'**. Verbal narratives – but works in other media as well – can absorb one, can make one get carried away, and "fictional devices are generally [...] constructed so as to maximize their immersion-inducing power" (Schaefer/Vultur 239). Thus, it can be observed that literary texts are capable of creating an emotionally charged storyworld which invites the reader's immersion and absorption, and it can be argued that without these basic capabilities – which certainly not all literary texts share – a myth based on a literary text is unlikely to arise. Thus, although a literary text may eventually be forgotten and remain unread by later generations, the existence of a powerful 'immersive' literary text at the start seems to be a strong precondition for a **'fertile' myth** or *Stoff* to emerge from such examples as *Don Quixote, Faust*, or *Tristan und Isolde*. An interesting observation is made by the *Routledge Encyclopedia* when it says, "the decisive plane [...] of the immersion-producing power [...] of verbal narratives is not that of the microstructural (linguistic) level, but that of the macrostructural level of the inferential logic of action" (ibid.). This is why it is the stage of the *Stoff*, at a middle position between concreteness and abstraction, between the abstract 'theme' and the concrete 'plot', which is the most productive agent in the intermedial adaptive process we are discussing.

To summarize my argument, it can be stated that in the adaptive process from a verbal text into a popular medium – as demonstrated by looking at Kate Bush's song based on Emily Brontë's novel *Wuthering Heights* – that process can often be seen as passing through a stage which is extramedial and is represented by a *Stoff* extracted from the verbal text and made powerful and 'fertile' by an 'immersive', 'storyworld'-building quality of that verbal text – which implies that there is extraordinary literary competence required on the side of its author to achieve this effect. (This is why it is meaningful that – as indicated at the beginning – Cervantes's *Don Quixote* first became a classic in literary terms and then a myth in cultural terms.)

Such a view of adaptation goes beyond the traditional view which generally thinks in terms of a direct transposition from one medium into another and tends to apply the category of fidelity of the target medium to the source medium as a central analytical tool. Eric Prieto has expressed himself similarly at the WMA Sydney conference in 2001 when he said that the aim of Intermedia Studies is "not the description of direct one-to-one correspondences between the arts" (51). With a modified view of adaptation, replacing the category of 'fidelity' by that of 'fertility', we are entering a far more interesting field, and any glance at contemporary cultural life demonstrates and proves what the prophetic André Bazin said as early as in 1948 – at a time, one should not forget, when adaptations were culturally anathemas –, namely that "we are moving toward a reign of the adaptation" (26). Consequently, as James Naremore asserts, adaptation study is moving from the margins to the centre of contemporary intermedia studies (cf. 15), which is confirmed by the fact that it has finally also become a central concern in the field of Word and Music Studies.

References

Andrew, Dudley (2000). "Adaptation" (1984). Naremore, ed. 28-37.
Bazin, André (2000). "Adaptation, or the Cinema as Digest" (1948; Engl. trans. 1997). Naremore, ed. 19-27.
Bluestone, George (1971). *Novels into Film*. Berkeley, CA: Univ. of California Press.
Brontë, Emily (1995). *Wuthering Heights* (1847). Pauline Nestor, ed. Harmondsworth: Penguin.
Fuest, Robert, Director (1970). *Wuthering Heights* (Film).
Herman, David (2005). "Storyworld". Herman/Jahn/Ryan, eds. 569-570.
Herman, David, Manfred Jahn, Marie-Laure Ryan, eds. (2005). *Routledge Encyclopedia of Narrative Theory*. London/New York, NY: Routledge.
Kayser, Wolfgang (1963). *Das sprachliche Kunstwerk* ([1]1948). Berne/Munich: Francke.
Kruse, Holly (1990). "In Praise of Kate Bush" (1988). Simon Frith, Andrew Goodwin, eds. *On Record: Rock, Pop, and the Written Word*. New York, NY: Pantheon. 450-465.
Lawrance, Jeremy (2005). "Still Readable". *Times Literary Supplement* 5325 (22 April): 6.
Miller, Lucasta (2005). *The Brontë Myth*. New York, NY: Anchor Books.
Naremore, James (2000). "Introduction: Film and the Reign of Adaptation". Naremore, ed. 1-16.

—, ed. (2000). *Film Adaptation*. London: Athlone Press.
Prieto, Eric (2002). "Metaphor and Methodology in Word and Music Studies". Suzanne M. Lodato, Suzanne Aspden, Walter Bernhart, eds. *Word and Music Studies: Essays in Honor of Steven Paul Scher and on Cultural Identity and the Musical Stage*. Word and Music Studies 4. Amsterdam/New York, NY: Rodopi. 49-67.
Ray, Robert B. (2000). "The Field of 'Literature and Film'". Naremore, ed. 38-53.
Rimmon-Kenan, Shlomith (1983). *Narrative Fiction: Contemporary Poetics*. London: Methuen.
Schaefer, Jean-Marie, Ioana Vultur (2005). "Immersion". Herman/Jahn/Ryan, eds. 237-239.
Shen, Dan (2005). "Story-Discourse Distinction". Herman/Jahn/Ryan, eds. 566-568.
Stoneman, Patsy (1996). *Brontë Transformations: The Cultural Dissemination of Jane Eyre and Wuthering Heights*. London et al.: Prentice Hall/Harvester Wheatsheaf.
Wilpert, Gero von (1961/1955). *Sachwörterbuch der Literatur*. Stuttgart: Kröner.
Wyler, William, Director (1939). *Wuthering Heights* (Film).

Online 1: Cosmo Landesman.
   http://www.independent.co.uk/stories/A1801927.html [18/01/99].
Online 2: Kate Bush. "Wuthering Heights" (lyrics).
   http://www.sing365.com/music/lyric.nsf/Wuthering-heights-lyrics-Kate-Bush/67A6699B7CAE2C4D482569A0002E01D8 [30/12/05].
Online 3: Kate Bush. http://gaffa.org/garden/kate1.html [02/08/05].
Online 4: Radio National Australia. 24/08/04. "Big Ideas: Great Lovers: Episode 5: Heathcliff and Catherine".
   http://www.abc.net.au/rn/bigidea/stories/s906676.htm [02/07/05].
Online 5: Kate Bush. http://gaffa.org/garden/kate18.html [03/08/05].
Online 6: Kate Bush. http://gaffa.org/garden/kate6.html [03/08/05].
Online 7: http://gaffa.org/garden/chrono.html [02/08/05].
Online 8: Clement Greenberg. "Avant-Garde and Kitsch", p. 4.
   http://www.sharecom.ca/greenberg/kitsch.html [02/01/06]. Orig. publ.: *Partisan Review* 6 (1939): 34-49.

From Novel into Film into Opera
Multiple Transformations of Emily Brontë's *Wuthering Heights*

Michael Halliwell, Sydney, NSW

The operatic adaptation of fiction usually follows the trajectory from novel into libretto into opera. Occasionally, a novel might be transformed into a spoken drama which later undergoes musical adaptation. Much rarer is the process whereby a 'canonical' novel undergoes an equally 'canonical' film adaptation which then strongly influences subsequent operatic versions. Such is the case with Emily Brontë's *Wuthering Heights*, made into a celebrated film directed by William Wyler (1939). Two operatic adaptations of the novel followed: Carlisle Floyd's opera (1958), and Bernard Herrmann's version (1965/1982). This paper explores the proposition that it is the film which is the impetus and model for both these operas rather than the original novel. The relentless concentration of the film on the tragic relationship between its two 'storm-tossed' central protagonists is mirrored in both operatic adaptations, a radical departure from the novel's much broader focus, and it can be argued that it is Wyler's film which has established the current romantic (stereotypical) view of the novel which can be seen to be 'filtered' through the prism of the film adaptation into its operatic form.

William Wyler's 1939 film of Emily Brontë's novel, *Wuthering Heights*, remains one of the most enduring literary adaptations in the film repertoire more than sixty years after its premiere[1]. Patsy Stoneman describes the film as enjoying "unprecedented success, drawing on a kind of cultural nostalgia and a factitious high-mindedness". (126) I would similarly argue that both operatic adaptations of the novel draw on what could be seen as both the prestige and familiarity with the novel, but more importantly, the considerable influence that the film has had on subsequent adaptations of the novel[2]. The reasons

---

[1] George Bluestone, while admiring of many aspect of the film adaptation, remarks that what transpires in the adaptation is that Brontë's story is forced into "a conventional Hollywood mould, the story of the stable boy and the lady" (99).

[2] Dudley Andrew uses the term "borrowing" in his discussion of film adaptation of literature where a well-known novel or play is the source of the adaptation. The gain from this, he argues, is that "the adapter hopes to win an audience for the adaptation by the prestige of its borrowed title or subject" (30).

for the film's success, particularly in its social and cultural context, is beyond the scope of this paper, but it is probably fair to say that one of the dominant images is that of Heathcliff and Catherine silhouetted against Penistone Crag, which was used as the poster for the film. This succinctly encapsulates the popular view of the pair of lovers as possessing a "cosmic, elemental dimension" (above 17) which is reflected in and by the surrounding landscape, as well as the "twin soul theme" (ibid.) which is contrasted with those other romantic lovers, Tristan and Isolde, with whom Catherine and Heathcliff are often compared[3]. Ironically, there is very little actual description of the two characters out of doors in the novel, and nature is not nearly as omnipresent as is the popular perception, but as Stoneman amusingly observes, the picture of Catherine and Heathcliff

> silhouetted against the sky which represents their mutual aspiration, has become a visual emblem of what the novel 'means'. By 1989 it was so well known that Monty Python's Flying Circus could assume that two lovers on a hilltop constituted a cultural icon to which a mass audience would respond. (127)

Stoneman cites Umberto Eco's argument that an image like this, "which becomes a repeated motif in the film, and was extracted from it for publicity purposes", becomes what Eco calls an 'intertextual archetype' – which has "the magic quality of a frame which, when separated from the whole, transforms the movie into a cult object" (127). Stoneman further notes that in dealing with a poster of the film adaptation of an earlier, written text,

> we have the added separation of film from written text. The still photograph transforms the original text in significant ways; it gives visual shape to the image which remains implicit in the novel, of Catherine and Heathcliff out of doors as adults, and it presents them in a pose and a physical situation which invites our direct participation in their experience and implicitly denies the existence of the framing, judging voices of the novel. (127-128)

As Stoneman concludes, "certain mythic texts become reduced, in the process of retelling, to their simplest memorable patterns", which become instantly recognisable for the audience. This aspect, in the case of the novel, "derives more from the Hollywood film than the original text" (129). In fact, the novel refuses to provide this image and this constitutes one of the many 'gaps' in the text. These observations are

---

[3] See Bernhart "From Novel to Song via Myth: *Wuthering Heights* as a Case of Popular Intermedial Adaptation" in this volume.

an illustration of what Walter Bernhart describes as the '*Stoff*' element in the process of intermedial transposition. In this process, Bernhart argues,

> [w]hat survives – if it *does* survive – is a *Stoff* in the form of a 'myth' or an 'icon' quite independent of its earlier literary manifestation, and frequently users of myths are quite unaware of their literary origins. (Above 24)

What is particularly interesting in the case of this image is that this 'Stoff' does not actually exist in the original literary work but has become embedded in popular imagination as a result of the Wyler adaptation. The film has created this powerful visual, not literary image, which most viewers assume originates in the novel, and which has become for many the dominant image of the novel and, as I shall discuss, is replicated in the two operatic adaptations of the novel[4]. Significantly, another image from the film which does not have an equivalent in the novel – Heathcliff with Catherine at the open window moments before her death – has also been incorporated into the dramaturgy of both operas, and this will serve as the basis of later discussion.

Furthermore, the relentless focus of the film on the two main characters to the virtual exclusion of all the other concerns of the novel, has influenced countless later adaptations for stage and screen[5]. The two operatic versions are by the American composers Carlisle

---

[4] George Bluestone, discussing film adaptation of novels, insists that the filmist does not adapt the novel but creates "a kind of paraphrase": the novel is "viewed as raw material". What remains are "characters and incidents which have somehow detached themselves from language and, like the heroes of folk legends, have achieved a mythic life of their own". (62) Stam, in his discussion of 'fidelity', however, warns of assuming that a novel contains an "extractable 'essence'", which he describes as a "kernel of meaning or nucleus of events that can be 'delivered' by an adaptation". He sees the literary text as an "open structure […] to be reworked by a boundless context. The text feeds on and is fed into an infinitely permutating intertext, which is seen through ever-shifting grids of interpretation." (57)

[5] Stoneman maintains that both operatic versions of *Wuthering Heights* "confirm, at the level of 'high culture' (but not so high as to be rejected by their audiences), the message of the film, namely, that this is a tragedy entirely focused on Catherine and Heathcliff, deriving from a mistaken marriage choice and gaining its intensity from the association of the adult lovers with the realm of nature". (166) I would argue that the version by Floyd has less of the relentless focus on the two protagonists but engages more fully with wider social issues.

Floyd (1958) and Bernard Herrmann (1965) respectively[6]. Neither, unfortunately, is part of the current operatic repertoire, but Herrmann's work has been commercially recorded, and Floyd's work was broadcast and has received several new productions – certainly not the norm in terms of contemporary opera!

A comparative analysis of the two operatic versions of *Wuthering Heights* offers some interesting insights into the discursive and adaptive practices of two post-war operatic composers, both strongly influenced by the conventions of romantic opera as well as contemporary trends, but composers who were certainly not part of the operatic avant-garde at the time of the composition of these two operas. Herrmann's opera falls strongly in the tradition of the 'number' opera, as evidenced by the many songs and closed musical forms which he employs. Floyd's opera, however, follows a divergent operatic tradition with its origin in the seamless music dramas of Wagner in which the division into discrete 'numbers' is concealed or disappears completely. This, of course, has been the dominant operatic form of the twentieth century. However, unlike Wagner, he makes extensive use of ensembles which grow organically from the dramatic situation. These two operas can, therefore, be regarded as representative of two major yet divergent operatic forms of the twentieth century, and both are early examples of a powerful trend in contemporary opera that was little apparent at the time of their composition: a movement away from atonalism and serialism towards what has subsequently sometimes been described as American *verismo* – a neo-romantic idiom which characterises much contemporary American opera[7]. In this paper I will focus on two scenes – the prologue and the closing scene – from both operas respectively, as these scenes seem to me to encapsulate much of the essence of both operas as well as illustrate some of the significant influence, particularly the dominant visual

---

[6] Herrmann is, of course, mainly celebrated as one of the most innovative and successful of film composers. Floyd is one of America's most productive operatic composers – his opera, *Susannah* (1955), is regarded as an American 'classic' and has a constant presence on American opera stages.

[7] Of course one cannot ignore the advent of minimalism, as exemplified by composers such as John Adams and Philip Glass, as an increasingly prominent operatic idiom which has added an important new and 'accessible' element into contemporary opera.

image discussed above, that the film has had on the final structure of both works.

Brontë's novel occupies a unique place in English literature and the difficulty in situating it comfortably within a narrowly-defined genre of the novel has long been recognised. Part of the problem from the beginning has been whether to regard it as a novel at all, and some have argued that it is more closely linked with the tradition of the tale, ballad and romance rather than the novel[8]. Of course there is much common ground between characters in romance and those in opera, a genre with its own origins traceable in romance and myth. Just as in opera, the novel can be seen as a work which combines within itself a number of different conventions.

The influence of German literature on Brontë's novel, particularly the works of E. T. A. Hoffmann, has frequently been noted, and this adumbrates another aspect of its suitability for operatic adaptation[9]. This period of European literature is also a significant source for the German *Singspiel* which strongly influenced composers such as Weber and Wagner[10]. One could argue that the novel's multiple literary antecedents assist the potential operatic adaptor in that these various literary genres have their loose equivalents in the multiplicity of styles and operatic discourses on which a contemporary operatic composer can draw and which constitute the operatic tradition. In both operatic adaptations of *Wuthering Heights* there are aspects of the drama of Verdi, the romanticism of Weber and Wagner, the lyricism of Puccini, and the tortured emotional outbursts of Berg, as well

---

[8] Cf. Frye (304-305).

[9] Cf. Knoepflmacher (28).

[10] Lyn Pykett perhaps best summarises the transgeneric nature of the novel: "*Wuthering Heights* straddles literary traditions and genres. It combines elements of the Romantic tale of evil-possession, and Romantic developments of the eighteenth-century Gothic novel, with the developing Victorian tradition of domestic fiction in a realist mode. Its use of ballad and folk material, romance forms and the fantastic, its emphasis on the passions, its view of childhood, and the representation of the Romantic quest for selfhood and of aspiring individualism, all link the novel with Romanticism. On the other hand, the novel's movement towards a renewed emphasis on community and duty, and towards an idealization of the family, seems to be more closely related to the emerging concerns of Victorian fiction. Emily Brontë's novel mixes these various traditions in a number of interesting ways, sometimes fusing and sometimes juxtaposing them." (73-74)

as a broader reflection of nearly four hundred years of operatic development. As previously suggested, there is also an evident reaction to the relentless high modernism of the post-Second World War avant-garde, particularly in its operatic manifestation.

Arising from the novel's heterogeneity and resistance to categorisation is its ability to resist any final interpretation[11]. A pervasive sense of some indefinable trans-generic primal energy – the *Stoff* – has surely contributed to the wide appeal of the novel and been a primary inspiration for its frequent adaptation into other genres. The amoral energy emanating from a character such as Heathcliff can be seen as essentially operatic in nature. An archetypal operatic character such as Don Giovanni, who functions as a disruptive yet fascinating force in Mozart's opera, has many parallels with the presentation of Heathcliff in the novel who, like Giovanni, resists to the end any form of repentance while retaining much of his appeal. Brontë's depiction of Heathcliff's relationship with Catherine has many essentially operatic elements as well, not the least being its embodiment of an intense, transcendental passion. Opera thrives on such relationships, and one needs only to look at some of the relationships in the operas of Wagner to find parallels with Catherine and Heathcliff (for example, the dubious relationship between Siegmund and Sieglinde in *Die Walküre*, not to mention Tristan and Isolde)[12].

---

[11] Graham Holderness remarks that without that "potentiality for plurality of meaning, the novel would not be able to survive beyond its own historical and cultural context" (83). Knoepflmacher maintains that while the Victorians tried "to tame the energies they recognize[d]", the modern trend is to "stress the novel's anarchic or libidinal powers", and it is surely these powers that have been the inspiration for adaptators. (108)

[12] Stoneman observes that the novel "has taken its place not only among the world's great love stories, but amidst our cultural heritage; the Hollywood hype, moreover, is not so far from the given structures of high culture. Olivier dying on Catherine's grave joins Tristan, who gains Isolde only in death, and Onegin, who dies for love of an inaccessible Tatiana; in each case the lamented woman is *la princesse lointaine*, held within the fastness of a husband's grasp. Sam Goldwyn may have been crude in expression, but he was in tune with the feeling of the age when he tried to call his film 'He Died for Her'." (133-134) However, Bluestone argues that the "theme of spiritual identity which, by later implication, cannot be fully realized until the soul is free of corporeal entrapment, is not sustained in the film version" (100). Herbert Lindenberger sees within Gothic fiction a reflection of the 'high style' which is so characteristic of opera, a style from which, with the exception of works such as *Wuthering*

Two essential elements of nineteenth-century romantic opera, Gothicism and melodrama, are also strongly evident in Brontë's novel. Despite much detailed description which gives the novel a concreteness and actuality over and above its metaphysical quality, its larger-than-life central characters are the life-blood of opera. Not only does the portrayal of Catherine have elements of the Gothic, but Heathcliff too is represented in a number of ways as a Gothic villain[13].

Of course the story of Heathcliff and Catherine is well known even to those who have not read the novel. Stoneman remarks that Wyler in his film creates a myth of "star-crossed lovers, who would willingly conform, by marrying, if only society would let them." (132) Interestingly, a popular twentieth-century novel, Daphne Du Maurier's *Rebecca* (1938), which owes much to the Gothic elements of its models, *Wuthering Heights* and *Jane Eyre*, has, in addition to the hugely popular film version, also been successfully adapted as an opera[14].

Within the pervasive Gothicism of the novel, its distinctively melodramatic quality goes a long way to explaining its relatively easy transformation into the profoundly melodramatic world of opera[15]. The melodramatic exaggeration and distortion inherent in the novel

---

Heights, literature has generally retreated: "the one form of fiction that pursued the high style systematically in the last two centuries was the Gothic novel, which, like opera, was a popular form whose public recognized its artifice and its distance from ordinary life, on the one hand, and, on the other, its power and immediacy of effect". (167)

[13] Pykett describes him as a "demonic, almost otherworldly figure" and remarks that this "fantastic, demonic version of Heathcliff is reinforced by the melodramatic scenes surrounding Catherine's death", particularly the last part of the novel where he appears to be "communing with the spirit of the dead Catherine in preparation for a removal to her sphere" (75-76). Bluestone argues that the filmmakers used "passion rather than brutality to advance their story line" but this forced them to face the problem of "how to transform the demonic Heathcliff into a conventional hero" for the film audience of the time. (108)

[14] Wilfred Josephs's opera, *Rebecca*, was premiered in Leeds in 1983. There has also been a recent operatic version of *Jane Eyre* by Michael Berkeley and David Malouf which was premiered in 2000 at the Cheltenham International Festival of Music and has also been recorded. (See Bernhart 2007)

[15] Peter Brooks remarks that life, in this kind of fiction, tends "toward ever more concentrated and totally expressive gestures and statements" (4).

accord well with operatic discourse. Probably the most important factor in terms of the novel's operatic viability lies in the presentation of the two central characters, as well as the triangular conflict between Catherine, Heathcliff and Edgar, which, of course, reflects the typically melodramatic operatic confrontation between soprano heroine, tenor lover, and baritone villain, with the soprano heroine as victim. Catherine Clément (33), in describing the subjugation of women in opera, locates the source of the soprano voice in "paternal violation", and the soprano thus inevitably in the role of victim. Therefore, it seems appropriate that both operatic adaptations under consideration here cast the role of Catherine with a lyric soprano thus situating her in a long line of soprano heroines/victims who die at the end of the opera[16].

Brontë's Heathcliff combines both Byronic and romantic elements with aspects of the demonic – an almost 'operatic' mixture of Othello, Don Giovanni, Mephistopheles and Iago! Heathcliff can also be seen as a threat from the 'outsider' to the family unit which receives him with violence and which will be the recipient of violence from him[17]. This 'outsider' figure has a long history in opera, featuring particularly in several Verdi and Wagner operas, for example, and embodied in two major twentieth-century operatic characters: Wozzeck and Peter Grimes. Both operatic versions of *Wuthering Heights*, significantly, cast Heathcliff with a baritone, the medium and lower voices usually being both the preserve of the villain as well as occasionally, the lover[18]. His vocal line in both operas lies relatively high, partially approximating that of the tenor. The brilliance of the high notes, but the general 'darkness' of this vocal range combines both the power

---

[16] Both operas also cast Isabella as a soprano – somewhat unusual to have two soprano leads – and their 'roles' are considerably expanded in importance when compared with the character's role in the novel.

[17] Holderness describes the popular conception of the Byronic figure as someone, "usually a wanderer, exiled from his native land, bearing the burden of some enormously wicked but nameless and mysterious crime [....] an early example of [...] an 'anti-hero' [...] a rebel, a criminal, a transgressor of moral codes and social conventions [....] embod[ying] an important experience of alienation, self-conscious separation from social norms, rejection of moral and social convention" (20).

[18] This accords with Pykett's view of Heathcliff in the novel as being "at once hero and villain, the oppressed and the oppressor, who is simultaneously the bearer of the novel's progressive forces and the embodiment of its contradictions" (113).

and virility of the romantic aspect of Heathcliff while emphasising the menace and ruthlessness which is traditionally the preserve of the lower voices.

It is obvious that the intrinsic dramatic qualities of the novel have long been recognised as evidenced by its many theatrical adaptations[19]. The author does not intrude and the novel combines the objectivity of impersonal narrative with the subjectivity of the first person. In a sense the subject of the novel is the act of narration itself. This curious mixture of subjectivity and objectivity in the novel parallels an important aspect of the nature of operatic discourse. Opera is perhaps unique in offering a synthesis of the apparently objective presentation of 'action' on stage in combination with the perception of an almost novelistic subjectivity created through the music, and can be seen as musical novel rather than musical drama; in some ways opera more effectively deals with psychological action rather than with physical action[20]. The complexity of the novel's discourse in which realistic details are evoked but which exist alongside romantic excess is immediately apparent. This is a central tension in opera where realism is striven for in many productions in terms of the staging, while the intrinsically 'artificial' nature of the genre itself resists this urge to realistic representation. One could argue that it is

---

[19] Hewish (141) observes that in *Wuthering Heights* "there is no direct comment by the author and a minimum of reflection divorced from action as 'scene' follows 'scene' and the characters are hastened to their various fates. There is nothing like this in nineteenth-century literature until Ibsen" (141). Allen relates this dramatic quality in the novel to the narrative method employed: "The device of plunging us into the action while it is well under way is as old as epic, but it always dramatizes it and keys up the suspense: our curiosity is piqued as Lockwood's was. We are compelled to identify ourselves with Lockwood, and the effect of our seeing everything partly through his eyes and partly through Nelly Dean's is, as it were, to see the action framed, almost as though on a stage." (198) According to Holderness, the self-conscious narrative method involves, on the one hand, an "emphasis on the devices of story-telling", and on the other, a story in which "every word is spoken by a character in the story" (5). Bluestone notes the fact that (as in the operatic adaptations) half the book has been cut in the film but, paradoxically, "roughly thirty new scenes [...] appear in the screen version" (94).

[20] See Halliwell, 1999. Robert Stam describes cinema as "both a synesthetic and a synthetic art, synesthetic in its capacity to engage various senses (sight and hearing) and synthetic in its anthropophagic capacity to absorb and synthesize antecedent arts" (58).

this tension which frequently enables the successful operatic adaptation of those works of fiction which are characterised by ambiguity and which are more difficult to adapt to the more 'literal' genres of the spoken stage and film[21].

* * *

Bernard Herrmann's *Wuthering Heights*, with libretto by Lucille Fletcher (Herrmann's wife), was completed in 1965, but only received its first staging in 1982[22]. It is divided into four acts and a prologue, and has, as epigraph, a quotation from Matthew Arnold:

> Unquiet souls!
> In the dark fermentation of earth,
> In the never idle workshop of nature,
> In the eternal movement,
> Ye shall find yourselves again!

Indeed, the whole flavour of the opera is self-consciously 'literary' or even 'poetic', librettist Fletcher having used much of the dialogue from the novel itself, modifying it only occasionally when absolutely necessary from a dramaturgical point of view. Fletcher has, furthermore, skilfully integrated several of Emily Brontë's poems into the opera, particularly when an aria or extended set-piece is called for, including one of her best-known poems, "Love and Friendship".

Carlisle Floyd's version, with libretto by the composer, was first performed in Santa Fe in 1958 and was revised in 1959 for performances at the New York City Opera. Consisting of a prologue and three acts, it is a gritty, 'veristic' version of the novel, retaining much of its plot structure and focusing strongly on its inherent conflicts. The opera has a libretto that is far less self-consciously poetic than that of Herrmann and makes much use of the text of the novel. It

---

[21] I have argued that opera is particularly suited to the adaptation of the fiction of Henry James which is characterised by a similar combination of melodrama and ambiguity as *Wuthering Heights* (cf. 2005). Lucasta Miller describes the ambiguity inherent in the novel and concludes that it is "this lack of closure that makes *Wuthering Heights* such a haunting book" (231).

[22] Stoneman notes that Lucille Fletcher claimed that Herrmann started working on the opera in the 1940s, "inspired directly" by Wyler's film, stating that "we more or less followed the adaptation used in the 1939 movie" (168). Herrmann was working on a film score for *Jane Eyre* in 1943, the date on the manuscript score of his opera.

retains many of the theatrically effective incidents that occur in the first part of the novel and is characterized by a less lyrical but more flexible musical language, and is structured in generally shorter and more swiftly-moving scenes than Herrmann's work[23].

Both operas follow the outline of the 'first' part of the story fairly closely and, in this, follow the outline of the film as well. The particular difficulty that any dramatic stage adaptation faces is that it is problematic to depict the lapse of time that is an important feature of the novel. In this the film is more successful as different actors are used to portray the young Catherine and Heathcliff. Their early developing relationship is not depicted in either opera and the events of the story 'proper' are picked up just before the disappearance of Heathcliff, a point where their relationship is already established.

It is remarkable how similar in structure, if not in musical idiom, these two operas are; it is the architecture of the novel combined with the influence of operatic convention which finally determines the dramaturgy. The dominant feature of the central act in both operas is an extended aria for Catherine, a fact which is dictated by the importance of the speech in the novel on which it is based, and which culminates in Catherine's exclamation: "I *am* Heathcliff", as well as its obvious verbal and dramatic suitability for operatic treatment (and the necessity for an extended 'set-piece' for the female protagonist). It is a moment of great crisis in the novel and a turning-point in the narrative: one of the two central characters disappears for three years and the circumstances at both Wuthering Heights and Thrushcross Grange change. The relationship between Heathcliff and Catherine is at a point of crisis and, in theatrical terms, the disappearance of Heathcliff and Catherine's anguish after her revelatory aria are emotional and dramatic highpoints and accord with the operatic convention of ending the central act with a suitably theatrical flourish, much in the style

---

[23] Naturally, the complexity of the narrative structure of the novel presents particular difficulties for operatic adaptation and a full analysis is beyond the scope of this essay. Terry Eagleton, in describing the complex narrative method of "texts-within-texts, narratives of narratives": explains the novel's form as "rigorously 'framed' in more than one sense of the term, by the dominative narrative control of Nelly herself. To narrate is to exercise power, not least when, as with Nelly, it involves a tendentious editing and revising of others' interpretations [...] Heathcliff, the 'Romantic' voice of the text, is himself 'uttered' and encompassed by that very different voice of sober bourgeois realism which is Nelly's." (xi-xii)

of nineteenth-century opera. Here both operas depart most radically from the novel as we are able to enter the mind of the character, which we never do to the same extent in the novel, and not at all in the film[24].

Particularly in Floyd's opera, the latent sexual passion which is never overtly depicted in the novel could be seen to find expression both visually (in the stage directions) and in the music which seems to be 'stating' what is only implicit in the novel. This is most apparent at the end of Act One where Heathcliff has been beaten by Hindley and his injuries are bathed by Catherine. The stage direction seems clear:

> As she continues to bathe him, Cathy begins to cry. Only her shoulders betray her tears. Then, she deliberately sets the cloth on the bowl, sits back on her heels, and, with her eyes closed against the tears which streak her face, she lifts her arms and slowly begins taking down her hair. An expression of infinite tenderness and gratitude comes into Heathcliff's eyes as her hair falls, dark and lustrous, to her shoulders. (107)

While the actions remain ambiguous, it is the warmth and intensity of the music which seems to powerfully convey the strength of the attraction between the two. This appears to follow the film where a similar physical attraction between them is frequently apparent. However, it can be argued that in the opera this is not explicitly conveyed as 'straightforward' sexual attraction and could be a representation of a relationship aptly described by Lucasta Miller as "far from the norm of adult heterosexuality": a relationship that is never consummated as it is "incapable of consummation, since it reaches back to the childhood time before the fall into self and other when Cathy and Heathcliff were surrogate brother and sister" (242). In the opera the music is bound up with the visual aspect but it is through the music that much of this relationship is established. However, the nature of this

---

[24] Indeed, in Herrmann's opera, at the end of Act Three there is a form of 'mad scene' for Catherine which owes much to the *bel canto* tradition. Both operas also make use of the scene of Catherine's delirium from the novel, and the film script had a similar scene which Bluestone describes as "reminiscent of the mad Ophelia; the feathers are Cathy's rosemary and columbine" (105). Bluestone notes Goldwyn's objection to this scene and argues that the film "is content merely with establishing the fact that Cathy is ill". He observes that the "significance of Cathy's self-imposed death, the *rendition* of it, which runs to some sixty pages in the novel, appears nowhere in the final movie version" (105).

relationship remains ambiguous as music does not possess the necessary specificity to dispel potential ambiguity[25].

In contemplating the novel as suitable for operatic adaptation it is immediately apparent that the complexity of the narrative structure of the novel presents particular difficulties[26]. Lockwood, who appears to be a conventional first-person narrator, is soon revealed to be an unreliable observer: he makes a series of mistakes in his initial encounter with Wuthering Heights and its inhabitants and his own perceptions are shown to be coloured by his assumptions and prejudices. Both Lockwood and Nelly appear to be 'normal', common-sense observers, but they are revealed as inadequate to their task.

It is virtually impossible to indicate in an opera in the same way as the novel that Lockwood is the initial narrator, that the narrative has various levels, or, indeed, that the narration passes from one character to another. In operatic terms we have a single narrator – the orchestra – and all complexities must be suggested by that single, albeit powerful narrative 'voice', and all characters are contained within this narrative act[27]. Obviously most of the effect and significance of the juxtaposed narrative levels, as well as much of the ambiguity and intricacy of the novel's narrative method itself, has had of necessity to be sacrificed. Herrmann has Lockwood already in Wuthering Heights as his opera opens, while Floyd depicts him "lurching and staggering" (2) up to the front door of the house, very similar to the opening of the

---

[25] Of course film frequently uses the music soundtrack for similar purposes, but characters in film are not 'immersed' in or 'constructed' by the music in the same way as in opera.

[26] Bluestone argues that the "density which Emily Brontë achieves by having Ellen function both as narrator and as actor at one and the same time is impossible in the film" (107). Shlomith Rimmon-Kenan's typology of narrators is useful in distinguishing the narrative function of the various narrators in the novel. Lockwood, who narrates the events which constitute the novel while also participating in these events, would be considered an "intradiegetic" narrator of the second degree. Nelly, who narrates the bulk of the events to Lockwood, but who is, in turn, 'narrated' by Lockwood, is a narrator of the third-degree – a "hypodiegetic" narrator. The other narrators: Catherine, Heathcliff, Isabella and Cathy, who narrate their own stories to Nelly, must be considered narrators of the fourth-degree: "hypo-hypodiegetic" narrators (94-96).

[27] See Halliwell, 1999.

film[28]. Lockwood's initial impressions are of great importance to the reader as he has a tendency to misinterpret what he sees and hears.

Herrmann has a brief orchestral prelude which functions as a narrative device. It deploys themes and musical figures, the significance of which later become apparent in the opera, in very much the way a narrator would set the scene in the opening of a novel which would then be expanded later. The vast dynamic range of the operatic discourse of the first two pages can be seen as a correlative of the emotional range of the novel.

Unlike Herrmann, who starts *in medias res* with Lockwood already describing his arrival and reception from Heathcliff, Floyd is intent on setting the scene more fully from the beginning. His opening pages have less of Herrmann's ominously portentous quality and there is the strong sense of a forward impulse in the structure of the music. Lockwood's arrival is accompanied by typically energetic music. Of interest is the fact that both librettists impose radical changes on the chronology of the novel: this scene is supposed to take place in 1801 but the stage direction in Floyd's opera describes it as a "winter evening in 1835" (1). According to the chronological structure of the novel, Isabella would have been dead four years (June, 1797) by the time Lockwood arrived at the house. As becomes apparent, Floyd has updated the setting some thirty-four years. (Fletcher's libretto states that her first scene takes place in 1840, indicating that the Prologue occurs twenty years later: 1860). Having Isabella there, however, makes good theatrical sense as well as creating a more theatrically viable role as the audience's knowledge of her 'present' situation will colour their reaction to the 'earlier' events of the opera which are still to be depicted.

Floyd overcomes the difficulties inherent in staging Lockwood's dream by having him being offered a blanket by the fire. The 'problem' of effectively conveying the crucial information contained in Catherine's diary is 'solved' by Isabella offering Lockwood "some books ... if you can't sleep", after which he "crosses to the window-seat and gets under the blanket" (11). Herrmann's opera follows the novel closely in that Lockwood's discovery of Catherine's diary

---

[28] This is significant. Kavanagh describes entrances as being very important in the wider context of the novel and observes that "our entrance to the novel coincides with Lockwood's entrance to Wuthering Heights" (17).

appears coincidental, although neither opera uses Lockwood's reading of the three names, "Catherine Earnshaw, Catherine Heathcliff, Catherine Linton", or his subsequent brief dream. Floyd also has Lockwood idly paging through several books until his eyes light on one which "arrests his attention". Herrmann has Lockwood intone his reading of the diary, initially on a repeated note, gradually falling in semitones. When he starts the account of Hindley's ill-treatment of Heathcliff, the singer is urged to "evoke the feeling that Cathy's grief still hauntingly pervades the room" and the musical indication for the following text is described as *andante con tristezza*, the voice supported by a plaintive string melody in the orchestra.

> How little did I dream that Hindley would ever make me cry. Poor Heathcliff! Hindley calls him a vagabond, and says we must not play together, and threatens to turn him out of the house ... Poor Heathcliff, my dearest one, goodnight. (9)

Here one sees an example of the voice not being used for verbal signification only, but the emphasis lying more on the utilisation of the quality of the singer's voice to create atmosphere. Floyd, however, has Lockwood speak his text from the diary:

> Tomorrow I shall become the bride of Edgar Linton and will leave my beloved Wuthering Heights to live with him and his sister, Isabella, at Thrushcross Grange. Edgar is sweet and gentle and loves me more than his own life and Isabella is pretty and worships me but she is very spoiled. I should be happy tonight but my heart is like lead. Heathcliff, where are you? Where are you? You are more myself than I am and you have left me. How am I to live without ... Heathcliff, wherever you are, come back! (13-14)

The text is spoken over a sparse musical accompaniment that gradually becomes more expressive and agitated, culminating in the sound of the wind outside. The orchestra, however, generally plays a more subservient role when compared with the equivalent moment in Herrmann.

One can perhaps draw some analogies regarding the narrative methods of the two composers. Herrmann seems to have responded to Lockwood as focaliser – the musical impulse seems to originate in his perception of the situation and frequently arises out of his description of his reactions and situation, while Floyd's method could be compared, in a limited way, to that of an authorial narrator who is, in a sense, 'above' the scene. Floyd distorts the chronology somewhat as Cathy's diary entries in the novel occur long before her marriage to Edgar. However, having Cathy voice her misgivings about her impending marriage functions proleptically as subsequent events in the opera are coloured for the audience by this knowledge.

Musically the methods of the two composers again differ significantly. Herrmann uses a rather lugubrious melody for Lockwood's reading from the diary. Floyd, however, has Lockwood speak his lines against an orchestral accompaniment – much in the tradition of melodrama. The musical discourse up to this point in Floyd's opera had been dominated by a flexible melodic recitative and this interruption of the dominant discourse and intrusion of a new discursive effect heightens the dramatic presentation of the information contained in the diary (as well as making it completely understandable for the audience). We are made both visually and aurally aware that this is a diary entry with the added advantage of the intelligibility of a spoken text. Paradoxically, these moments of apparent musical stasis or even absence, either where the vocal utterance reverts to speech, or more particularly when the orchestral accompaniment altogether ceases, can also be seen as dramatic climaxes. These discursive shifts arrest the audience's attention and signal the importance of this particular dramatic moment. As well, the importance of the text is underlined by this change in mode which, through juxtaposition, deliberately 'points' that particular section of text – a device frequently employed in opera.

The methods used by the two composers to suggest the ghostly presence of Catherine also differ significantly. Herrmann uses predominantly orchestral means to indicate this collision of the real and the supernatural (as a composer renowned for his film-scores for Alfred Hitchcock such as *Psycho, Vertigo, Marnie,* and *The Man Who Knew Too Much,* effects such as these pose few problems). He employs drum-rolls followed by jagged orchestral outbursts to create an ominous feeling of suspense, very much in the idiom of film music. The visual images he stipulates remain rather vague – the stage directions state that the "fir-tree outside the lattice window throws grotesque shadows about the room – its branches wildly tossed by the storm, rattle against the panes" (10). Rather than attempting to stage this visitation, Herrmann has Lockwood cry out in his sleep, uttering broken phrases that suggest what he is experiencing: "No...No... Begone Catherine Earnshaw. Begone! No! Not for twenty years! No! Take your hand away" (11-12). Lockwood finally screams out in terror and "in great agitation awakes and rushes to the window and peers searchingly into the storm" (12). Heathcliff immediately storms in and Lockwood recounts what has happened (his words taken verbatim from Chapter Three), but with Heathcliff as his audience:

> I was lying there. I heard the gusty wind and the driving of the snow. I heard the fir-bough repeat its teasing sound. And I must have dreamt, but it seemed to me I rose and tried to unhasp the casement. The hook was soldered to the staple. Knocking my knuckles through the glass, and stretching an arm out to seize the branch, my fingers closed on an ice-cold hand ... I tried to draw back my arm, but the hand clung to it, and a voice sobbed – "Let me in. Let me in." "Who are you?" I asked. Catherine Linton. I've come home. I've lost my way on the moor." As it spoke, I saw a child's face looking through the window ... Terror made me cruel. I pulled its wrist onto the broken pane, and rubbed it to and fro, till the blood ran down, and the fingers relaxed. "Begone!" I shouted. "Begone. I'll never let you in. Not if you beg for twenty years." (15-19)

Comparing the narrative method at this point in the novel with that in the opera, we see that Lockwood in the novel recounts his experience to the 'implied reader' who functions as his 'audience'. Lockwood uses a mixture of direct speech and descriptive passages which the librettist then adapts fully into direct speech but significantly retaining the occasional reporting verbs, which enhance the narrational aspects of this experience with Heathcliff (and the 'real' audience) as the fascinated listener.

This is an example of what Carolyn Abbate describes as "a subject's distancing reformulation [...] the ordering and reordering discourse of a subject-voice" (26). This narrative process Abbate explains further as "the composer's silhouetting of a phenomenal object" and poses the question whether the music itself can be said to be narrative "or does the narrative quality not instead reside in what is adjunct or outside the music, the thing that the music traces?" (27) Much operatic discourse would fall into this latter category as the musical accompaniment can be seen in effect to be 'tracing' the physical events depicted by the characters on stage. Yet, paradoxically, these characters are themselves 'narrated' by the music; in this sense operatic discourse can be regarded as essentially diegetic[29]. This is an aspect of operatic discourse that has become characteristic of much

---

[29] See Halliwell, 1999. One could argue that the actors on stage in opera are part of what is known in narratology as the 'surface structure', while the orchestra-narrator could be seen as the 'actant': as at the level of narrative 'deep structure'. See Prince (1).

twentieth-century opera where frequently this 'tracing' of events by the musical accompaniment can become mannered and often an end in itself. Opera has tended to oscillate between two poles of musical representation: from the one extreme of *bel canto* melody or highly decorated, virtuosic *fioritura*, which, superficially, appears to have little to do with the drama of the situation, to the opposite extreme of music imitating and underlining every action on stage where the vocal line approximates the inflections and rhythms of speech. There is the danger of creating what Joseph Kerman ironically describes as "enervated" music which "contorts itself so strenuously at every detail of action that one loses interest in discriminating between the tremendously dramatic, the stupendously dramatic, and the merely earth-shakingly dramatic" (222).

The violence of Lockwood's reaction to his dream in the novel has frequently been noted[30]. The two dreams in the novel each function in a different way: the first being seen as a 'realistic' and hardly a disturbing one, while the second is one that seems almost genuinely supernatural[31]. Herrmann demands that the singer imitate the voice of Catherine "in a ghostly voice – quasi falsetto", the vocal effect being bizarre and estranging with a certain, unfortunate, comic element as well.

Floyd opts for the more theatrical (yet perhaps more difficult to achieve) depiction of what actually happens during the dream. The stage directions state that

> the shutter of the window above the window-seat bangs against the pane. Lockwood starts and raises himself to a sitting position. As the banging continues, Lockwood gets to his knees and raises the window to fasten the shutter. As he does so, a chalk-white hand and arm reach through the open space and the outstretched fingers convulsively clutch at the warm air of the room. Lockwood screams and jerks away from the window. Then there is the unearthly sound of a woman's voice, near, then distant, like the sound of wind. (15)

All this occurs to the accompaniment of rushing scales in the orchestra. The actual physical depiction of what happens is perhaps more effective in Floyd's opera than Lockwood's account of his dream in

---

[30] See Van Ghent (177), Knoepflmacher (90) and Kavanagh (22).

[31] Lucasta Miller argues that this is the "most memorable ghost scene in literature" and its success "depends in part on its ambivalence: we are left in a radically unsettled state of not knowing whether the ghost is real – as Heathcliff wants to believe – or a dream" (231).

Herrmann's opera in that, as well as the brevity he achieves in physical representation as opposed to narration, Floyd actually uses the voice of Cathy rather than the slightly grotesque effect of a bass voice imitating a female voice, which Herrmann calls for. The sound of Cathy's voice is also 'fixed' in the audience's aural memory even though ghost-like effects are used to 'estrange' it somewhat. Floyd also has Lockwood briefly recount to Heathcliff what has happened, thus doubly reinforcing the impact of this event in the audience's minds and indirectly conveying an aspect of the narrative process of the novel.

The dramaturgy of the final part of the Prologues of both operas differs substantially. In Herrmann's opera Heathcliff wrenches the window open and calls out to Cathy (as in the novel). The composer uses thematic material which first occurred in the opening pages of the opera and which will again occur at the very end. In the conclusion of the Prologue to Herrmann's opera, the stage directions are explicit:

> Heathcliff holding the lantern aloft, vainly searches out into the storm. The winds echo his cries. The lantern light is blown out. Darkness engulfs the room, except for the window which remains constantly radiant through which the whirling snow can be seen. Only Heathcliff's silhouette is seen, as the curtain slowly falls. (23-24)

The question is left hanging in both operas: has there really been a ghost or is it a figment of Lockwood's imagination? Certainly the operatic 'reality' might seem to tend towards the authenticity of the ghost rather than suggesting Lockwood's ironic view, especially as the audience can hear a voice in Floyd's opera which seems to indicate a ghostly presence of some kind. However, the 'reality' of the portrayal of the ghost can depend greatly on the imaginative staging of this scene[32].

Both *Wuthering Heights* operas, of course, omit the last part of Chapter Three which deals with Lockwood's final hours at Wuthering

---

[32] In productions of Britten's *The Turn of the Screw*, for instance, where the physical presence of the ghosts appears to sacrifice some of the essential ambiguity of the tale, staging effects sometimes are used to suggest a view of the ghosts as manifestations of the governess's overheated mind. However, it can be argued that it is Britten's music in all its structural complexity which most effectively sustains this ambiguity. Miller argues that attempts to reproduce that essentially literary quality of this kind of ambiguity "in the cinema or on the stage have been fraught with difficulty" (231).

Heights and his return to the Grange; events which would not have added much to the theatrical effectiveness of these scenes. Herrmann has Heathcliff staring imploringly out of the "radiant" (23) window, a visual image that is restaged almost exactly at the end of the opera. The importance of the structural and symbolic use of windows in the novel has provoked much critical comment[33]. The window, of course, also acts as a frame – a visual representation of the complex literary framing devices that characterise this novel. As one shall see, the use of the window is of great significance in the film as well and, indeed, 'frames' the final image of the film.

Herrmann's Prologue conveys a similar sense of Heathcliff's realization that his identity lies outside in the storm rather than in the room with Lockwood – 'reality' is with Catherine, and Herrmann has obviously realized the drama inherent in ending the scene with Heathcliff calling out into the night after Cathy. In both operas, but more particularly in Herrmann's, the prologue acts as a formal framing device both musically and dramatically, with both visual images and motivic musical material being repeated at the end of the opera – an equivalent of Lockwood's 'framing' role in the novel.

Floyd has a different stage set design in mind and he exploits this by having Heathcliff rush out of the house in pursuit of this ghostly presence. We have the theatrically melodramatic image of Heathcliff standing, "arms outstretched, silhouetted against the sky over the moors" – an image that will also bring the curtain down at the end of the opera. Again there is a visual echo of the dominant image which emerges from the film. Herrmann's scene comes to a formal musical ending using musical material that will end the opera as well, thus sustaining the sense of a frame. Floyd employs the same whirling orchestral motifs during this action of Heathcliff's as those employed during Lockwood's earlier dream. These motifs continue without a break into the next scene, gradually modulating into lighter, more playful musical phrases and creating a stronger impression of the continuity of the action than Herrmann's closed-form Prologue – a dramaturgical illustration of the difference in overall conception of the essence of musical drama between these two operas. However, the frame-like construction of both of these operatic prologues incorporate a scene-setting function in much the same way as do the first

---

[33] See Van Ghent (178) and Vogler (12).

three chapters of the novel. Lockwood then disappears from both operas whereas in the novel he is still prominent but not as the primary narrator, a role he surrenders to Nelly.

Of course the limited knowledge to which each narrator is privy is difficult to suggest in a visual and aural medium such as opera and any ambiguity can only obliquely be suggested by the orchestra through technical devices such as tonal ambivalence and lack of musical resolution. Thus it is apparent that the narrative complexity of the novel is necessarily simplified for the different imperatives of the lyric stage.

* * *

Stoneman notes that in the first three weeks after the release of Wyler's film more copies of the novel were sold than in any five-year period since the novel's publication. The Pocket Book edition printed in 1939 has a cover illustration showing Heathcliff carrying Catherine to the open window to die. As Stoneman observes, "this scene, which does not appear in the novel, was nevertheless henceforth a part of the mythology of the story" (155). This is another example of Bernhart's concept of *Stoff* arising out of what in this case could be seen as an intentional 'misreading' of the novel. It is certainly one of the most enduring images from the film and has influenced both operatic adaptations as they both incorporate this 'mythical' scene into their dramaturgy.

The final scenes in the two operas are similar in many ways, both obviously following the film rather than the novel; the dominant and potent image being the death of Cathy and the despairing yet defiant Heathcliff alone on stage. Herrmann's opera has Cathy enter as Heathcliff is engrossed in staring out at the falling snow. (How the dying Cathy finds herself at Wuthering Heights is not explained, however, and does strain logical credibility.) Heathcliff tries to embrace her but she pulls away, singing his name on a familiar falling semitone phrase that has become directly linked with her, and he echoes her name using the same musical material. Cathy asks him to take her in his arms and she embraces him. The composer calls for a curious musical effect to illustrate how Cathy envisages the future once she is dead. The instruction: "to be sung in the manner of a plain chant", creates an estranging yet quasi-religious effect. The discursive shift at this stage results in the listener recognizing a musical style which may be extremely far removed from the operatic, however with its 'meaning' and purpose being immediately identifiable. This 'plain chant' passage functions proleptically – the words indicate the way Catherine sees the future after her death: the music has a dirge-like quality, powerfully suggestive of her approaching death. However, the 'normal' discourse is soon resumed with a passionate duet between Catherine and Heathcliff. Finally Heathcliff urges her, "Kiss me and don't let me see your eyes. I forgive what you have done to me" (238). They embrace as the sound of the intensifying storm, achieved both in the orchestra and through stage effects, grows louder. Catherine is drawn to the window and begs Heathcliff to open it: "Open the window. Let me breathe the wind. It comes straight from the moors." (239) She sees an escape beckoning to her as she sings of being "enclosed" in a "shattered prison". The window, which has functioned symbolically throughout, is the means of final escape for Catherine into that outside "glorious world". She envisages a final transcendent escape into this new world "incomparably beyond and above" all.

Heathcliff interrupts her and the scene nears its end with Catherine's final utterance. The music takes on a more tranquil character, conveying the final peace that she yearns for. There is a downward movement in Catherine's vocal line as her strength gradually ebbs – a typical romantic operatic trope. Heathcliff becomes aware that she is dead but he continues gazing into her face. Suddenly, he breaks the mood with a tormented outburst which gradually subsides, and slowly and solemnly he makes a vow:

> Catherine Earnshaw, may you not rest as long as I am living. You said I killed you. Haunt me, then! Be with me always! Take any form! Drive me mad! Only do not leave me in this abyss, where I cannot find you! Oh, God! I cannot live without my life. I cannot live without my soul! (246)

Then the sound of an off-stage organ is heard which accompanies a soprano voice also off-stage which "should match that of Cathy" to "create a supernatural effect" (248). Heathcliff rushes to the windows calling out into the storm, a direct repetition of his cries in the Prologue. The voice calls on Heathcliff to let it in while Heathcliff cries out for Catherine to come to him. The voice sings, "I have lost my way on the moors", and Heathcliff's final words gradually die away as the voice disappears. Heathcliff sinks down beside the window which "remains radiantly white with the swirling snow" (254), the final visual image in the opera being the glowing window. This ending, with its repetition of musical and visual motifs from the Prologue, frames the opera, which, in a sense, completes the circular structure.

Floyd's ending follows a somewhat different path. In contrast, it is set as in the novel, at Thrushcross Grange, seven months later (April, 1821). Herrmann obviously opted for the visual and dramatic symmetry inherent in having his final scene set at Wuthering Heights with its unmistakable echoes of the opening of the opera despite the dramatic implausibility. Floyd's ending has much more dramatic coherence and a stronger theatrical impact. In Floyd's final scene, the change in Catherine's appearance is sudden and startling; "her skin is ashen and there are hollows in her cheeks" (266) and it is apparent that she is close to giving birth. This follows the equivalent scene from the novel more closely than Herrmann. Floyd, however, also uses the same passage from the novel that Herrmann used and there is a wistful atmosphere, rather than a sense of a mental breakdown which Herrmann attempts to evoke. Her train of thought leads her to recall her days with Heathcliff on the moors and she pleads with Nelly to open the window. Nelly resists, remarking: "Be patient, now. You'll be delivered soon." Catherine's reply displays her state of mind: "I don't want this child; I only want to die!" (269)

Nelly realizes that the end is near and at that moment Heathcliff enters, enquiring from Nelly whether it is true that Catherine is sick. Nelly attempts to prevent Heathcliff from seeing her: "It could mean her life if she's excited at all! Would you kill her, Heathcliff?" (273), but Heathcliff strides into the living room and he and Catherine embrace rapturously. Her first concern is whether Heathcliff will remember her when she is dead. The music takes on a renewed intensity as Catherine, taking Heathcliff's face in her hands, sings: "I will die very soon. No don't protest. And before I die, I must tell you this: I've loved you and only you all my life." (275-276) The crux of this exchange occurs on her line, "I only want us together again and death is the only way I know" (277-278) – strongly suggestive of Wagner's *Tristan und Isolde*. As Nelly announces the arrival of Edgar, Catherine asks Heathcliff to take her to the door again to look at the moors. Heathcliff clasps her in his arms and flings the door open and, accompanied by warmly passionate music, Catherine sings ecstatically: "Oh,

Heathcliff, I can breathe again! My lungs are not enough to drink the air" (281) (both a musical and verbal echo of the earlier scene in the opera). Heathcliff sings a short expressive arioso which develops musically out of Catherine's previous music and is punctuated by words of affirmation from her.

Suddenly, there is a large downward leap in the vocal line suggestive of his disbelief as he realises that Catherine is dead (a similar musical trope to that used by Herrmann). He tenderly places Catherine down on the sofa as Nelly looks on and Edgar falls sobbing on her body. Heathcliff rushes from the room and the final visual image in the opera is of Heathcliff, "with arms upraised and fists clenched ... silhouetted against the sombre and cloud-massed sky":

> May you never find peace as long as I live. If I killed you then haunt me the rest of my life. Take any form, even drive me mad, but just don't leave me, don't leave me here! Haunt me, Cathy for the rest of my life! (287-288)

This is virtually the exact image that ended the Prologue of Floyd's opera, both Floyd and Herrmann achieving symmetry of visual and musical effects at the end of their respective operas. Of course this is an image which owes its origin to the film and not the novel.

Naturally it is significant and to be expected that both operas end with the death of Catherine and a final defiant image of Heathcliff. This is a powerful and typically operatic image, the dead soprano in the arms of the lover (usually the tenor but in this case the baritone), and this follows the dramaturgy of the film rather than the novel – it is the film, and perhaps to a lesser extent, operatic tropes and not the novel, which provides the essential *Stoff*. Three of the most popular operas in the repertoire, *La Traviata*, *Carmen* and *La Bohême*, end in similar fashion and it certainly accords with Clément's view of the soprano as victim: "opera concerns women [...] they suffer, they cry, they die [...] Not one of them escapes with her life, or very few of them do ..." (11). Both operas have little choice but to end where they do, given the structural and dramaturgical imperatives of opera. Interestingly, most of the film and stage versions of the novel also end at this point, which indicates the problematic nature of the second half of the novel in terms of its dramatic suitability for adaptation regardless of its importance in the overall 'meaning' of the novel.

For the operas to end where they do obviously makes dramatic and theatrical sense as well as from the purely practical one of length – to dramatise the second half of the story is not really practicable and would inevitably be an anticlimax[34]. In Herrmann, the final image is of Heathcliff "hopelessly searching out into the storm", and the final stage direction: "only the windows remain radiantly white with the swirling snow" has an open-ended, enigmatic quality, with the symbolism of the radiant window remaining ambiguous (254). There is no resolution to this relationship, even in death, and we have in the Prologue seen the aftermath of these events. Floyd's ending achieves a similar effect in a perhaps more traditionally operatic way with the figure of the defiant Heathcliff. Herrmann's Heathcliff ends "broken and desperate" and the music reflects the visual image as well as his emotional state and there is little sense of closure in the music: Heathcliff is denied emotional or musical resolution. Although the ending of Floyd's opera seems more conventional, with a final ringing high note from the singer and crashing chords in the orchestra, there is an equivalent lack of resolution. The operas offer two contrasting final views: one is of a broken Heathcliff, the other of a defiant one, yet we are aware of the tormented future that awaits both of them[35]. As previously suggested, there is a strong suggestion of a romantic, Wagnerian *Liebestod* quality in the ending of both operas where the death of Cathy does not mean the end of their relationship but suggests that their love now exists on a metaphysical level, transcending the everyday world.

The difference in dramaturgy as regards the ending of the two operas in many ways reflects the different aesthetic approaches of the two composers. Not only do their individual musical discursive practices differ considerably, but so do their conceptions of the novel and the adaptive strategies themselves. Herrmann chooses to focus on the

---

[34] As in the book, the movie ends on a tragic note. Heathcliff is unable to unite with Cathy, but in a departure from the book, Heathcliff and Cathy are shown walking hand in hand in their afterlife, visiting their favourite place, Penistone Crag. Miller argues that Wyler has "literalised the idea of haunting in its final image of Cathy and Heathcliff's transparent forms." (231f.)

[35] Apter maintains that Heathcliff in the novel becomes a "Tristanesque figure, longing for the union with Catherine which will be his death. When he feels himself close to the realization of his desire he calls himself happy, but it is clear that he is tormented by a mingling of excitement and pain. [...] Death provides for that impossible Romantic combination: ecstasy and peace. Heathcliff's longing has grown to such a pitch that only in death can he rest. His longing makes life an impossible torment [...] only in death is there satisfaction for this devouring Romantic passion." (218f.)

romantic aspects, with the relationship between Catherine and Heathcliff as the central dramatic and musical focus (he has several extended duets for them), much like the film, and most of the wider social issues are underplayed. To this end he employs predominantly 'closed' operatic forms. Floyd, however, seems to be more concerned with the wider world around these two: their relationships with the other characters are more fully explored, and a range of theatrical possibilities arising out of these additional relationships is exploited. There is a sense that Herrmann has concentrated on creating a primarily poetic version of the novel while Floyd is more concerned with expanding its inherent dramatic possibilities. It could be said that Herrmann is more the poet, Floyd the dramatist.

Herrmann seems more conscious of tradition; there is a strong sense of intertextuality in his opera in its many musical and even structural allusions to the operatic repertoire such as the many songs he incorporates into his work, which deliberately call attention to the art form itself. Floyd, significantly, does not use discrete song in his opera and employs a consistently 'through-composed' style, and his primary focus is on the drama with musical invention for its own sake playing a subservient role. This is not to say that he does not exploit conventional operatic devices, but they are less self-consciously employed. Both operas offer valid, though differing responses to the novel and reveal interesting aspects of the process of recent operatic adaptation itself.

If recent trends are significant, it seems that there could be a growing sub-genre of operas that identifiably owe their origin, or exhibit considerable influence, as much to the (often more famous) film adaptation of the literary work on which they are based than the 'original' work itself. Some recent examples include *The Great Gatsby* (John Harbison, 1999); *Sophie's Choice* (Nicholas Maw, 2002); *A Streetcar Named Desire* (André Previn, 1998); *The End of the Affair* (Jake Heggie, 2004). How this 'fluidity' will influence the more 'traditional' operatic adaptation of literary works is an area of potentially fruitful research. In fact, opera based on film itself could also be seen as constituting a 'new' trend: Elliot Carter's opera, *What Next* (1999), is based on the Jacques Tati film, *Traffic*; William Bolcom's opera, *The Wedding* (2005), has Robert Altman's film of the same name as its source; and Gerald Barry's opera of Rainer Werner Fassbinder's movie, *The Bitter Tears of Petra von Kant* (albeit itself based on a play by Fassbinder), received its premiere in 2005. As André Bazin, whose 1948 essay foreshadows many later theoretical paths, perceptively remarked: "it is possible to imagine that we are moving toward a reign of the adaptation in which the notion of the unity of the work of art, if not the very notion of the author himself, will be destroyed." (6) Robert Stam sees adaptation more in the sense of "intertextual dialogism" in which there is little "attempted resuscitation of an originary word than a turn in an ongoing dialogical process" (63). Bazin's formulation of the possibility of an original novel spawning a play and then a film still seems to me to be a useful way of viewing this 'multiple' adaptation trend. As Bazin notes, the result would be a

> single work reflected through three art forms, an artistic pyramid with three sides, all equal in the eyes of the critic. The 'work' would then be only an ideal point at the top of this figure, which itself is an ideal construct. The chronological precedence of one part over another would not be an aesthetic criterion any more than the chronological precedence of one twin over the other is a genealogical one. (26)

This view is echoed by Linda Hutcheon, who concludes her recent fascinating study of the process of adaptation, with the comment that "[t]emporal precedence does not mean anything more than temporal priority [...] there are precious few stories that have not been 'lovingly ripped off' from others" (177). The whole area of adaptation studies has a compelling breadth and range with contemporary operatic adaptation a relatively unexplored sub-genre. Of course operatic adaptation from literary sources is central to the more than 400-year development of the art form, but the influence of film (and television, not to mention new technologies such as DVD, music-streaming etc.) on the adaptive process seems to me to be one of the more interesting and fruitful developments in recent times. The influence of film on opera, and vice versa, has received considerable attention, and Bazin's 'artistic pyramid' – in the case of opera being the relationship between the literary source, the film version, and the final operatic product – is worthy of more thorough investigation.

References

Abbate, Caroline (1991). *Unsung Voices: Opera and Musical Narrative in the Nineteenth Century*. Princeton, NJ: Princeton University Press.
Allen, Walter (1986). *The English Novel*. Harmondsworth: Penguin.
Allott, Miriam, ed. (1970). *Emily Brontë: Wuthering Heights. A Casebook*. London: Macmillan.
Andrew, Dudley (2000). "Adaptation". Naremore, ed. 28-37.
Bluestone, George (1957). *Novels into Film*. Berkeley, CA: University of California Press.
Apter, T. E. (1976). "Romanticism and Romantic Love in *Wuthering Heights*". Smith, ed. 45-67.
Bazin, André (2000). "Adaptation, or the Cinema as Digest". Naremore, ed. 9-27.
Bernhart, Walter (2007). "Myth-making Opera: David Malouf and Michael Berkeley's *Jane Eyre*". Margarete Rubik, Elke Mettinger-Schartmann, eds. *A Breath of Fresh Eyre: Intertextual and Intermedial Reworkings of* Jane Eyre. Internationale Forschungen zur Allgemeinen und Vergleichenden Literaturwissenschaft 111. Amsterdam/New York, NY: Rodopi. 317-329.
— (2008). "From Novel to Song via Myth: *Wuthering Heights* as a Case of Popular Intermedial Adaptation". In this volume: 13-27.
Brooks, Peter (1976). *The Melodramatic Imagination*. New Haven, CT: Yale University Press.
Clément, Catherine (1989). *Opera, or the Undoing of Women*. Trans. Betsy Wing. London: Virago Press.
Floyd, Carlisle (1961). *Wuthering Heights: A Musical Drama in a Prologue and Three Acts*. London: Boosey and Hawkes.
Eagleton, Terence (1988). *Myths of Power: A Marxist Study of the Brontës*. London: Macmillan.
Frye, Northrop (1957). *The Anatomy of Criticism*. Princeton, NJ: Princeton University Press.
Halliwell, Michael (1999). "Narrative Elements in Opera". Walter Bernhart, Steven Paul Scher, Werner Wolf, eds. *Word and Music Studies: Defining the Field*. Word and Music Studies 1. Amsterdam/Atlanta, CA: Rodopi. 135-153.
— (2005). *Opera and the Novel: The Case of Henry James*. Word and Music Studies 6. Amsterdam/New York, NY: Rodopi.

Herrmann, Bernard (1965). *Wuthering Heights: An Opera in Four Acts and a Prologue*. London: Novello and Company.
Hewish, John (1969). *Emily Brontë: A Critical and Biographical Study*. London: Macmillan.
Holderness, Graham (1985). *Wuthering Heights*. Milton Keynes: Open University Press.
Hutcheon, Linda (2006). *A Theory of Adaptation*. New York, NY/ London: Routledge.
Kavanagh, James (1985). *Emily Brontë*. Oxford: Basil Blackwell.
Kerman, Joseph (1988). *Opera as Drama*. Berkeley, CA: University of California Press.
Knoepflmacher, U. C. (1989). *Wuthering Heights*. Cambridge: Cambridge University Press.
Lindenberger, Herbert (1984). *Opera: The Extravagant Art*. Ithaca, NY: Cornell University Press.
Miller, Lucasta (2005). *The Brontë Myth*. New York, NY: Anchor Books.
Naremore, James, ed. (2000). *Film Adaptation*. London: The Athlone Press.
Prince, Gerald (1982). *A Dictionary of Narratology*. Aldershot: Scholar Press.
Pykett, Lyn (1989). *Emily Brontë*. London: Macmillan.
Rimmon-Kenan, Shlomith (1983). *Narrative Fiction: Contemporary Poetics*. London: Routledge.
Smith, Anne, ed. (1976). *The Art of Emily Brontë*. London: Vision Press.
Stam, Robert (2000). "Beyond Fidelity: The Dialogics of Adaptation." Naremore, ed. 54-78.
Stoneman, Patsy (1996). *Brontë Transformations: The Cultural Dissemination of* Jane Eyre *and* Wuthering Heights. London: Prentice Hall/Harvester Wheatsheaf.
Van Ghent, Dorothea (1970). "Dark 'Otherness' in *Wuthering Heights*". Allott, ed. 45-61.
Vogler, Thomas A., ed. (1968). *Twentieth-Century Interpretations of* Wuthering Heights. Englewood Cliffs, NJ: Prentice-Hall.

Adaptations of *Othello*
Shakespeare – Verdi – Zeffirelli

Ulla-Britta Lagerroth, Lund

This essay deals with multiple adaptations of a specific source text, Shakespeare's *Othello*. In an introductory discussion of the concept of 'adaptation' it is argued that adaptation belongs to intermedia studies and, consequently, that adaptation criticism is an intermediality discourse. A brief orientation follows of the ways by which composer Giuseppe Verdi, in close co-operation with librettist Arrigo Boito, transformed Shakespeare's play into an opera, *Otello*, first performed in Milan at La Scala on 5 February 1887. The essay's main focus, however, is on the nature and function of director Franco Zeffirelli's cinematic adaptation, his screen opera *Otello* (1986). Examined are the ways by which Zeffirelli achieved a synthesis of cinematic realism and operatic theatricality, the means by which he balanced musical excess and visual excess, and the importance of his choice of singers. Finally, the question is posed: why has Shakespeare's play *Othello* become such a strong incitement to adaptation over the centuries?

I

This is a study of multiple adaptations of Shakespeare's *Othello*, of how in the 1880s the play was transformed into an opera, Verdi's *Otello,* and one hundred years later the opera into a screen opera, *Otello* by Franco Zeffirelli. But first, as a frame to such an investigation, let me offer some reflections on the concept of adaptation.

Promoted by film theoreticians in particular, a more systematized approach to adaptation has replaced the so-called fidelity discourse, according to which an adaptation is judged in relation to how 'faithful' or 'unfaithful' it is to the source text. This rhetoric is prejudiced since it usually hints at a deplorable 'loss' in the transition. The terms employed, such as 'infidelity', 'violation', 'betrayal' or 'deformation', imply that the adaptation has somehow done a disservice to the original.

However, the fidelity discourse seems to have been abandoned, at least in modern film criticism where adaptation studies have become a dynamic research area. This is well demonstrated by Robert Stam in a recent (2005) essay on "The Theory and Practice of Adaptation", an introductory essay included in a three-volume publication devoted to studies of film adaptations of novels. Stam here surveys the kind of structuralist and post-structuralist theoretical currents which, by offering alternative perspectives on the benefits of cross-fertilization between texts, have undermined the moralistic and judgmental ideas of fidelity, and so have come to influence the reshaping of adaptation criticism. Stam lists Kristeva's intertextuality theory and Genette's transtextuality theory, both of which stress "the endless permutation of textualities rather than the 'fidelity' of a later text to an earlier model", as well as Derridean deconstruction, which "also dismantled the hierarchy of 'original' and 'copy'", in addition to Bachtin's dialogism and conception of the author as the 'orchestrator' of pre-existing discourses (8-9; cf. 26-31). Stam finally mentions further trends which, in his opinion, have directly or indirectly influenced adaptation criticism: cultural studies, modern narratology, reception theory, and performance theory (cf. 9-11).

Referring to Wolfgang Iser's conception of a text's 'indeterminacies', Stam suggests that an adaptation, too, may be seen as a 'filling in' of the "lacunae" of the source work (10). Personally I find the trope of filling in gaps less than adequate for the process of adaptation and will rather argue that at the base of an adaptation lies a personal interpretation of the **totality** of the source text, an interested reading in search of its spirit or creative energy.

On the other hand, I fully agree with Robert Stam when he asserts that "crucial to any discussion of adaptation is the question of media specificity" (16). Stam is not the first film scholar to stress that each adaptation automatically **is** different and original due to the change of medium. But he also demonstrates how this change of medium involves hundreds of crucial choices as to mode of production, technology and performance, focalization and point-of-view, spatio-temporality, and potential spectator/listener positions.

As previously mentioned, questions of the basic personal interpretation and of medium-specificity are essential in adaptation studies. But so too are observations of the kind of social, political, and ideological contexts to which the adapted work is related, and which explain the adaptation's function in its contemporary society. Each adaptation reveals not only the time and culture of the source text, but also the time and culture of the adaptation. To quote Stam: "Adaptation, in this sense, is a work of reaccentuation, whereby a source work is reinterpreted through new grids and discourses" (45).

Since an adaptation is the result of an intermedial process, i. e., a very complex transformation from one specific medium into another specific medium, adaptation studies obviously belong to the field of intermedia studies. And it is precisely there where Werner Wolf, in his pioneering work on a theory of intermediality, also situates adaptation. Consequently, it seems accurate to speak of theoretically updated adaptation criticism as a case of **intermediality** discourse.

II

As is underlined by Michael Halliwell in his book, *Opera and the Novel: The Case of Henry James*, little theoretical discussion concerning the process of operatic adaptation of fiction has been published so far. However, in his book Halliwell lays a solid foundation for further studies of operatic adaptation of fiction, and of novels in particular. The aim of his investigation is to see "how far meaning, structure and other aspects of the fictional form influence the form of the operatic adaptation, and whether certain intrinsic operatic structures as well as theatrical or performance conventions and imperatives are decisive in determining the main thrust and final form of the adaptation" (11-12).

Turning to Shakespeare and Verdi's *Otello*, and thus to the operatic adaptation of a play, it is an astonishing fact that more than 200 operas have been based on Shakespeare's plays, a testimony indeed of their adaptability for opera. No wonder there are books which from varying aspects discuss this one subject: they include *Shakespeare and Opera* (Schmidgall), and *The Opera and Shakespeare* (Klein/ Smith).

In addition, there are a host of studies which deal exclusively with Verdi's operatic adaptation of Shakespeare's *Othello*. Julian Budden and James Hepokoski in particular have contributed substantially to an understanding of this opera: its genesis in relation to Shakespeare's play and to the Italian opera culture, the close co-operation over the years between the librettist Boito and composer Verdi, the total vocal and orchestral structure of the work, and the content of the production book (*disposizione scenica*), published by Ricordi. But other scholars, among them Ulrich Weisstein in his pioneering studies in librettology, have also contributed valuable studies of adaptation aspects of *Otello*[1]. In the following I refer to more common observations by scholars and critics which shed light on the main characteristics of the operatic adaptation, but which also, in my opinion, facilitate an understanding of Zeffirelli's screen adaptation of Verdi's opera.

That Shakespeare's *Othello* is especially apt for transformation into opera is stressed by both opera and Shakespeare scholars. *Othello* has been appointed Shakespeare's 'best' play, with reference to the theatre. It has a simple and theatrically effective plot, no sub-plot, and only a few characters. The transformation of a text's linguistic signs into theatrical spatio-temporal signs, visual as well as verbal and aural, is certainly a complex process (cf. Fischer-Lichte 191-206). But being a play (i. e., containing a dramatic structure built on dialogue and stage directions), this kind of structure probably also facilitates the adaptation of *Othello* to operatic as well as theatrical stage performances[2]. Besides, as a domestic tragedy, *Othello* relentlessly grips the emotions of the public, its main theme, jealousy, being so human and therefore so strongly affecting. *Othello* is often characterized as a drama of passion – the passion of love turned into the destructive passion of jealousy for Othello, but also the passion of envy as the driving force for Iago, all ending in inevitable death.

This combination of passion and death has also explained why Shakespeare's play responded so well to the demands of nineteenth-century Italian opera, the important cultural context to Verdi's *Otello*. And obviously this theme of passion met Verdi's particular need in the 1880s of an emotionally intense (and thus audience-gripping) topic for yet another opera late in his life. Judging from his correspondence and his comments on the opera, published in the production book, there is no doubt about Verdi's personal interpretation of *Othello* as a drama of passion.

Boito's libretto, an 'intermediate' text dependent mainly on a French translation, closely follows Shakespeare's text. But his adaptation of the text also reflects the opera aesthetics of its time as well as

---

[1] In an essay on Zeffirelli's opera film *Otello*, André Lorant, too, gives some detailed examples of the ways in which Boito adapted Shakespeare's text (cf. 113-119).

[2] For a survey of the tendency among certain critics and scholars to treat Shakespeare's *Othello* as an in itself 'operatic' text, see Lisa Hopkins (61-70).

more general codes and conventions for opera. Considering the medium specificity of opera, Boito had to make several cuts and alterations, most drastic among them being the omission of the entire first act. Cuts were necessary due to the well-known fact that singing words needs more time than speaking them. Music requires time to function successfully as a dramatic discourse – to express emotions, develop characters, and create suspense in effective climaxes (arias, duets, ensembles). Such medium-motivated alterations of the source text in *Otello* are the tender "Love Duet" between Otello and Desdemona, Iago's horrifying, God-mocking "Credo", and the "Ave Maria" prayer, sung by Desdemona after her "Willow Song".

Further significant changes made to meet the medium specificity of opera are heard in Boito/Verdi's composition of the type of spectacular scenes which were standard conventions in nineteenth-century opera. There is the marvellous opening storm scene in the harbour of Famagusta in Cyprus, with a chorus singing in agitation over Otello's still-missing ship, followed by hailing the victorious hero. Finally arriving safely, Otello makes one of the most glorious stage entries in the world of opera. There is, further, a drinking song (sung by Iago), one of opera's categories of songs for special occasions, as well as an extravagant crowd scene for the arrival of the Venetian ambassador. There are also a couple of elaborate ballet scenes, in opera representing entertainment for dignified on-lookers ('performances within the performance'). The already-mentioned love duet and the prayer, too, belong to the traditional features of nineteenth-century Italian opera.

Opera scholars and critics have generally considered Boito/Verdi's operatic adaptation of Shakespeare's play to be a magnificent musico-dramatic achievement. Though following Shakespeare's text fairly closely, Boito created an original libretto where the conflict of emotions is central. Verdi's control of dramatic pace through a continuous musical score has been praised as masterful, brilliantly capturing the passionate emotions in both the vocal and the orchestral music. The music expresses the text, and at the same time brings out what the words alone cannot communicate. The orchestra develops the dramatic situations, yet it, too, has become an autonomous force as narrator.

But critical complaints have also been voiced, in line with the fidelity discourse, arguing that the adaptation has affected the characters in an unfortunate way. It has been claimed that the magnificence and nobility of Shakespeare's Othello is sacrificed in the opera, his character 'flattened', since he becomes a gullible victim of Iago's manipulations much more quickly than in the play. Iago is considered to have become too devilish a villain, turned into the supreme tempter in the opera, reminiscent of the main character in Boito's own opera, *Mefistofele* (1868/1876). Desdemona's role is vocally expanded in the opera, yet she represents only a **type** of woman, in Verdi's own words, "the type of goodness, resignation, self-sacrifice" (qtd. Budden 322).

However, the study of a play's transformation into an opera and of the means by which the operatic adaptation might generate meaning when meeting the public, cannot exclude questions of intrinsic performativity and of the theatrical context. As to performativity, the dialogue of the source text signifies direct speech of the dramatic characters, but the dialogue and the stage directions also contain signs that point to theatrical signs such as actors' bodies and movements, masks, hair, costumes, decoration, props, lighting, sound and music. Operatic singers are also actors, and the songs composed for them are meant to be performed not only in vocal but also with bodily action. From Verdi's correspondence and from the production book we know that the composer himself attached great importance to the choice of singers, to their movements and costumes, and to setting and light. It has to be remembered that when the première took place on 5 February 1887, it was after intense rehearsals supervised by the elderly composer himself.

As to the theatrical context of Verdi's operatic adaptation, Hepokoski underlines that "*Otello* was conceived during the crest of a general Italian enthusiasm for Shakespeare, a period when Shakespeare was the 'new' dominating and liberating force in the reform of the nineteenth-century Italian theatre" (163). This was a time when the influential Italian actors Ernesto Rossi and Tommaso Salvini performed Othello (as well as other Shakespearean characters) in such a spectacular way that "the floodgates finally opened for the Italian acceptance of staged Shakespeare" (166). In Rossi's interpretation *Othello* was emphasized as a drama of violent jealousy, while it became a drama of deep, idealistic love in Salvini's interpretation. According to Hepokoski, there is no doubt that the ways of staging Shakespeare's *Othello* in the contemporary Italian theatre and, consequently, both Rossi's and Salvini's acting manners, "are reflected in the opera" (169).

This notion of performativity and theatricality, intrinsic in the libretto and the musical score and realized in the scenic performances of *Otello* seems, in turn, to have been of importance for Zeffirelli in his cinematic adaptation of the opera.

III

Verdi's *Otello* has been presented several times on film and telecasts. But Franco Zeffirelli's screen adaptation of 1986 is probably the most famous version for cinema, the cast including tenor Plácido Domingo as Otello, soprano Katia Ricciarelli as Desdemona, baritone Justino Diaz as Iago, with the orchestra of La Scala directed by Lorin Maazel.

By 1986 Zeffirelli had long since established strong credentials as a director of theatre and opera as well as of film. His particular fondness for Shakespeare in all three media is also well documented. In 1976 he made his first stage production of Verdi's *Otello*, at La Scala with Plácido Domingo in the lead, and their close co-operation and friendship dates from that successful event. Zeffirelli has later staged *Otello* in other opera houses.

However, his screen opera *Otello* is not based on any performance of an opera house production, shot by cameras placed at different angles of the stage, which before the 1980s was the most common way of producing screen or TV operas. Already in the 1970s, opera films betrayed a strong directorial or auteurist presence, and so indeed does Zeffirelli's *Otello*, based on his own carefully prepared screenplay, produced by the team of Golan and Globus, and a great success at the box office.

Opera on screen is a fairly new area of scholarly investigation, somewhat amazingly so as opera has been captured on film for more than one hundred years, as is explained in Ken Wlaschin's huge *Encyclopedia of Opera on Screen*. But the genre is gaining more and more critical attention, as is demonstrated in such books as Jeremy Tambling's *Opera, Ideology and Film*, Richard Fawkes's *Opera on Film*, and Marcia J. Citron's *Opera on Screen*. Citron's study is informed by a musicological perspective, and it offers the first serious attempt to survey the field and to theorize its study. Zeffirelli's *Otello* is one of the screen operas she discusses.

From the perspective of medium specificity, what happened to the music when Verdi's opera *Otello* was adapted to the film medium? To quote Citron: "As in staged opera, music naturally functions as a major discourse in screen opera. Yet the presence of the camera, and the prominence of the visual inevitably effect the role of music and how it shapes narrative and meaning." (17) Just as Boito and Verdi were obliged to make omissions in Shakespeare's play with regard to the **musical** development, so Zeffirelli had to make significant cuts in Verdi's continuous music in order to enhance cinematic pace, and to give more room and time for the cinematic image, for **visuality**.

As to the pace, some 30 minutes had to be omitted from the score, some re-ordering and re-composition of the music made, all this motivated by the need of tailoring the music to the film medium. To a certain extent this affected the musical continuum in Verdi's opera. According to Citron, the result is somewhat similar to music's function in mainstream Hollywood film: heightened moments, separated by pauses (cf. 75-77). But Zeffirelli's elimination of Desdemona's "Willow Song" especially caused some critics, evidently supporters of the fidelity discourse, to speak of a 'vandalism' of the source opera.

As already mentioned, medium-specific needs of additional time for visuality were also responsible for Zeffirelli's revisions in the musical score. Music in opera often tends to become excessive, particularly in nineteenth-century Italian opera. Since Zeffirelli's screen adaptation is characterized by visual excess, a constant negotiation between powerful music and flamboyant scenery was necessary in order to attain an interaction between the two.

To balance visual richness and musical richness, Zeffirelli applies what seems to be his overall adaptation strategy: a synthesis of cinematic realism and theatrical artificiality. While opera performed in the opera house establishes a theatrical world of representation (usually framed by a proscenium arch), cinema, in contrast, gives the illusion of a space without limits – landscapes and skies, nature and architecture, etc. –, which promotes a sense of realism. As mentioned by Zeffirelli in his autobiography, he filmed his exteriors at the port of Heraklion in Crete, and at the castle of Barletta in southern Italy, while more intimate interiors were shot afterwards in the studios of Cinecittá in Rome (cf. 333). The outdoor locations, often rich panoramas, stress **cinematic realism**, long and medium shots and zooms, pans and tracking shots emphasizing realistic depth. The indoor locations, on the other hand, stress **theatricality**. The camera swiftly moves between the two types of space. And in contrast to an opera performance, cinema has the possibility of multiple perspectives, a montage technique where scenes of different times and places can be realistically presented as parallel.

As to the medium-specific technological basis of film, it is the camera which all the time decides what we see and hear, controls how long we see and hear it and, consequently, also guides our interpreting response. In Zeffirelli's *Otello* the camera frequently brings us intimately close to the singers, in facial close-ups making their appearance even more 'larger than life' than on a stage, and their vocal action is seemingly even more powerful[3].

To give an example, the camera brilliantly captures Justino Diaz's Iago as a *voyeur*. From more or less hidden positions he furtively observes, and ironically reacts to, what he sees, not only vocally but also by facial expression. This is an equivalent to Iago's asides in Shakespeare's play. But in the film he glances in secret understanding in the direction of the camera, and once even, intimately, straight into the camera in a facial close-up. In doing so, he represents the spectatorial drive, forcefully influencing **us** as viewers. He makes us align ourselves with **his** point of view, a good example of how the medium structures our interpretation.

But visuality is also enhanced through a dominant theme with brilliant visual possibilities, Roman Catholicism. We approach Zeffirelli's basic personal **interpretation** of the Othello-story. In his autobiography, he explicitly states that "my *Otello* is a very Catholic affair. Otello's struggle is in a very real sense a religious one" (339). The dynamics of a drama of passion, of devastating jealousy – in Shakespeare's play and, still, in Verdi's operatic adaptation, a psychological, human struggle going on within Othello/Otello himself – is re-interpreted by Zeffirelli in the direction of a monumental religious

---

[3] In this context there is yet another aspect of medium specificity to be taken into consideration: the circumstance that in Zeffirelli's *Otello*, as in most screen operas, the sound was pre-recorded, and later lip-synchronized to playback when the film was shot. The sound we hear appears to originate simultaneously from the singers, while in reality they only mouth the words on the screen.

conflict between good and evil, embodied in the figures of Desdemona and Iago, with religious icons and rituals constantly appearing.

The most striking religious image imposed is the crucifix, first visible in a short glimpse during the opening storm scene, and there evidently indicating hope of rescue for the seafarers. Then the tall crucifix is seen hanging in a subterranean chamber of the castle, and it is in front of this crucifix, which shows Christ as a tormented, miserable figure, that Iago sings his highly blasphemous "Credo". The camera rapidly moves between the suffering face of Christ and the triumphant face of Iago, and so the words and the music achieve a much more ominous dimension.

Exactly the same setting with the dominant crucifix reappears later, when Iago and Otello pledge loyalty to their common mission of revenge, a duet sung while they kneel in front of the crucifix in a ritual of male bonding. Finally the cavern-like room with the crucifix appears again at the beginning of the last act. Here Otello, now completely blinded by jealousy, is regressing into paganism, back to his African roots, in a magic ritual (a strikingly Eurocentric staging of the event, which has been criticized). Sitting on the floor, bare-chested and in an orange glow, he conducts a ritual over candles, removes the cross hanging around his neck, dangles it over the flames, and finally drops it into the fire. Having in this way ostentatiously abandoned his Christian faith, Othello is prepared to commit the horrible deed of murdering his wife.

But the visual impact is also matching the music's impact in other ways. Fires are constantly flaming high in all the rooms, symbolizing the jealousy which burns so devastatingly in Otello's soul and mind, and the obstacles, piling up against Otello's and Desdemona's love, are symbolically visualized by a constant use of partitions or barring elements behind which the characters move, thus separating them: a lattice wall, arrays of weapons etc. A still more significant expansion into the visual setting is that of a Shakespearean language symbol: **jealousy as a green-eyed monster**. Otello and Iago are seen indoors, moving around in Otello's spectacular studio, filled with such Renaissance scientific instruments as an educated navigator of the period would have gathered around him, among them magnifying glasses (symbolic of the increasing of the passions). Iago sings the fatal words, warning Otello of jealousy as a green-eyed monster, and he and Otello watch through a window – another kind of partition between indoors and outdoors – what is happening in the garden. They see how Desdemona walks in the **green** garden, followed by a singing group of children, and how all of a sudden she is met by a smiling Cassio, dressed in a **green**, or gray-green, suit. At the later festivities for the Venetian ambassador, Desdemona appears in a **green** dress, and when she has been thrown to the floor by Otello, the green cloak draped over the back of her body reminds us of an ensnaring animal.

Also striking is the medium-specific use of flashbacks. In the Love Duet in Verdi's opera, Otello and Desdemona only **sing** about their courtship in the past (a kind of musical flashback, substituting for some lines in Shakespeare's first act, omitted in the opera). Since in Zeffirelli's screen adaptation the Love Duet is made the emotional pivot of the opera, the happy memories they sing of are directly visualized in four extravagant flashbacks. Evidently their function is to stress the sad fact that only the idealized past meant total happiness for them, while their present life rests on a fragile ground.

But how significant is the presence of the actual performers, their voices and their physical appearance in the screen opera *Otello*? Zeffirelli has said that an important rule for screen opera is that the performers, besides of course being outstanding singers, are good-looking and capable of acting for the camera in a believable way. In this respect, Plácido Domingo – probably the opera singer with the most extensive experience of film-making – was irreplaceable in the cast. With his rich, flexible voice, his attractive, masculine appearance, and his extraordinary theatrical abilities, he has been since long considered **the** Otello of his generation. He had performed the role numerous times on the opera stage, before the film was made, and in his autobiography, where he devotes a whole chapter to "The Moor of Venice", he also acknowledges that Otello became the role of his life.

It is obvious that in attire, manners and appearance Domingo's Otello is interpreted as a dignified person. In Zeffirelli's words: "We both saw Otello, not as some black savage with a veneer of western civilization easily ripped away by Iago's poison but as a truly cultured man of the Renaissance whose goodness makes him blind to the sheer force of evil that is brought to bear on him" (294; cf. 334). Again, Zeffirelli underlines how his interpretation of the Othello theme is a religious one. However, it is also obvious that the bearded, blackened face and grandiose gestures of Domingo's Otello strongly remind one of Orson Welles's magnificent appearance as Othello in his legendary expressionistic film, *Othello*, of 1951. The subterranean caverns and corridors in Zeffirelli's screen opera are also reminiscent of the same kind of gloomy interiors in Welles's film, the interiors mirroring the darkening mind of the male character.

In line with Zeffirelli's religious interpretation, Justino Diaz's Iago – according to many critics appearing in such a magnificent way that he nearly steals Otello the show – both musically and visually performs as a true incarnation of the sheer force of evil, or as the devil himself. Wherever he moves in the castle, he is always **descending**, moving downstairs into weird tunnels and caverns, a sign of his connection with the underworld, with hell. Down there his demonic laughter is heard, echoing against the walls.

Katia Ricciarelli's Desdemona, in Zeffirelli's religious interpretation, represents goodness – as did most sopranos in nineteenth-century Italian opera. But in order to balance her strong vocal action, Zeffirelli stages her much more visibly and much more actively than in Shakespeare's play or in Verdi's opera. Desdemona already appears in the opening storm scene, where we get a glimpse of her face as she waits in anguish to catch sight of Otello's still missing ship. Later, during the festivities in Otello's honour, we see her seated by his side as his equal, talking, laughing, even smiling a little flirtatiously in the direction of the approaching Cassio.

On the one hand, Ricciarelli's Desdemona appears as the pure and innocent angel, with accentuated pale skin and blonde tresses, backlit and resembling a halo. In this respect she fulfils the same Madonna identification as in Verdi's opera. But on the other hand, Ricciarelli's Desdemona is also sexualized. In Zeffirelli's words: "[…] my interpretation of the role envisages Desdemona, not as the wilting virginal girl sometimes portrayed, but as a full-blooded sensual young woman". Consequently, he moved the Love Duet from the outside into their bedchamber, and turned the duet into "a highly passionate, almost erotic scene" (338). Here Desdemona, waiting for Otello, is lying in a tempting position on their bed, in a white gown with bare shoulders, and her hair now brushed out. While Otello and Desdemona tenderly sing of how they once fell in love, he joins her on the bed, and they kiss and caress each other, the camera capturing their intimacy in close-ups, with his black face tight over her white face. This is love made physical, typical for contemporary trends in European art cinema. But Otello interrupts the act, as if overwhelmed by his feelings rising from the bed, and still singing he and Desdemona instead move upstairs, and so outdoors, to look at the star of Venus, which is the closing scene of the first act. It will be on the same stairs, and **not** while she is lying on their bed – the traditional setting for the death scene, also chosen by Verdi and Boito – that Otello later strangles Desdemona and stabs himself to death with a dagger.

IV

But how comes it that Verdi's late-nineteenth-century opera was transformed into a screen opera one hundred years later? The heyday of filmed musicals was over by the 1980s. Zeffirelli, anxious to promote a new interest in the art of opera, had expressed the idea of replacing musicals with screen operas, which would make opera available to large numbers of audiences. His real intentions were to popularize opera in our media-intensive age.

What matters, too, is that all the way through the media transformations of Shakespeare's *Othello* there remains the fascination of a thought-provoking theme. Zeffirelli has said that the very first rule for filmed opera is that "the story must be universally understood", and that was exactly what he found in the Othello story. As he said, it "is known to millions and it combines intense passion with high drama and adventure on an epic scale" (331).

To the more general question of how Shakespeare's *Othello*, of all literary texts or dramatic plays, has become such a strong incitement to adaptation, the answer must evidently be that it represents a story which over the centuries has attracted new directors and actors, just as it always appeals to new audiences[4]. And it is remarkable that throughout the varying re-interpretations of the source text, and the different medium-specific transformations and changing contexts for the adaptations, the creative energy of the source text is never sacrificed, its spirit never damaged. The adaptations never diminished the power at the core of the source text: **the drama of passion**.

---

[4] Another notable adaptation of Shakespeare's *Othello*, which could not be discussed here, is Rossini's opera *Otello* (built on Berio's libretto), which had its premiere on 4 December 1816 at Teatro del Fondo in Naples, and which immediately was a great success.

References

Budden, Julian (1992). *The Operas of Verdi. Vol. 3. From Don Carlos to Falstaff*. Rev. ed. Oxford: Clarendon Press.

Citron, Marcia J. (2000). *Opera on Screen*. New Haven, CT/London: Yale University Press.

Domingo, Plácido (1983). *My First Forty Years*. New York, NY: Knopf.

Fawkes, Richard (2000). *Opera on Film*. London: Duckworth.

Fischer-Lichte, Erika (1992). *The Semiotics of Theater*. J. Gaines, D. L. Jones, transls. Bloomington/Indianapolis, IN: Indiana University Press.

Halliwell, Michael (2005). *Opera and the Novel: The Case of Henry James*. Word and Music Studies 6. Amsterdam/New York, NY: Rodopi.

Hepokoski, James A. (1987). *Giuseppe Verdi: Otello*. Cambridge: Cambridge University Press.

Hopkins, Lisa (1994). "'What did thy song bode, lady?' *Othello* as operatic text". Klein/Smith, eds. 61-70.

Klein, Holger, Christopher Smith, eds. (1994). *The Opera and Shakespeare*. A Publication of the Shakespeare Yearbook, vol. 4. Lewiston, NY/Queenston/Lampeter: The Edwin Mellen Press.

Lorant, André (1994). "From *Othello* to *Otello*: Zeffirelli's Opera-Film (1990)". Klein/Smith, eds. 113-142.

Schmidgall, Gary (1990). *Shakespeare and Opera*. Oxford: Oxford University Press.

Stam, Robert (2005). "Introduction: The Theory and Practice of Adaptation". Robert Stam, Alessandra Raengo, eds. *Literature and Film: A Guide to the Theory and Practice of Film Adaptation*. Oxford: Blackwell Publishers. 1-52.

Tambling, Jeremy (1987). *Opera, Ideology and Film*. New York, NY: St. Martin's Press.

Weisstein, Ulrich (1954). *Studies in the Libretto: 'Otello', 'Der Rosenkavalier'. Prologomena to a Poetics of Opera*. Ph.D. Dissertation, Indiana University.

Wlaschin, Ken (2004). *Encyclopedia of Opera on Screen: A Guide to more than 100 years of Opera Films, Videos and DVDs*. New Haven, CT/London: Yale University Press.

Wolf, Werner (1999). *The Musicalization of Fiction: A Study in the Theory and History of Intermediality*. Internationale Forschungen zur Allgemeinen und Vergleichenden Literaturwissenschaft 35. Amsterdam: Rodopi.

Zeffirelli, Franco (1986). *The Autobiography of Franco Zeffirelli*. London: Weidenfeld and Nicholson.

Zeffirelli, Franco (1986). *Otello*. DVD, MGM 2003.

Since Linda Hutcheon's book *A Theory of Adaptation* (Rodopi, 2006) appeared **after** my essay was delivered for publication in WMS 9, I have not been able to include references to her discussion of adaptation.

The Spoken Opera-Film *Fedora* (1942)
Intermedial Transposition and Implicit Operatic References in Film

Bernhard Kuhn, Lewisburg, PA

The influence of opera on film can be observed since the beginning of cinema. All categories of intermediality (plurimediality, transmediality, intermedial reference, and intermedial transposition) are relevant for this broad phenomenon and present opportunities to generate new understandings of individual films and film genres as well as of the relationship between word and music in film. This paper presents an overview of the development and different forms of opera in film and explores the manner in which the intermedial categories relate to the subject matter. It then focuses on the particular genre of the spoken opera-film by applying the relevant theories of intermediality and Genette's theories of hypertextuality to the particular media of opera and film in order to analyze the spoken opera-film *Fedora*. This paper comes to the conclusion that this film presents a relatively true adaptation of the libretto of the opera *Fedora*. While both libretto and film focus on the opposition 'love-revenge' as the main paradigm, the film adds the contrast 'love-loyalty' to the dominant paradigm. In addition, through the use of implicit intermedial references, the film imitates the medium of opera by 'partially recreating' and 'simulating' its *discours*.

Opera in Cinema

Since the earliest days of cinema, attempts have been made to incorporate opera into film. During the first decade of the so-called silent film period, famous opera scenes were filmed and were often accompanied by corresponding operatic music (cf. Fawkes 1-25)[1]. In addition to these early silent opera-films, many silent feature films include

---

[1] According to Richard Fawkes, one of the first examples of a silent opera-film is a two minute scene of Gaetano Donizetti's *La Fille du Régiment*, filmed in 1898 in New York (cf. 8).

inter- and transmedial references to opera. Examples are silent biopics of opera composers, or feature films incorporating operatic elements. The relationship between opera and film grew stronger once sound film was invented and, at the beginning of the 1930s, the first attempts were made to present complete operas in films. In these first opera-films of the sound film period, actors mostly spoke and did not sing their operatic roles. The film score generally incorporated selected parts of the opera score, usually the vocal line of famous arias, important orchestral motifs, or excerpts of the overture. Film-operas, which adapted not only the libretto but also the opera score, were not produced until after the Second World War[2]. In the post war period, operatic films were quite popular and many opera-films and film-operas were produced, particularly in Italy. Starting with the mid 1950s, however, increasingly fewer operas were adapted for the cinema. Nonetheless, operas continued to be filmed, although mainly for television. The genre 'film-opera' was revived for the cinema in the middle of the 1970s by directors like Jean-Marie Straub and Danièle Huillet, Ingmar Bergman as well as Joseph Losey[3].

This paper is primarily concerned with the genre of the 'spoken opera-film', which was popular mainly from the 1930s until the 1940s, and hence ought to be seen as a precursor to the film-operas of the post-war period (cf. Kuhn 85-118). It is the goal of the second part of this study to highlight the importance of these early attempts of sound cinema to transpose opera into film. The next section of this paper is concerned with the theoretical framework of intermediality between opera and film, which will inform the analysis of the film *Fedora* that is then presented.

---

[2] *Il Barbiere di Siviglia*, directed by Mario Costa, was first screened in 1946. It is considered to be the first film-opera (cf. Fawkes 117).

[3] Famous film-operas of the 1970s and 1980s are for example *Moses und Aron* (Jean-Marie Straub and Danièle Huillet, 1974), *Trollflöjten* (Ingmar Bergman, 1975), *Don Giovanni* (Joseph Losey, 1979), *La Traviata* (Franco Zeffirelli, 1982), *Parsifal* (Hans Jürgen Syberberg, 1982), *Carmen* (Francesco Rosi, 1983), *Otello* (Franco Zeffirelli, 1986). Cf. also Ulla-Britta Lagerroth's contribution to this volume.

Intermediality between Opera and Film

Opera and film have influenced each other since the beginning of cinema and relations between the two media can be observed up to the present day. All four categories of intermediality, developed by Irina Rajewsky and Werner Wolf, are relevant for an analysis of these intermedial relations (cf. Rajewsky; Wolf, "Intermediality Revisited"; Kuhn 19-48). In the following discussion of transmediality, intermedial transposition, intermedial reference, and plurimediality, the focus is on operatic aspects in film, and not on the phenomenon of filmic aspects in opera[4].

The first form of intermediality applicable to the study of the relationship between opera and film is 'transmediality'. Transmediality is by definition not media specific (cf. Wolf, "Intermediality Revisited" 18f.). It describes the occurrence of formal or content elements in different media without establishing an exclusive relationship between them. This means that transmedialities of opera and film not only create a relationship between the two media, but build bridges to other media (such as literature) as well. Significant examples of transmedialities relevant for opera and film are, for instance, biblical references, the combination of spectacle and narrative[5], the use of melodramatic elements, and motivic repetition or thematic variation[6].

For the analysis of opera in film, the category 'intermedial transposition' is certainly very important. In contrast to transmediality, intermedial transpositions take place mostly between entire works and a clear origin of formal or content elements can be recognized. In our case, opera is the medium of origin and film the target medium. If we consider the films created through intermedial transposition of an

---

[4] For filmic aspects in opera cf. e. g. Tambling, *Opera, Ideology and Film*, 68-90; Joe, "The Cinematic Body in the Operatic Theater". For a definition of intermediality cf. Wolf, "Intermediality Revisited" 17.

[5] This transmediality is particularly relevant for the analysis of early silent cinema. Cf. Theresa.

[6] Werner Wolf notes correctly that "some transmedial devices such as 'variation' may have acquired the connotation of a specific medium" ("Intermediality Revisited" 27). If such a relation to a specific medium can be unmistakably identified, it should be interpreted as intermedial reference.

opera, the spectrum reaches from the filming of a live stage performance to a feature film transforming the operatic texts[7]. The end points of this continuum have been defined as 'performance documentation' and 'opera-film' (see Kühnel). As the term suggests, a performance documentation presents the portrayal of an opera presentation. An opera-film, on the other hand, realizes an opera with filmic means. In the literature, however, not only the term 'opera-film', but also the term 'film-opera' has been used to describe opera adaptations. Since the results can be aesthetically very different, it makes sense to differentiate between the two terms. The filmic adaptation of one libretto and opera score can be best described as 'film-opera'[8]. The filmic adaptation of just an opera libretto (or other parts of an opera) should rather be considered as 'opera-film'. The first attempts of filmic opera transpositions, which are at the heart of this paper, transformed, for example, the operatic voice into a speaking voice, and consequently actors spoke for the most part instead of singing

---

[7] Helmut Schanze describes four different techniques which define the spectrum of theater in television: transposition, adaptation, transformation, and transfiguration. These categories can also be used to portray the spectrum of opera in film. Schanze defines 'transposition' as the filming of a performance. The category of 'adaptation' is reserved for productions which attempt to remain faithful to the source. As 'transformation', Schanze defines the realization of the theatrical (in our case operatic) *sujet* with primary attention to the possibilities and means of the audiovisual medium. Through 'transfiguration' a "pure film" is created, in which the theatrical (operatic) *sujet* is no longer recognizable. With regard to the categories of intermediality, however, a 'transfigured' medial product cannot be seen as result of an 'intermedial transposition'. Instead, the relationship between an opera and a film in which the operatic *sujet* is not recognizable ought to be considered as a transmedial phenomenon instead. In addition it is useful to combine Schanze's categories of 'transformation' and 'adaptation' under the concept of 'adaptation' because newer studies suggest that fidelity to the source should not be the dominant criterion for a good adaptation (cf. Stam).

[8] In the older literature the term 'film-opera' has sometimes been restricted to operas exclusively written for film, such as Menotti's *The Medium* (1951). It is however useful to broaden the term and to include opera adaptations. I follow here also Marcia Citron's approach, which seems to favor the term 'film-opera'.

their roles. These films should thus be categorized as 'spoken opera-films'[9].

The following diagram illustrates the different forms of intermedial transposition of opera into film[10].

```
┌─────────────────────────────────────────────────────────────────┐
│  ┌ ─ ─ ─ ─ ─ ─ ─ ─ ─ ─ ─ ─ ─ ─ ─ ─ ─ ─ ─ ─ ─ ─ ─ ─ ─ ─ ─ ─ ┐  │
│     opera texts (libretto and written score)                   │
│  └ ─ ─ ─ ─ ─ ─ ─ ─ ─ ─ ─ ─ ─ ─ ─ ─ ─ ─ ─ ─ ─ ─ ─ ─ ─ ─ ─ ─ ┘  │
│          │                   │                    │            │
│          ▼                   ▼                    ▼            │
│  ┌ ─ ─ ─ ─ ─ ─ ─ ┐   ┌──────────────┐    ┌──────────────────┐ │
│   opera performance     film-opera         (spoken) opera-film│
│      on stage                                                  │
│  └ ─ ─ ─ ─ ─ ─ ─ ┘   └──────────────┘    └──────────────────┘ │
│          │                                                     │
│          ▼                                                     │
│  ┌──────────────┐                                              │
│   performance                                                  │
│   documentation                                                │
│  └──────────────┘                                              │
└─────────────────────────────────────────────────────────────────┘
```

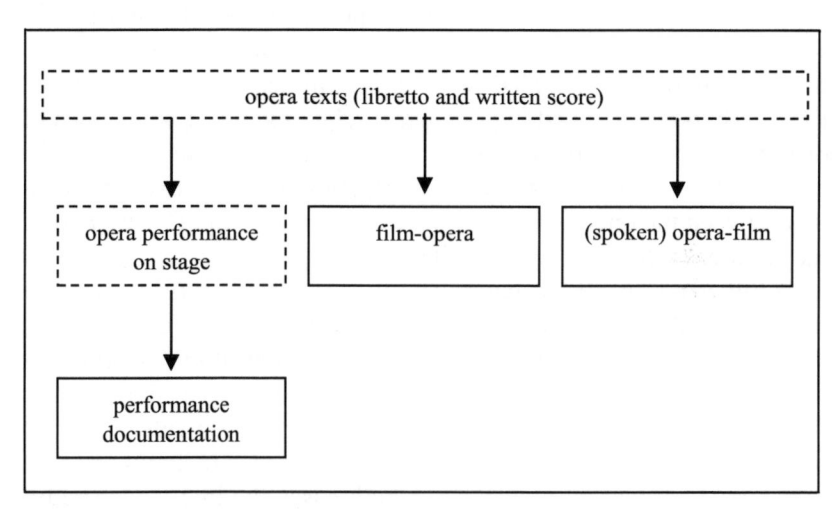

Figure 1: Intermedial transposition of opera into film

Generally speaking, there are therefore three different categories which describe the intermedial transposition of opera into film: performance documentation, film-opera, and opera-film. Performance documentation is the result of the intermedial transposition of a stage production; film-opera and opera-film present filmic interpretations of opera texts. A film-opera offers an adaptation of a libretto and score, an opera-film transforms the opera by adapting only parts of the opera texts. One significant sub-genre of the category opera-film is the spoken opera-film.

For an analysis of this intermedial transposition, Gérard Genette's categories developed to define hypertextual relations will prove useful. Genette defines hypertextuality as "any relationship uniting a text

---

[9] In all spoken opera-films a 'prosification' of the libretto takes place. Therefore, this genre is sometimes referred to as 'opera in prose' (e. g. Citron, *Opera on Screen*). Regarding the concept of 'prosification' cf. Genette 219-225.

[10] Film genres are depicted by boxes with continuous lines, while other art forms (texts and stage performances) are depicted by boxes with broken lines.

B ([...] the *hypertext*) to an earlier text A ([...] the *hypotext*)" (5). He also acknowledges that the concept of hypertextuality is not limited to literary texts and that his theory may be applied to other art forms as well (384-394).With regard to intermedial transpositions of opera into film, his categories are therefore appropriate to describe hypermedialities in films which are based on hypomedialities of operas (libretto and written score). Included in hypermedialities between opera and film are hypertextual and hypermusical relations. Since boundaries of distinct media of communication (opera-film) are transgressed, the hypertextuality (between the libretto and film text) and hypermusicality (between the opera score and the film score) are in this case part of the broader category of hypermediality.

Another intermedial category significant for the analysis of opera in film is that of the 'intermedial reference' (cf. Wolf, "Intermediality Revisited" 23-26). Intermedial references are part of the signifiers of the 'dominant' medium, in our case film, and refer to one specific 'non-dominant' medium, in our case opera. Film can refer either to one specific opera ('individual reference') or to the medium of opera in general ('system reference'). For both cases the intermedial reference can be either explicit or implicit. An explicit reference 'thematizes' one opera or the medium of opera in general, whereas an implicit reference 'imitates' the semiotic system of opera within the film's *discours*. Through the use of intermedial references, operatic elements thus become explicitly part of the film's *histoire* or implicitly part of its semiotic structure. Since the semiotic structure of film is different from the semiotic structure of opera, the implicit reference can only 'simulate' the operatic *discours* with means characteristic to film or 'partially recreate' the operatic *discours* with semiotic elements that film has in common with opera (cf. Rajewsky 83-85).

In order to recognize implicit intermedial references, identifiers or 'markers' are necessary (cf. Rajewsky 200). Such markers may appear within the narrative as 'explicit references', in the paratext, or the context. Also, frequent intertextual or intermusical citations in films, which point to one or more operas, may establish the relationship between the two media and hence function as 'marker' (cf. Helbig 135).

Finally, the concept of 'plurimediality' is defined as the overt presence of at least two distinct media on the surface of a given work in at least one instance (cf. Wolf, "Intermediality Revisited" 22). Since both opera and film are plurimedial art forms, plurimediality is always present as an intermedial concept in each of the two media. Of particular importance for the intermedial transposition from opera into film is the distinction between 'medial combination' and 'medial fusion' (cf. ibid.). A performance documentation, for example, is the result of the intermedial transposition of a medial fusion (an opera performance) while film-operas or spoken opera-films are adaptations of medial combinations (the opera's texts, or parts of them).

In short, all four categories of intermediality are important for the analysis of opera in film. Of particular importance for the following analysis of the spoken opera-film *Fedora* are the concepts of intermedial transposition and intermedial reference.

The Spoken Opera-Film *Fedora*

The film *Fedora*, which was produced in 1942 under the direction of Camillo Mastrocinque, can be considered a typical example of a spoken opera-film[11]. As the title suggests, the film offers an adaptation of the libretto of Arturo Colautti's and Umberto Giordano's opera *Fedora*. During the production of this film, Giordano himself worked alongside Nucio Fiorda, who is credited with the music of the film (cf. Rossellini).

The storyline of the film is based both on the 1882 play *Fédora* by Victorien Sardou as well as on the libretto of the opera *Fedora*, which was staged for the first time in 1898[12]. At the center of the film's story is the Russian princess, Fedora Romazoff. Vladimir Andrejevich, Fedora's fiancé, is murdered in St. Petersburg on the eve of his wedding to Fedora. Fedora swears that she will find the murderer to avenge the death of her fiancé. She moves to Paris and meets a painter by the name of Ivan Petrovich. After a while, Petrovich confesses that his real name is Loris Ipanoff and that he had murdered Vladimir.

---

[11] In addition to *Fedora*, Mastrocinque directed two other spoken opera-films: *Don Pasquale* (1940, based on the opera by Donizetti/Accursi) and *Il Matrimonio Segreto* (1943, based on the opera by Cimarosa/Bertati).

[12] For the opera adaptation of the Sardou's play cf. Girardi; Viale Ferrero.

Fedora then goes to the Russian secret service and reveals the identity of Loris. She later learns from Loris that he murdered Vladimir because Vladimir had an affair with Loris's wife. Fedora subsequently falls in love with Loris and convinces the police of the innocence of her lover and points to Valeriano, Loris's brother, as the real murderer. The brother is then apprehended and dies, together with his mother, in a Russian prison. When Loris finds out what Fedora has done, he distances himself from her. Fedora then poisons herself. The last scene of the film shows Fedora dying in the arms of Loris. As she dies, Loris forgives her for her deeds.

Like the opera, and in contrast to the play, the film is divided into three parts[13]. The first takes place in St. Petersburg, the second in Paris, and the third in Switzerland. If one compares the film's storyline to Sardou's play and Colautti's libretto, several formal and thematic transformations are observable, of which I would like to point out the most significant.

Like in almost all filmic adaptations, we find here 'expansions' and 'concisions'[14]. As far as concisions are concerned, when compared to Sardou's play the film excludes several political and historic references. It is, however, fair to say that the political and historic context is portrayed rather weakly in the libretto as well. For example, the conflict between the Czarists and the so-called nihilists, which plays a rather significant role in Sardou's play, is treated only in passing in the libretto (cf. Girardi). The film, in turn, omits the whole conflict entirely.

The most important expansion takes place at the beginning of the film in the form of a prologue. This prologue consists of two parts: in the first part, Vladimir introduces Fedora to his father, Jariskin. The second part documents the evening Vladimir is murdered. Of note in this prologue is a cross, which Jariskin hands to Fedora. Vladimir explains to Fedora the significance of this cross. He tells her that it has been in his family for generations and is a symbol of loyalty and

---

[13] *Fédora* by Sardou is divided into four acts. The first takes place in St. Petersburg, the other three in Paris. Giordano and Colautti combined the second and the third acts of the play into the second act of the opera.

[14] The concepts developed by Genette and applied to describe the hypermedialities between the film *Fedora* and its hypomedialities are marked with single quotation marks, when used for the first time.

faithfulness. Musically, this gesture is accompanied by the orchestral score of "Su questa santa croce" (Fedora I, 46+1), which introduces one of the main motifs of the opera. In the opera, it is heard for the first time when Fedora swears to avenge her fiancé's death and therefore represents the motif of revenge. Vladimir's words in the prologue, however, add an additional meaning to the music and the cross. They become symbols for Fedora's faithfulness to Vladimir and his family.

Example: "Su questa santa croce" (Fedora I, 46+1)

The prologue of this film includes another formal characteristic, which Genette defines as "transmodalization regarding distance", i. e. the transformation of the narrative mood with respect to the distinction between "telling" and "showing" (287). Here, the film presents characters which are only implied in the text and are not supposed to be incorporated into a performance. For instance, in the prologue the film brings Vladimir and Jariskin to life in a manner that extends beyond other characters speaking about them. Another example of a transmodalization regarding distance is Vladimir's murder, which is likewise shown during a flashback in the second part of the film.

A rather significant thematic transformation involves the 'devaluation' of Russians. In the libretto as well as in the play, Loris retains his real name and identity. The changing of his name in the film (Loris Ipanoff to Ivan Petrovich) makes him appear false and cowardly. Jariskin, Vladimir's father and head of the Russian police, is introduced as a weak and unpredictable alcoholic. Furthermore, in the libretto and the play, Loris's mother dies of sorrow after the death of her son, Valeriano, who drowns in prison, while in the film the mother is imprisoned as well. By depicting the death in prison of the innocent mother, the film emphasizes the horrors of the Russian justice system, which is another example of a devaluation. The reason for these devaluations might have been political and a reflection of the fascist ideology of the time, in which the film was produced (1942).

Apart from ideological differences, however, the film stays relatively true to the meaning of the libretto, preserving its primary structure and building on the love-revenge paradigm, which is reflected in Fedora's character[15]: During the first part of the film, Fedora is in love with Vladimir, who is then murdered. She swears that she will avenge his death. In the second part she finds the culprit and denounces Loris and his brother to the Russian police (= revenge). As Fedora learns of the reasons for the murder, she falls in love with Loris. At the end of the third part, she concedes that she had acted out of love for Vladimir, as well as hate and rage. As in the opera, she takes poison and begs Loris for forgiveness and love.

Regarding the music, the film score uses only excerpts of the opera score and also contains newly-composed music. Several film scenes are even presented without the accompaniment of music and, for the most part, the music plays only a secondary role. The film score therefore does not present an adaptation of, but makes only reference to the opera score[16]. This is particularly true with regard to the main musical motifs and themes of the opera[17]. The opening credits of the film for example are accompanied by an instrumental version of the aria "Amor ti vieta", whose vocal line in the opera is associated with

---

[15] Characteristic for many opera librettos (and operas) in general is a contrast structure which often presents a central opposition of two irreconcilable principles. The paradigmatic level of the text is hence crucial for its meaning (cf. Gier 6-14).

[16] The relationship between this film and the medium of opera is clearly established, since the film is an adaptation of an opera libretto and the film's title is identical to the title of an opera. Hence all references to opera ought to be interpreted as intermedial references.

[17] Regarding the musical structure of the opera cf. Bernardoni.

Loris's love[18]. In congruence with the opera score, this theme is repeated three times during the film. Also the above-mentioned motif, which in the opera is associated with Fedora's revenge (Fedora I, 46+1), plays a crucial role in the film's narrative and functions as a reminiscing motif. These implicit references to the opera score can be described as 'partial recreations', because structural elements of the operatic *discours*, specifically the narrative function of recurring motifs, are recreated by the film score.

Another example of a partial recreation is the evocation of *couleur locale* through diegetic and non-diegetic music. In a manner similar to the opera, we hear local folk songs several times throughout the film and a shepherd boy at the end. Also, the music which accompanies the first scene of the third part fulfills a function comparable to the music in the opera.

The first shots of the third part show a pastoral scene under blue skies, replete with fruit trees, mountains, a waterfall, and finally dancing peasant women picking flowers. This idyllic Alpine panorama is accompanied musically as reflected in the score of the opera (III, 1-8). As in the opera, a chorus of peasant women, singing about the spring, joins in. In this scene the setting of the events is introduced through shots of the Swiss countryside, accompanied by diegetic and non-diegetic music that evokes the Alps. The film thus makes use of cinematic, musical, and theatrical elements to introduce the setting of the events in Switzerland. The non-diegetic music and the songs of the peasant women establish the *couleur locale*. Accordingly, this scene can be interpreted as a remarkably close adaptation of the opening scene of the third act of the opera.

The closeness to the libretto is evident also during the last sequence of the film, which presents Fedora's suicide. The setting is Fedora's chalet in the Berner Oberland. At the beginning of the sequence, Fedora and Loris sit on a bench on the veranda and converse. The following dialogue between Loris and Fedora in the film demonstrates this close relation to the libretto of the opera:

L: Una spia dunque. Ma Boroff saprà il suo nome.
F: No, no, forse non è una spia.

---

[18] This instrumental variation of "Amor ti vieta" is adapted from the Intermezzo of the second act (Fedora II, 37-38).

L: Ma che dunque?
F: Forse è una creatura disgraziata.
L: Un essere abietto che non merita nessuna difesa.
F: No, oh certo. Troppo grande è la sua colpa. Ma quello che ha fatto è così orribile che cerca di capirne il perché e di volerle un po' di perdono.
L: Perdono?
F: Di compassione se posso.
L: Nessuna compassione.
F: Ascolta, se una donna avesse amato Vladimiro ... tu le hai ucciso l'uomo che essa amava ... e allora per vendicarsi ... e se ignorava che l'uomo amato era indegno, ignorava i torti che aveva commesso contro di te.
L: E si vendica su due innocenti? Che colpa avevano loro?
F: Ma essa forse sarebbe pronta a piangerli con te? Ascolta, se tu la vedessi disperata per il male che ti ha fatto, se tu sappía (sic), scongiurassi (sic) di salvarla? La perdoneresti?
L: Mai.
F: Ma se te lo chiedessi in nome del tuo amore per me? Avresti pietà, vero? Dimmi, avresti pietà?

(direct quotes from the film)[19]

Libretto text of Fedora III, 47-53:
L: Fedora, quella donna è a Parigi .../ Partiam per rintracciarla .../ O spia, la maschera le strapperò!
F: È veramente, quella una spia?
L: Tu la difendi!
F: Se quella sciagurata/ perdutamente avesse amato/ Vladimiro?/ Tu le uccidi il suo diletto./ T'odia;/ e l'odio non perdona,/ e non ragiona amor.
L: Ma che le avean fatto/ mia madre e mio fratello?
F: Forse con te li piange,/ forse per essi prega./ Nella sua cieca rabbia,/ nel suo fatale inganno,/ alle innocenti vittime/ la stolta non pensò!
L: Una carozza!/ È Boroff.

---

[19] 'L: A spy then. But Boroff will know her name. F: No, no, perhaps she is not a spy. L: But what then? F: Perhaps she is an unfortunate person. L: A mean being who does not deserve any defense. F: Surely not. Too grave is her crime. But because what she has done is so horrible, try to understand her reasons and to grant her some forgiveness. L: Forgiveness? F: Compassion if I may. L: Not any compassion. F: Listen, if a woman had loved Vladimir ... you killed the man she loved ... and then for revenge ... and if she didn't know that the lover was unworthy, didn't know about the injustice he had committed against you. L: And her revenge falls on two innocent lives? What did they do to deserve it? F: But she would perhaps be ready to mourn them together with you? Listen, if you saw her desperate for the evil she committed against you, if you knew, that I would implore you to save her? Would you forgive her? L: Never. F: But if I asked you in the name of your love for me? You would have pity, right? Tell me, would you have pity?' [My translation]

F: Dio! Lui!
L: No, non ancora ...
F: Ascoltami!/ Se fosse pentita,/ o cuor generoso,/ pietà non avresti?
L: Pietà? No, giammai!
F: Se quell'infelice/ qui stesse ai tuoi piedi,/ di lagrime intrisa,/ languente, morente,/ perdono invocando,/ chiedendo pietà,/ gridandoti:/ grazia, grazia!/ Loris, io ben ti conosco,/ mio dolce, mio buono,/ mio grande fanciullo:/ clemente saresti./ Non dire di no .../ non dire di no./ Dimmi che tu le perdoni[20].

During the dialogue in the film, as in the libretto, Fedora tries in vain to explain her treacherous behavior and to beg for forgiveness. Even though the text is not incorporated word for word and is stylistically transposed, its meaning remains within the confines of the libretto. The spoken film text even incorporates identical or similar key words, such as *pietà* (pity) and *perdono* (forgiveness). Musically this dialogue is accompanied in congruence with the opera score[21].

In comparison to the hypotext, Fedora's reasoning for what she has done is only slightly 'transmotivated'. In the libretto, Fedora emphasizes, in addition to her love for Vladimir ("perdutamente avesse amato Vladimiro" – 'passionately had loved Vladimir'), 'hate' ("odio") and 'blind rage' ("cieca rabbia") as primary reasons for her behavior. In the film, Fedora says that she had acted out of revenge ("per vendicarsi" – 'for revenge').

Immediately after this scene, the camera focuses on Fedora's suicide. After showing Fedora's face from her chin to her hairline, the camera pans slowly down to her hands. She grasps the chain around her neck, on which hangs the cross containing the poison. She lifts the

---

[20] 'L: Fedora, that woman is in Paris ... Let's depart to find her ... O spy, I will rip the mask off her face! F: Is she really a spy? L: You defend her! F: If that unfortunate person had passionately loved Vladimir? You kill her happiness. She hates you; and hate does not forgive, and love does not reason. L: But what have my mother and my brother done to her? F: Perhaps she mourns them together with you, perhaps she prays for them. In her blind rage, in her fatal error, the stupid person did not think of the innocent victims! L: A carriage! It is Boroff. F: God! Him! L: No, not yet ... F: Listen to me! If she regretted, o generous heart, wouldn't you have pity? L: Pity? No, never! F: If that unhappy person was here in front of your feet, in tears, desperate, destroyed, imploring forgiveness, asking for pity, crying to you: mercy, mercy! Loris, I know you well, my sweet, my good, my noble person: you would be merciful. Do not say no ... do not say no. Tell me that you forgive her.' [My translation]

[21] The conversation is accompanied by the orchestral score to Fedora III, 49-52.

cross slowly. The cross is here at the center of the frame and is shown through a close-up shot. After a cut, Loris and Fedora move towards each other and she falls into his arms. Not one word is spoken during the entire scene. The scene draws life exclusively from the images and the music, which corresponds to the opera score (Fedora III, 53-55).

Particularly interesting in this suicide scene is the function of the cross. Through being shown in close-up, the cross has implications on the meaning of Fedora's suicide. It reminds the viewer of the prologue, in which the cross has been portrayed as a symbol of faithfulness and loyalty towards the Jariskin family. Through this paradigmatic relationship, delivered through the images, a different reason for Fedora's suicide is communicated: Fedora has been unfaithful to the Jariskin family because she got involved with Loris. By having accepted the cross and having promised to be loyal to the family, she is almost required to make use of the poison. This interpretation modifies also the overall meaning of the opera in that the love-revenge paradigm (which is certainly also dominant in the film) is augmented by the contrasting love-loyalty[22].

From a technical point of view, through repeated shots of the Byzantine cross with visual (filmic) means the film 'imitates' the effect an opera would have achieved through the musical technique of a recurring motif. Hence, this technique ought to be interpreted as implicit operatic reference and more specifically as operatic 'simulation'.

In conclusion, this spoken opera-film presents a relatively true adaptation of the libretto to the opera *Fedora*. Although the opera score is incorporated only in excerpts and mostly in a non-diegetic manner, the film score includes the main musical motifs and themes. In addition, the film makes use of operatic techniques on the *discours* level, which conveys an operatic impression to the viewer. Examples of these 'implicit intermedial references' include the communication of *couleur locale* through Alpine music or typical folk songs. Also the use of recurring motifs can be regarded as operatic reference. This

---

[22] The last scene of the film, which shows Fedora's death, supports this interpretation. By contrast to the opera, Fedora appears to interpret her end as fate ("È stato il destino" – 'It has been destiny'). Since Fedora had been disloyal to the Jariskin family through her affair with Loris, destiny had decided her death.

technique is also extended to images by showing, hence the film imitates the medium of opera not only by 'partially recreating', but also by 'simulating' its *discours*.

Spoken opera-films like *Fedora*, which were popular during the 1930s and 1940s, demonstrate cinema's continuous attraction to the older plurimedial art form of opera, and document the first attempts of sound cinema to transpose opera into film. The decline in the production of spoken opera-films in the 1950s may be attributed to the invention of more sophisticated forms of operatic adaptations such as film-operas and television-operas.

Although for all intents and purposes the genre of the 'spoken opera-film' died in the second half of 1950s, operas continue to be realized in film in several ways. Today, the most popular form is the performance documentation. In addition, feature films continue to make reference to single operas or the medium of opera in general. Recently, attempts have been made to create new multimedial productions of operas by staging and filming operas at the historic settings outlined in the libretto and then broadcasting them over television and the internet[23]. It will be interesting to see how the relationship between opera and film continues and further develops during the twenty-first century and what new intermedial experiments will be realized in the future.

References

Bernardoni, Virgilio (1999). "Il linguaggio musicale della *Fedora* di Umberto Giordano". Johannes Streicher, ed. *Ultimi splendori: Cilea, Giordano, Alfano*. Roma: Ismez. 347-361.

Bourre, Jean-Paul (1987). *Opéra et cinéma*. Editions Artefact. Paris: Veyrier.

Bragaglia, Cristina, Fernaldo di Giammatteo (1990). *Italia 1900-1990. L'opera al cinema*. Firenze: La Nuova Italia.

---

[23] Cf. Giuseppe Patroni-Griffi's productions of *Tosca* (1992, directed by Brian Large) and *La Traviata* (2000, directed by Pierre Cavassilas).

Callegari, Giuliana, Nuccio Lodato, eds. (1984). *L'ultimo mélo. La vita cantata tra set e scena lirica*. Pavia: Amministrazione Provinciale di Pavia.

Casadio, Gianfranco (1995). *Opera e cinema. La musica lirica nel cinema italiano dall'avvento del sonoro ad oggi*. Ravenna: Longo editore.

Citron, Marcia J. (1994). "A Night at the Cinema. Zeffirelli's *Otello* and the Genre of Film-Opera". *The Musical Quarterly* 78/4: 700-741.

— (2000). *Opera on Screen*. New Haven, CT/London: Yale University Press.

Fawkes, Richard (2000). *Opera on Film*. London: Duckworth.

Genette, Gérard (1997). *Palimpsests: Literature in the Second Degree*. Trans. Channa Newman, Claude Doubinsky. Lincoln, NE/ London: University of Nebraska Press.

Gier, Albert (1998). *Das Libretto. Theorie und Geschichte einer musikoliterarischen Gattung*. Darmstadt: Wissenschaftliche Buchgesellschaft.

Giordano, Umberto (1941). *Fedora. Dramma di V. Sardou. Ridotto in tre atti per la scena lirica da Arturo Colautti. Riduzione per canto e pianoforte*. Milano: Sonzogno.

Girardi, Michele (2000). "Fedora, una prima donna sull'orlo di una crisi di nervi". *Fedora di Giordano, Stagione d'opera 2000*. Torino: Teatro Regio di Torino. 9-20.

Helbig, Jörg (2001). "Intermediales Erzählen. Baustein für eine Typologie intermedialer Erscheinungsformen in der Erzählliteratur am Beispiel der Sonatenform von Anthony Burgess' *A Clockwork Orange*". Jörg Helbig, ed. *Erzählen und Erzähltheorie im 20. Jahrhundert. Festschrift für Wilhelm Füger*. Heidelberg: Winter. 131-152.

Joe, Jeongwon (1998). "Opera on Film, Film in Opera. Postmodern Implications of the Cinematic Influence on Opera". Ph.D. Dissertation. Northwestern University, 1998.

— (2002). "The Cinematic Body in the Operatic Theater". Jeongwon Joe, Rose Theresa, eds. *Between Opera and Cinema*. New York, NY/London: Routledge. 59-73.

Kuhn, Bernhard (2005). *Die Oper im italienischen Film*. FORA: Studien zu Literatur und Sprache 9. Essen: Die Blaue Eule.

Kühnel, Jürgen (2001). "'Mimesis' und 'Diegesis' – szenische Darstellung und filmische Erzählung. Zur Ästhetik der Oper in Film und Fernsehen". Peter Csobádi et al., eds. *Das Musiktheater in den audiovisuellen Medien: '...Ersichtlich gewordene Taten der Musik': Vorträge und Gespräche des Salzburger Symposions 1999.* Anif/Salzburg: Müller-Speiser. 60-79.

Marchelli, Massimo, Renato Venturelli, eds. (2001) *Se quello schermo io fossi.* Genova: Le Mani.

Miceli, Sergio, ed. (1987). *L'opera in film.* Quaderni dell'I.R.Te.M. 5. Roma: I.R.Te.M.

—, (1988). *Opera e cinema.* Quaderni dell'I.R.Te.M. 6. Roma: I.R.Te.M.

Rajewsky, Irina O. (2002). *Intermedialität.* Tübingen: Francke.

Rossellini, Renzo (1942). "Schermi Sonori: 'Fedora', 'Bengasi'". *Cinema* 21/154: 681.

Sardou, Victorien (1908). "Fédora: Drame en quatre actes". *L'Illustration Théatrale* 2/88: 1-32.

Schanze, Helmut (1996). "Theater und Fernsehen im Kontext 'Neuer Medien'". Rolf Bolwin, Peter Seibert, eds. *Theater und Fernsehen: Bilanz einer Beziehung.* Studien zur Kommunikationswissenschaft 18. Opladen: Westdeutscher Verlag. 45-52.

Simpson, Alexander Thomas, Jr. (1990). "Opera on Film: A Study of the History and the Aesthetic Principles and Conflicts of a Hybrid Genre". Ph.D. Dissertation. University of Kentucky.

Stam, Robert (2005). "Introduction: The Theory and Practice of Adaptation". Robert Stam, Alessandra Raengo, eds. *Literature and Film: A Guide to the Theory and Practice of Film Adaptation.* Malden: Blackwell. 1-52.

Tambling, Jeremy (1987). *Opera, Ideology and Film.* New York, NY: St. Martin's Press.

—, ed. (1994). *A Night in at the Opera. Media Representations of Opera.* London: John Libbey.

Theresa, Rose (2002). "From Méphistophélès to Méliès: Spectacle and Narrative in Opera and Early Film". Jeongwon Joe, Rose Theresa, eds. *Between Opera and Cinema.* New York, NY/London: Routledge. 1-18.

Viale Ferrero, Mercedes (1995). "Da 'Fédora' a 'Fedora': smontaggio e rimontaggio di uno scenario (melo)drammatico". *Il Saggiatore musicale* 2/1: 93-104.
Wolf, Werner (1999). *The Musicalization of Fiction. A Study in the Theory and History of Intermediality*. Internationale Forschungen zur Allgemeinen und Vergleichenden Literaturwissenschaft 35. Amsterdam/Atlanta, GA: Rodopi, 1999.
— (2002). "Intermediality Revisited: Reflections on Word and Music Relations in the Context of a General Typology of Intermediality". Suzanne M. Lodato, Suzanne Aspden, Walter Bernhart, eds. *Word and Music Studies: Essays in Honor of Steven Paul Scher and on Cultural Identity and the Musical Stage*. Word and Music Studies 4. Amsterdam/New York, NY: Rodopi. 13-34.

Literary Mediations of Baroque Music
Biber, Bach, and Nancy Huston

Frédérique Arroyas, Guelph, Ont.

The renewed popularity of Baroque music has been a clearly visible trend in Western cultures ever since the mid-nineteenth century. This revival is apparent in various works of fiction and not only shows that writers have been inspired by Baroque music, but that they continue to shape the contours of its appeal. My study of two novels by Nancy Huston demonstrates that musical compositions of a revived historical era can be made to contribute elements of their medium's specificity to a literary work, and that they may also be brought to resonate with contemporary issues of culture, power, class, and gender. In this way, we see the novels as literary mediations of Baroque music, an interface between music and literature, between the past and the present.

The renewed popularity of Baroque music has been a clearly noticeable trend in Western cultures ever since the mid-nineteenth century. The excavation of the past's musical compositions, a legacy of the Romantic period, initiated a new appreciation for these forgotten relics. By the mid-twentieth century, early music specialists fervently researched and studied Baroque music, restoring its original vitality and specificity. Since that time, Baroque music has become known to ever-wider audiences and it is no surprise to see manifestations of its influence in contemporary literary works.

Canadian-born (and Paris-based) novelist Nancy Huston has cultivated through her fiction a fruitful and dynamic relationship with the musical domain. As a child, she studied the piano and in later adolescence took up the harpsichord[1]. Having become a resident in Paris in

---

[1] In an interview with Marcus Robinson, Huston states: "I think I fell in love with the harpsichord and the French language at the same time and for the same reason. So, it was about age seventeen, and I was in high school in New Hampshire […] and there was a harpsichord concert in the museum, and I just literally was blown away by the beauty of this instrument and I decided to study it, if I could […] The first book I wrote in French, the first book I wrote, the first novel I wrote, period [sic], was *The Goldberg Variations* […] I told myself, and my husband, that I wanted to use the royalties from the book to buy a harpsichord. So there was always that dream that I

1973, she started incorporating musical characters, themes and structures in several of her novels. In 2002, she recorded for the CD *Les Pérégrinations Goldberg* a reading of her first novel, *The Goldberg Variations*, with musical accompaniment. Of particular interest to us here, however, are two novels that present intriguing intermedial adaptations of Baroque compositions: *Instruments of Darkness* (1996), and The *Goldberg Variations* (1981) can be considered literary adaptations of Heinrich Biber's *Sonaten über die Mysterien des Rosenkranzes* (ca. 1670) and J. S. Bach's *Goldberg Variationen* (ca. 1741) respectively. As we will see, the adaptation of these musical works from the Baroque era is a deliberate choice that conveys the particular significance which Baroque aesthetics and Baroque music hold for this author.

One can consider the following definition of adaptation: "[…] a specific process involving the transition from one genre to another: novels into film; drama into musical; the dramatization of prose narrative and prose fiction; or the inverse movement of making drama into prose narrative" (Sanders 19) and ask whether *The Goldberg Variations* and *Instruments of Darkness* can in fact be deemed adaptations. On one level, we witness in these two novels a cross-modal transfer where novels, via a verbal medium, exploit and transform the technical and stylistic characteristics of the particular Baroque musical works they refer to. This is an inherent feature of what has been called 'intermediality', to be understood as the "direct or indirect participation of two or more media in the signification of a human artefact" (Wolf, *Musicalization of Fiction* 37). On another level, however, adaptation, as a transpositional device, is "an act of re-vision in itself" (Sanders 18) and is often culturally loaded. Our study of these two novels will show that the original works, musical compositions of a revolved historical period, not only contribute elements of their medium's specificity to a literary work but are also brought to resonate with contemporary issues of culture, power, class, and gender. In this way, we see the novels as literary mediations of Baroque music, an interface between music and literature, between the past and the present.

---

was going to be able to have one of my own, and I indeed did buy one, although not with the royalties, that's for sure." (Robinson, online)

1. Twentieth-Century Neo-Baroque Poetics

Although the Baroque compositions in the two novels are exploited to specific ends and reflect themes that are prevalent in Huston's work, they also convey concepts that have been shaped by a retrieval of Baroque aesthetics in mid-twentieth-century Europe. As we will see, there is a strong correlation between Huston's literary adaptations of these musical works and the symbolic values attributed to Baroque aesthetics by French intellectuals of the 1960s. Thus, a brief look at this renewed interest and appropriation of Baroque art and music will help elucidate the significance of the Baroque compositions that have been adopted and adapted in the context of Huston's novels.

The early-music revival can be said to parallel the emerging popular interest in Baroque art and architecture that took hold in European avant-garde cultural circles in the mid-twentieth century. Of conesquence here is the enthusiasm it created amongst French cultural theorists, art historians, artists and novelists. Between 1950 and 1970, a significant number of French publications and artistic productions attest to the interest generated by Baroque art and architecture[2]. Transposed to a contemporary context, Baroque art came to signify an opposition to accepted "universal" and "objective" norms and the questioning of principles of rationality and hierarchy. Baroque aesthetic principles were considered representative of such post-modern concepts as decentred perspectives, mobility, openness, multiplicity of reality, and subjectivity.

While it would take too long here to retrace the many instances where the Baroque became a supporting structure for post-modern thought, it can be said that the impassioned representation of Baroque art and architecture by the Swiss art historian Heinrich Wölfflin was instrumental in launching a renewed interest in things Baroque and in shaping their portrayal. Through his books and teachings, Wölfflin demonstrated how Baroque art had evolved from the classical style of the Renaissance. He established a binary relationship between the two periods. To Wölfflin, the Baroque was dramatic, theatrical, full of contrasts, and above all dynamic, whereas sixteenth-century classical

---

[2] For an overall description of this phenomenon, see Pierre Charpentrat's *Le Mirage Baroque*. This renewed popularity of Baroque art was such that Charpentrat came to denounce the overuse and the dissolution of the concept of Baroque art.

style was linear, static, and closed. As the antithesis to the centered symmetrical art of the late Renaissance, the Baroque preferred curved lines, fleeting and unstable perspectives, and an open form. Wölfflin's representation of Baroque painting, sculpture and architecture hit a sensitive chord with the rebellious era of the 1960s where a general movement to dislodge conservative, patriarchal structures was underway. The Baroque aesthetic, as presented by avant-garde intellectuals, was a transhistorical state giving voice to artistic freedom and allowing flight from the conventions of authoritarian regimes. Consequently, it came to symbolize a revolt against what was seen as the oppressive control and overbearing authority of political, religious and cultural institutions on the new generation.

Among the theoretical essays in which the Baroque was taken to support avant-garde principles, is Umberto Eco's highly influential *The Open Work*. Published in France in 1965, it presented itself as a manifesto of the avant-garde, in which its author outlines concordances between experimental art works and those of the Baroque period. The antithetically paired Renaissance/Baroque periods are used as an overarching framework for opposing aesthetic concepts such as determinacy/indeterminacy, closure/openness, stasis/movement, circumscribing Baroque aesthetics and establishing parallels with contemporary art works. With respect to the 'open form' in Baroque art, Eco writes:

> [...] it is precisely the static and unquestionable definitiveness of the classical Renaissance form which is denied: the canons of space extended round a central axis, closed in by symmetrical lines and shut angles which cajole the eye toward the centre in such a way as to suggest an idea of "essential" eternity rather than movement. Baroque form is dynamic; it tends to indeterminacy of effect (in its play of solid and void, light and darkness, with its curvature, its broken surfaces, its widely diversified angles of inclination); it conveys the idea of space being progressively dilated. Its search for kinetic excitement and illusory effect leads to a situation where the plastic mass in the Baroque work of art never allows a privileged, definitive, frontal view; rather, it induces the spectator to shift his position continuously in order to see the work in constantly new aspects, as if it were in a state of perpetual transformation. (7)

It is these effects of disequilibrium and perpetual transformation, where spectators are required to move around and change their angles of vision, and where perception itself becomes an object of inquiry, that are sought out in the avant-garde art works Eco is defending. Eco continues by indicating that Baroque and contemporary visions converge through a common valorization of the imagination and through the stimulation of human intellect.

> Now if Baroque spirituality is to be seen as the first clear manifestation of modern culture and sensitivity, it is because here, for the first time, man opts out of the canon of authorized responses and finds that he is faced (both in art and in science) by a world in a fluid state which requires corresponding creativity on his part. The poetic treatises concerning '*maraviglia*', 'wit', '*agudezas*', and so on really strain to go further than their apparently Byzantine appearances: they seek to establish the new man's inventive role. He is no longer to see the work of art as an object which draws on given links with experience and which demands to be enjoyed; now he sees it as a potential mystery to be solved, a role to fulfill, a stimulus to quicken his imagination. (7)

Aware that "it would be rash to interpret Baroque poetics as a conscious theory of the 'open work'" (ibid.), Eco nonetheless observes that the Baroque traits described above are taken up by the avant-garde because of a concordance in philosophical outlooks. It is in this sense that, for Eco, Baroque aesthetics reflect the *Zeitgeist* of the new era ushered in by the 1960s. Affinities between the two periods, according to Eco, are rooted in the function of the art work, and particularly in its ability to promote creative activity. Whether in the Baroque or the contemporary avant-garde periods, art reflects the instability of the universe, the indeterminacy of absolute knowledge, and calls for an examination of individual perception and the acceptance of multiple interpretations. Each of these conditions, according to Eco, makes the individual "the focal point of a network of limitless interrelations" (4).

This portrayal of Baroque aesthetics was also echoed in the musical domain. Here, the Renaissance/Baroque opposition came to bear upon the definition of Baroque music as a liberating force from the controlled and restrained compositions of the late Renaissance. For example, Suzanne Clercx' *Le Baroque et la musique*, published in Brussels in 1948, describes the birth of Baroque music as 'the irruption of human personality' with melody taking on 'the contours of human passion'. This development is seen as a rupture in the serenity and equilibrium of the fluid and forward motion of Renaissance melodic lines where 'something has irrupted in the musical form, inflating it with intentions, lifting it and conferring to it new meaning: it is in fact a devastating current that saps it and takes it apart.'[3] Clercx describes Baroque music as a reaction to the order and harmony characteristic of Renaissance music, something that was initiated with the use of chromaticism, the insertion of a semi-tone whose effect disturbs expectations:

> A note that was expected, in the envisaged melodic unfolding, is withheld, a harmony whose plenitude and permanence were initiated by a system of perfect intervals, is dissolved into unknown relations. In this calm homorhythmic unfolding, a voice, suddenly, recites its chant, accentuates syllables, attracting attention to a text[4].

Another example of a contemporary representation of Baroque musical style is Rémy Stricker's 1968 *La Musique du Baroque*, which advances an analysis of musical ornamentation aligned with the functions of architectural ornaments. Stricker comments on the abundance and the nature of ornamentation in Baroque music and, especially, its 'dialectical relationship with form' ("ses rapports dialectiques avec la forme"; 39). He notes that if musical ornaments enrich the melodic line, better translating and reflecting the range of emotions and passions, they also reveal an inclination to play with appearances and question the boundary between illusion and reality. Ornamental ostentation or surface decorations offer to the listener the 'illusion of deployed forces in nature. The reality game is depicted in "flamboyant displays" and "surfaces" to better lure the senses, provoke doubt and thus liberate the imagination'[5].

Both Stricker and Clercx demonstrate that during the Baroque era music changed from a mimetic ideal (art as a mirror held up to nature or emotion) to an expressive one (art as expressing one's unique inner feelings). They diligently apply to Baroque music the criteria initially

---

[3] My translation of : "[...] quelque chose a fait irruption dans la forme, la gonfle d'intentions, la soulève et lui confère une signification nouvelle: un esprit dévastateur, en réalité, qui la sape et la désagrège." (92)

[4] My translation of : "Une note que l'on attendait, dans un déroulement mélodique prévu, ne se produit pas; une harmonie dont la plénitude et la permanence étaient annoncées par un système d'accords parfaits, se dissout en rapports inconnus. Dans ce calme déroulement homorythmique, une voix, soudain, récite son chant, accentue des syllabes, attire l'attention sur un texte." (92)

[5] My translation of : " [...] l'illusion d'un déploiement des forces de la nature. Le jeu de la réalité s'offre en 'fastes' et en 'surfaces' pour mieux tromper les sens, provoquer le doute et ainsi libérer l'imagination." (55)

laid out by Wölfflin, which allow them to emphasize the propensity for Baroque music to represent individual freedom and the liberation of creative impulses. Baroque musical devices and aesthetics thus become symbolically salient and, as such, useful models for transmitting issues of contention.

To that effect, the retrieval of Baroque music becomes linked to a debate that equates the term 'classical' (initially attributed to the classical style of the Renaissance) to 'classical music'. The French sociologist Antoine Hennion, reflecting on the Baroque revival, remarks: '[…] as early as ca. 1965-1970, this movement becomes a pretext […] to call into question the state of classical music altogether, "from Bach to Debussy"' [6]. Hennion places the term 'classical music' in the context of its social function and specifically a type of 'class' music inscribed within a particular social hierarchy. Classical music is thus equated with bourgeois ideals of order, control and repression. In contrast to this, the theatrical and individualistic orientation of the Baroque seem to speak to a contemporary sensibility that came into being after World War II and that saw the emancipation of the individual from imperialist or religious manipulations.

One manifestation of this extended meaning is the symbolic representation of Baroque music as a purposeful counterweight to the grandiose, large-scale symphonic works of the late nineteenth century. It stands out in opposition to the symphonic performances directed by celebrated conductors like Furtwängler or Stokowski, whose performances followed a course set by the Romantic tradition[7]. The intimate and historically informed performances of Baroque ensembles like those of the Concentus Musicus[8] offer a humble yet critical contrast

---

[6] My translation of: "[…] dès les années 65-70 environ, ce mouvement s'affirme comme pré-texte […] à une remise en cause de l'état de la musique classique en bloc, 'de Bach à Debussy'." ("Le Baroque, un goût si moderne" 24)

[7] Nikolaus Harnoncourt writes: "Conductors like Furtwängler or Stokowski, whose ideal was grounded in the late Romantic period, presented all earlier music from this perspective. Bach's organ works, for example, were scored for Wagnerian orchestras and his Passions were performed in an overly romantic way, with a gigantic ensemble." (*Music as Speech* 14)

[8] One must remember that for the early-music movement, not only was there considerable effort expended in retrieving forgotten works and composers as well as in the reconstruction of period instruments and historically informed performances, but that these new interpretations also stirred up controversy as they went against the

to the maestro cult in Romantic, and modern, resolutely hierarchical models where the conductor's dictatorial manner would relegate the musician's role to that of a passive medium[9].

As we will see in the following discussion of Huston's *Goldberg Variations* and *Instruments of Darkness*, the Baroque musical works evoked in these novels offer both a structural foundation and thematic substance that serve to support a decidedly post-modern ideology. Fictional characters embark on a quest to emancipate themselves from stifling social structures. An underlying voice of dissention pushes to overturn traditional hierarchies and categorisations. The characteristic Baroque elements of Bach's and Biber's musical compositions, transposed into the literary medium, become ideologically charged, thus building up the path of resistance that will ultimately liberate individual initiative and diversity from the tyranny and subordination of social conventions.

---

established conventions of the Romantic symphonic interpretations of old masters. In 1953, Harnoncourt founded the Concentus Musicus Wien, a laboratory for works of early music. In the beginning, the ensemble's repertoire consisted mainly of little-known works of Austrian Baroque music. The year 1962, however, marked an important date when the ensemble performed Bach's *Brandenburg Concerti* on period instruments. Whereas the ensemble's previous performances had been graciously received as heritage projects worthy of national pride, the performance and reinterpretation of a major work of the musical canon set off a polemic. Not only was the number of musicians greatly reduced, but Harnoncourt had 'corrected' the score. It can be said that Harnoncourt and others like him saw in Baroque music a new repertoire that allowed for a renewed personal investment. "We have lost the 'unselfconsciousness' necessary to use the present as the ultimate standard", he wrote in his introduction to *Music as Speech* (5). Rather than continuing to uphold the cult of beautiful music, his approach to historical music was to understand its discourse by reconstituting the context in which it developed. The neo-Baroque movement of the twentieth century echoes the cultural and aesthetic values of its time. In essence, it can be said to have wanted to reinstate a truth value to music, opposing the overbearing notions of classical music (large concert hall, tyrannic conductor) that denatured Baroque musical works.

[9] See Philippe Beaussant's *Vous avez dit Baroque?*, in which the author retraces the important concert dates and publications that punctuated the early-music revival.

2. Bach's and Huston's *Goldberg Variations*

Nancy Huston's first novel, *The Goldberg Variations* (or *Les Variations Goldberg*, originally published in French in 1981), bears witness to the author's keen interest in early music. With an obvious emphasis on narrative structure through its interfacing with J. S. Bach's 1741 *Goldberg Variationen* it aligns itself with the formal experimentations of the French *nouveau roman*. *The Goldberg Variations* does not attempt to tell a story, rather, the author adapts the theme and variations form in order to account for the diverse attitudes performer and listeners entertain with the musical medium[10].

The novel follows the structure of Bach's *Goldberg Variationen* with its opening and closing arias framing thirty intervening variations. The first and final chapters of the novel are given the title "Aria" and are narrated by the harpsichordist Liliane Kulainn. In the thirty chapters that follow the opening "Aria", Liliane imagines the thoughts running through the minds of each of the thirty friends and acquaintances she has invited to her home to listen to her performance of Bach's illustrious composition. Each chapter thus constitutes a variation and is, in turn, 'interpreted' by what could be considered a 'guest' narrator.

The multiplicity of discourses and preoccupations in these variations bears witness to the diverse thoughts and attitudes of audience members in the course of attending a concert. With this diversity of commentary, the musical work is taken off its pedestal and placed within the sociological framework of its users. Commentaries offered by the guests encompass subjects such as sexual politics, the social value of classical music, the classical/popular music divide, or the pressures placed on performers. Yet the guests' thoughts also drift to mundane preoccupations of everyday life ("did I turn off the lights before leaving for the concert?", 98, "what still needs to be done to prepare for the up-coming children's trip?", 102; there are also cravings for food, cf. 164, a cigarette, cf. 134, or a more comfortable chair, cf. 38).

---

[10] As a possible motivation for novelists adapting the theme and variation form Werner Wolf points to the "rejection of traditional storytelling" ("From Sign to Signing" 308) as well as "the use of a musical form as a correlative to the vagaries of consciousness" (ibid. 312).

In *The Goldberg Variations*, Huston takes a reactive stance to what has been termed the "sacralization" of musical works (Dahlhaus 76). She takes what is considered one of the 'Great Works' of our musical canon and anchors it within the realities of its production and reception. By having the harpsichordist speak of the stress of performance, of her "sausages" running across the keys (13) and her page turning assistant articulating her efforts in concentration and the frustration of needing to stay 'invisible', Huston accounts for the physical and mental work involved in its performance. She demonstrates that the musical work cannot exist independently but requires an invested human presence for its realization. Furthermore, by registering the listening experiences of individual audience members, she also accounts for the diversity of an audience's engagement with a musical performance. The musical work is not uniquely represented by the discourse of specialists (although two of the variations, 13 and 15, do indeed provide for some professional commentary). The freely flowing narratives, in a non-hierarchical manner, blur the dividing lines between highbrow and lowbrow culture, thus reinstating a discourse that, since the establishment of a classical musical canon and the measures that maintain it, has traditionally been silenced.

Indeed, in the world of classical music, an idealized musical work overshadows the less glamorous aspects of its production. The musicologist Suzanne Cusick has argued that the performance of classical music is in essence "a ritual for disappearing Selves" (85). In the concert hall, performers and audiences must adhere to a strict social code. The audience is to remain seated and quiet and only manifest its presence at the end of the piece with applause to indicate its appreciation. The performer, too, is expected to follow the musical score and adhere as much as possible to the composer's intentions. Both listener and performer should in fact be as inconspicuous as possible so that the music itself may fill one's consciousness and ideally bring about the elation expected from great works of art. Thus the ideal musical performance is one where the musical work comes to life unhindered by material restraints[11].

---

[11] This notion is overtly present (although uncontested) in Thomas Bernhard's novel *Der Untergeher* (*The Loser*) in which a character named Glenn Gould expressly wishes that, when playing the *Goldberg Variations*, he could himself become the piano. He would thus be "Glenn Steinway" (Bernhard, 82) and, by annihilating his own body and soul, would come to embody the music itself.

It is through this implied criticism of the sacralization of the musical work that Huston's *Goldberg Variations* entertains an ideological link to Baroque aesthetics. Huston's exploitation of Baroque music is driven by the binary opposition of the authoritative and elitist versus the individual, more personal means of expression it has come to represent in the twentieth century. In the novel, particular elements representative of a neo-Baroque aesthetic stand out and are symbolically charged.

First, **polyphony**, representing multiple points of view, stands in opposition to monody. In Huston's *Goldberg Variations*, musical polyphony is (intermedially) transposed into the multiple narratives of the performer and her guests. Ostentatious narratives that serve to sacralize the musical work (those present in Variations 10 and 20) are buried within a multitude of other voices. Although these alternate voices are communicating more mundane preoccupations, their substantial presence nevertheless has the effect of valorizing difference and choice. The polyphony towards which this novel gestures can be seen as an attempt towards emancipation from a reductive hierarchy and silencing social order[12].

Similarly, the **theme and variations** form, virtually endless and open-ended, conveys movement, exploration and change. In the opening "Aria", the harpsichordist admits her inability to enjoy the music she plays for fear of landing on a false note, or losing her place in the music (cf. 13). Also, both she and her assistant are aware that they must make themselves invisible for the music to take on its full beauty. However, by the end of the piece, a transformation has taken place. Registering the voices of her guests has modified her attitude to the music. If, at the beginning of the concert, Bach's music was presented as dry and abstract, a music "that touches neither them or me" (14), by the end, it has been infused with human qualities. This transformation furthermore occurred under a magical aura. The concert, as Liliane points out, was held on June 24, Saint-Jean Baptiste day, *Walpurgisnacht*, the night of spells (cf. 89). She also relates it to

---

[12] Nikolaus Harnoncourt echoes this sentiment when he explains that monody can be seen as a reduction of complexity: "Melodies had to be simple and ingratiating, their accompaniment as simple as possible. The listener was to be addressed on the level of his emotions, so that no specialized knowledge was required as was the case in Baroque music." (*Baroque Music Today* 123)

Shakespeare's *A Midsummer Night's Dream* "for the understanding that's been bestowed upon me" (171). Transformation or metamorphosis, instability of form, attributes of a Baroque aesthetic, are exploited and adapted by the author to facilitate the alteration of the work of art into a more humanized artefact. Huston's *Goldberg Variations* takes on as its mission the transformation of the idealized or 'sacralized' work of art into music that is closer to its listeners and performers[13].

Finally, the **harpsichord**, a period instrument, is paramount in this performance of the *Goldberg Variations*. One of the guests, a fervent enthusiast, explains that Bach had intended the variations to be played on a two manual harpsichord rather than a piano. But this defence of the harpsichord is really secondary to the important role it plays in the performer's psyche. The harpsichord's understated subtlety allows for more nuanced and personal expression whereas the piano, "a revolting instrument" (15) in the context of this novel, is considered melodramatic and manipulative, used to "lead [listeners] by the nose through the whole gamut of intensities" (ibid.). The hammers hitting the strings remind Liliane of the sobs (*piano*) and screams (*forte*) of her parents arguing in the middle of the night (cf. ibid.). In contrast, the harpsichord's plucked strings convey an intimacy and gentleness that ultimately allow her to connect with her own emotions. Liliane states:

> I'd succeeded in reducing the dynamic possibilities of music by switching from the piano to the harpsichord. And I wanted something narrower still. I wanted the melodic range to shrink as well, to close in around me. The E: *do, re, mi*. An instrument that would play nothing but me's. Me and nobody else. (170)

According to this performer, the harpsichord contrasts with the pretence and social affectations she associates with the piano. As a peri-

---

[13] Let me address here the observation that the novel falls short of being a true intermedial adaptation of the theme and variation form because the initial "Aria" (the novel's first chapter) is not deemed to offer a central organizing principle regulating the development of the ensuing variations. This observation is legitimate in the sense that the content of the novel's initial "Aria", mainly the performer's reticence and discomfort toward musical performance, is not taken up again until the final "Aria". One could argue, however, that it is the overarching concept of musical performance that is present throughout the variations and, in the true spirit of the variation form, each guest's intervention brings about the transformation of the performer's attitude toward musical performance.

od instrument, the harpsichord stands as a guarantee of authenticity. By extension here, it represents authenticity to the self allowing for the expression of deep personal truths[14].

Contrary to supporting the performance of music as a "ritual for disappearing Selves" (Cusik, 85), Huston's narrative is one of embodiment and resistance. Huston enlists the Baroque qualities of Bach's *Goldberg Variationen*, namely the theme and variation form, polyphony and the harpsichord, and uses them as ideological tools to thwart the cultural supremacy of the traditional classical music performance. Instead of dissolving the presence of musician and audience in order to celebrate the essential, timeless qualities of the work itself, it is the human, 'extramusical' elements that are accentuated. As the musical performance of Liliane Kulainn is transposed into a narrative performance, the flow of words infiltrates and subverts the idea of a pure, disembodied music. Rather than submitting to Romantic notions of genius or of the artwork as timeless perfection, Huston performs their dismantlement, empirically grounding the work in actual musical praxis.

3. Biber's "Resurrection Sonata" in Huston's *Instruments of Darkness*

Instruments of Darkness, published in French in 1996 and in English in 1997, links the sacred in Counterreformation art to the stories of two women, an ill-fated maid-servant in seventeenth-century France,

---

[14] In *Losing North: Musings on Land, Tongue and Self*, Huston confirms that the harpsichord played an important role in her own struggle toward self-determination: "It so happened that I became fluent in French at almost exactly the same time as I discovered the harpsichord (1971). And that, two years later, when I abandoned my mother tongue, I also abandoned the piano. A strange and secret paradigm has come to form and deform my thinking about these things for the past quarter of a century. I see English and the piano as motherly instruments: emotional, romantic, manipulative, sentimental and crude. In both, variations in dynamics are emphasized, exaggerated, imposed, flagrantly and unavoidably expressed. French and the harpsichord, on the other hand, are neutral, intellectual instruments. They require control, restraint and delicate mastery; their expressivity is infinitely more subtle, discreet and refined. Speaking French or playing the harpsichord, in other words, there are never any violent surprises or explosions. What I was running away from when I turned my back on English and the piano seems quite clear. (50)

and a cynical novelist living in late-twentieth-century New York. In the novel, the remarkable particularities of Heinrich Biber's "Resurrection Sonata" come to contribute to the thematic and structural elements of the novel. Biber's sonata, composed ca. 1670, is present throughout the novel and becomes instrumental in establishing the novel's manifest feminist agenda.

Instruments of Darkness is composed of alternating chapters titled "The *Scordatura* Notebook" and "The Resurrection Sonata". In "The *Scordatura* Notebook", Nadia (or Nada as she contemptuously calls herself) is a divorced and bitter New York writer engaged in researching and writing the story of Barbe Durand, a young French maiden put to death in 1712 on the suspicion of witchcraft. As Barbe's tale unfolds within the chapters titled "The Resurrection Sonata", Nada confides in her journal ("The *Scordatura* Notebook") the childhood memories and past events that now haunt her. Writing Barbe's tale, she hopes, will help her "come to terms with the death at birth of [her] twin brother and the disaster of [her] parents' marriage" (27). In both narratives, powerful themes of exclusion and alienation of women are interwoven with references to Heinrich Biber's "Resurrection Sonata", a favourite piece of the novelist's mother. As we will see, the novel and musical work possess structural and thematic parallels that work together to elucidate these themes and ultimately activate, for its protagonists, a reversal of fate.

Over the course of both the servant girl's story and the writer's deliberations, the social constructs that establish binary oppositions are criticized: the sacred and the profane, artistic creation and biological procreation, male domination and female submission. While the women's tales in the two narratives portray hardship and exclusion from salvatory musical activities, Biber's "Resurrection Sonata" stands to represent the sublime expression of Man's devotion to God and the ability, through high art, to elevate oneself to the realm of the divine. As the narrator's violinist mother attested, performing Biber's *Mystery Sonatas* "had given her a glimpse into the very essence of the divine" (29). Yet the sonata's presence in the narratives, being aligned with the sacred, stands in opposition to a common feature in both stories – women's exclusion from the musical world. Nada's mother's career as a violinist was interrupted by her marriage to an abusive husband, and by the numerous pregnancies she endured. Nada feels guilt for being the cause of her mother's unhappiness, her spiritual death. She knows that before having children, her mother had been able to soar on the music she played. Once married with children, she was continually weighted down with bags of groceries, children hanging on her skirts, and tormented by her husband's drunken tantrums. Similarly, in the story of Barbe Durand, Barbe's mother, gifted with an angelic voice, dies in childbirth. Barbe's twin brother, who inherits his mother's beautiful voice, is coached by his mother's ghost. Barbe's harsh fate as an abused maid-servant seems all the more bitter as she wonders why she has been denied the privilege of her mother's visitations.

Music in this novel is part of an idealized, ethereal realm from which women are excluded. Huston's female protagonists are rooted in terrestrial, visceral matters. They must tend to domestic duties and forgo higher intellectual or spiritual pursuits. Nada's mother's hardships made a deep impression on her eldest daughter. Before her marriage, she had been a violinist in a quartet and her future had been promising. After marriage, her body was no longer her own. Nada recalls:

> Being the eldest child, and being, to boot so to speak, a female, it was I who was privy to the regular bedroom carnage, miscarriage after miscarriage as my father continued to knock her catholically up and she in obedience to the pope, Pius XII at the time, refrained from taking measures to prevent it and the sheets filled with blood and trembly velvety black clots of something like human flesh more than once a year, yes, more often than once a year though seven mouths gaped around the dining-room table already. (30)

This legacy of guilt and anger has resulted in the narrator's present dysfunctional state. She confides that she has undergone a number of abortions, that she has distanced herself from her partners and family and that she requires the assistance of a *daemon* to help her write her novel. Biber's "Resurrection Sonata", so closely aligned with her mother's past, offers a metaphor for describing her own condition.

The sonata's peculiarity is its *scordatura*, an unusual and bold practice among Baroque composers who would modify the standard tuning of string instruments in order to create relationships between strings which would otherwise not be possible with a conventionally-tuned instrument. Biber's "Resurrection Sonata" is known for "the most unearthly, the most inhuman *scordatura* in the history of the violin" (28). In order to play the piece, the strings of the instrument must undergo a change in tuning as indicated in the tablature at the beginning of the piece. Instead of the violin's standard tuning of g-d'-a'-e", the strings are tuned to g-g'-d'-d". The effect of this modification is that when the violinist reads the music, her instrument produces an entirely unexpected sound. This is explained by one of the characters in the novel:

> "So," Stella went on, "the piece being notated as if the violin were normally tuned, the sound that comes out of the instrument bears no resemblance to what is written on the page. For instance, your eyes can be following a series of ascending notes on the stave while your ear hears them descending. Or you can read a major chord and produce a minor one [...]." (Ibid.)

The discrepancy between the music seen and the music heard reinforces the symbolism of divergence and nonconformity. In the Baroque era, it could have transmitted a message of humility, indicating that not all one's perceptions are what they may seem. In the novel, however, it becomes a metaphor for the novelist's inability to conform. Her mental state, Nada finds, is best represented by this musical technique. When the term *scordatura* is explained to the narrator, she exclaims:

> "That's me, I'm the mistuned instrument". Somehow I had always known this. People kept trying to play me, fiddle with me, saw me this way or that – they could never get what they wanted out of me. Squawks and screeches. I didn't function the way I was supposed to. (27f.)

Nada's cynicism and alienation are the product of both her own rebellious nature and the weighty burden of her mother's unhappiness. The *scordatura*, in the case of this individual, cannot produce the astonishingly divine sounds it is made to generate in Biber's sonata. This defective human being does not have access to the celestial summits that music can be made to elicit. The inability to reach the higher plateaux of artistic fulfillment is made even more apparent in the story of Barbe.

In the chapters titled "The Resurrection Sonata", both the orphaned girl and her mother are excluded from music and salvation. Barbe's mother, the young shepherdess with "the silvery voice" (17), dies in childbirth. Barbe is continually passed along from household to household. Her hardships are contrasted with the life of her twin brother, who at birth had been placed in a monastery and thus escaped the destiny of poor orphaned children. Motherhood, just as in "The *Scordatura* Notebook", is portrayed as increasing hardships and in the case of Barbe and her mother can even result in death. Barbe's mother dies in childbirth and Barbe's own pregnancy, a product of forced relations with her employer, is a drawn out ordeal that will ultimately lead to her mental breakdown. To begin with, her pregnancy must be hidden from her employers for fear that she will once more be driven away. When she finally gives birth, it is ironically on Christmas Day and Barbe, having lost both the baby and her senses, is found by the villagers who decide to have her tried as a witch and put to death.

The hardships of childbirth and the mutual exclusion of creation and procreation are insistent themes in both stories. In each, the mothers have abandoned their daughters, Nada's through mental collapse, Barbe's through death. *Instruments of Darkness* advances the troubling notion that legacies of the past, for women, have dire consequences that lead to instability and despair, ultimately resulting in the inability to pass on a feminine heritage. "My mother Elisa never talked to me about music. The pleasure she took in music was as private and sacred to her as her belief in God; in a sense the two were the same thing." (28) In the novel's dual storyline, music is depicted as a state of grace and linked to a sacred space. Yet God and music, aligned together as they are, seem to remain out of these women's reach.

Consequently, and despite the fact it is not revealed in the pages of the novel, the historical context in which Heinrich Biber composed "The Resurrection Sonata" becomes quite pertinent. The "Resurrection Sonata" is the eleventh of 15 Rosenkranz Sonatas (known in English as the *Mystery* or *Rosary Sonatas*) composed by Biber and dedicated to the Austrian archbishop Max Gandolf von Khuenberg, Biber's employer and a member of a Rosenkranz (Rosary) society. Marian veneration was central to the ideology of Rosary fraternities and Biber's sonatas are designed as a meditation on the 15 mysteries of salvation in the Catholic faith, events in the life of Jesus Christ as seen through the eyes of his Holy Mother. (The first mystery is The Annunciation to Mary, and the fifteenth is Mary's coronation as Queen of Heaven and Earth.)[15] Given the problematic nature of the

---

[15] Likewise, a large portion of Biber's music has a Marian agenda: apart from the *Mystery Sonatas*, his earliest surviving composition was a setting of the Marian text *Salve regina*; his *Vespers* publication from 1693 includes a group of *Psalms of the Blessed Virgin Mary*; and he also wrote a *Stabat Mater*, another text about Mary (cf. Clements).

figure of Mary in post-modern feminist thought, one might ask how Marian veneration in Biber's "Resurrection Sonata" contributes to the novel's overt feminist agenda. Julia Kristeva, in a 1984 essay, "Stabat Mater", examines the maternal function of the Virgin Mary as a construct of a patriarchal order. According to Kristeva, Mary's immaculate conception negates female anatomy. As the mother of Jesus Christ, she is a symbol of suffering and sacrifice, leading to masochism.

> The Virgin especially agrees with the repudiation of the other woman (which doubtless amounts basically to a repudiation of the woman's mother) by suggesting the image of A Unique Woman: alone among women, alone among mothers, alone among humans since she is without sin. But the acknowledgement of a longing for uniqueness is immediately checked by the postulate according to which uniqueness is attained only through an exacerbated masochism: a concrete woman, worthy of the feminine ideal embodied by the Virgin as an inaccessible goal, could only be a nun, a martyr, or, if she is married, one who leads a life that would remove her from the 'earthly' condition and dedicate her to the highest sublimation alien to her body. (Kristeva 181)

One must ask then whether, in the context of this novel, the Virgin Mary is being reclaimed as an important symbol of motherhood, reinforcing the legitimate place of women in religious cult or, on the contrary, whether Huston is using Biber's "Resurrection Sonata" and its association with the Virgin Mary to criticize and subvert Christian orthodoxy? This ambiguity, I believe, is best examined in light of the structural symbolism inherent in the "Resurrection Sonata's" singular *scordatura*.

In studying the "Resurrection Sonata" closely, there are indications that Biber incorporated symbolic formal elements in his composition. Musicologists have pointed out that the *scordatura* called for in this piece requires that the two middle strings be crossed over each other between the bridge and the peg box thus forming the image of a Christian cross (cf. Chafe 35, Schmid 197)[16]. This particular tuning, moreover, results in the high notes being rendered by a lower string and inversely the low notes by an upper string, implying a reversal of

---

[16] See also Andrew Manze's CD recording of the Biber *Rosary Sonatas*. The CD includes a photograph of the violin with the D and A strings crossed to achieve the desired *scordatura* retuning for the Biber "Resurrection Sonata". In the G-G'-D'-D" retuning of the violin strings, where the middle two strings are crossed before the bridge of the violin and again in the peg box, one can clearly see the resulting cross shape.

the cycles of life and death. In Biber's time, the symbolic crossing of the strings and reversal of high and low registers would have been conceived as a celebration of the Resurrection of the Son of God. In Huston's novel, however, the reversal symbolism and the notion of Resurrection are more likely to support another type of reversal, an attempt to circumvent a traditional patriarchal and religious order. Given the hardships endured by the women protagonists and their exclusion from the religious and artistic realms, this notion of reversal seems to operate in opposition to the relegation of women to the functions of procreation, as a breaking down of the traditional mind/body divide and as paving the way for women to gain access to the spiritual and divine orders, to be creators and not only procreators.

In this sense then, the appropriation of the Biber Sonata and its resurrection symbolism serves to reinforce the reversal of darkness and despair that occurs at the end of the novel. Huston seems to have been inspired by the sonata's ingenious structural design and its ability to musically capture religious symbolism. While Heinrich Biber's striking use of *scordatura* structurally reverses the cycles of life and death, Huston creates a narrator who sees herself as a 'mistuned' instrument and whose emotional affliction and inability to conform will eventually lead her to action. By the end of the novel, this narrator/writer has undergone a significant transformation. She refuses to accept her protagonist's demise as inscribed in the seventeenth-century archives of France's Berry province: although the maid-servant's condemnation and burning at the stake are matters recorded in these historical annals, Nada decides to alter the outcome. She writes:

> In the second part of the book, Barbe will find her way to Paris, she'll learn to read and write, Louis XIV will die and be replaced by Louis XV, Barbe will become famous throughout the capital as a healer, consoler, spell-lifter, angel-maker and broken-heart-repairer [...]. (315)

No longer incapacitated by remorse and despair, the once-cynical New York writer in the end refuses to accept the tragic fate of her heroine and, at least in a fictional world, is able to create a promising future for her. Lastly, in the novel's final pages, Nada dismisses her *daemon* and decides to reinstate the "i" in her name, a sign of agency and reconciliation with herself. The reversal symbolism of the "Resurrection Sonata" is thus apparent in the two final chapters of the dual fictional worlds of the novel as the two women's negative trajectories are overturned.

Hence, the association of the novel with the *Rosenkranz Sonatas*, originally written to celebrate Catholic worship and the cult of the Virgin Mary, is an important element that points to the novel's endeavour to 'adapt' a musical work. The structural symbolism of the "Resurrection Sonata" is 'intermedially transposed' and operates in opposition to the traditional patriarchal and religious order where women are essentially defined by their maternal function and discouraged from participating in spiritual and creative endeavours. This is an especially potent example of cross-modal adaptation whereby a musical composition is deployed and reinscribed with the author's agenda.

4. Conclusion

Huston's *The Goldberg Variations* and *Instruments of Darkness* are exemplary cases of intermedial adaptation. In both novels, the musical composition is present in the form of structural elements that have been 'transposed' into the literary domain. Thus the theme and variations form, as well as the reversal symbolism present in Biber's *scordatura* are adapted into a verbal medium. Furthermore, we see that these musical elements are symbolically charged in the sense that they support an ideology of resistance to hierarchical and exclusionary social structures. The theme and variations form, through its endless possibilities of transformation of a central theme, and the reversal symbolism particular to the *scordatura* of the "Resurrection Sonata" thus carry with them an ideological weight that has a basis in what we have described as neo-Baroque poetics. In addition to these symbolic formal elements, Huston has integrated into these two narratives the thematic potency of Baroque instrumentation. The harpsichord and Biber's mis-tuned violin, as period instruments, play an important role. Their physical properties are isolated as significant sensory features. These instruments in fact are 'instrumental' in carrying the author's messages of authenticity to the self. Just as the instruments themselves "correspond perfectly to the tonal ideal of their age" (Harnoncourt, *Musical Dialogue* 13), they are present in the narratives under scrutiny to support the aesthetic and ethical ideals of the author. In bringing to play Baroque musical compositions within the lines of their respective fictions both *Instruments of Darkness* and *The Goldberg Variations* have not only reinforced their message via the musical medium but have also shed a new light (just as successful adaptations do) on musical works of a distant past.

References

Bach, Johann Sebastian (1741/1968). *Goldberg Variationen.* New York, NY: Kalmus.

Beaussant, Philippe (1988). *Vous avez dit Baroque?* Paris: Actes Sud.

Bernhard, Thomas (1991). *The Loser.* Trans. Jack Dawson. New York, NY: Knopf. [German original: *Der Untergeher.* Frankfurt/ Main: Suhrkamp, 1983.]

Biber, Heinrich (1980). *Sonaten über die Mysterien des Rosenkranzes.* Wyton, Huntingdon, Cambridgeshire: King's Music.

Chafe, Eric Thomas (1987). *The Church Music of Heinrich Biber.* Ann Arbor, MI: UMI Research Press.

Charpentrat, Pierre (1967). *Le Mirage Baroque.* Paris: Editions de Minuit.

Clements, James (Online). "Biber Mystery Sonatas". http://www.aam.co.uk/index.htm [06/08/2007].

Clercx, Suzanne (1948). *Le Baroque et la musique.* Brussels: Librairie Encyclopédique.

Cusick, Suzanne (1994). "Gender and the Cultural Work of a Classical Music Performance". *Repercussions* 3/1: 77-110.

Dahlhaus, Carl (1989). *The Idea of Absolute Music.* Chicago, IL: University of Chicago Press.

Eco, Umberto (1989). *The Open Work.* Cambridge, MA: Harvard University Press.

Harnoncourt, Nikolaus (1989). *Musical Dialogue: Thoughts on Monteverdi, Bach, and Mozart.* Trans. Mary O'Neill. Portland, OR: Amadeus Press.

— (1988). *Baroque Music Today: Music as Speech.* Trans. Mary O'Neill. Portland, OR: Amadeus Press.

Hennion, Antoine (1997). "Le Baroque, un goût si moderne". François Borel et al., eds. *Pom pom pom pom: musiques et caetera.* Neuchâtel: Musee d'Ethnographie. 21-38.

Huston, Nancy (1996). *The Goldberg Variations*. Montreal: Nuage Editions. [French original: *Les Variations Goldberg*. Paris: Editions du Seuil, 1981.]
— (1997). *Instruments of Darkness*. Toronto: Little, Brown and Company.
— (2000). *Pérégrinations Goldberg*. CD. Paris: Actes Sud.
— (2002). *Losing North: Musings on Land, Tongue and Self*. Toronto: McArthur & Company.
Kristeva, Julia (1986). "Stabat Mater". Toril Moi, ed. *The Kristeva Reader*. New York, NY: Columbia University Press. 160-186.
Manze, Andrew, Richard Eggar (2004). *Heinrich Ignaz Franz von Biber: The Rosary Sonatas*. CD 907321.22. Arles: Harmonia Mundi.
Robinson, Marcus (Online). "In Dialogue: Nancy Huston". *Pagitica* 1/2: http://www.pagitica.com/issues/vol_01_no_02/index.html [06/08/2007].
Sanders, Julie (2006). *Adaptation and Appropriation*. New York, NY: Routledge.
Schmid, Manfred Hermann (1995). "Surrexit Christus hodie: Die Sonate XI aus den Mysterien-Sonaten von Heinrich Ignaz Franz Biber". B. Edelmann, M. H. Schmid, eds. *Altes im Neuen: Festschrift Theodor Göllner zum 65. Geburtstag*. Münchner Veröffentlichungen zur Musikgeschichte 51. Tutzing: Schneider. 193-208.
Stricker, Rémy (1968). *Musique du Baroque*. Paris: Gallimard.
Wölfflin, Heinrich (1915/1999). *Kunstgeschichtliche Grundbegriffe: Das Problem der Stilentwicklung in der neueren Kunst*. Munich: Bruckmann. English transl.: *Principles of Art History: The Problem of the Development of Style in Later Art*. Trans. Marie Donald Mackie Hottinger. New York, NY: Dover, 1932/1950.
Wolf, Werner (2002). "Intermedial Iconicity in Fiction: Thema con variazioni". Wolfgang G. Müller, Olga Fisher, eds. *From Sign to Signing: Iconicity in Language and Literature*. Amsterdam: Benjamins. 339-360.
— (1999). *The Musicalization of Fiction: A Study in the Theory and History of Intermediality*. Amsterdam: Rodopi.

Interart Contraband
What Passed between García, Liszt and Sand in "Le Contrebandier"[1]

Peter Dayan, Edinburgh

It was common in the nineteenth century for works of instrumental music to present themselves as transpositions or paraphrases of literary texts. However, the converse was relatively rare. Although literature endlessly described itself as musical in general terms, specific works of music did not normally serve as pre-texts for translation or transposition into complete works of literature. Sand's "Contrebandier" is a striking exception, a unique form of music-word adaptation. It describes itself as a "paraphrase fantastique sur un rondo fantastique de Franz Liszt" (Sand 266). The paraphrased piece is Liszt's *Rondeau fantastique sur un thème espagnol*, for piano; the 'thème espagnol' is Manuel García's song "Yo que soy contrabandista". Sand tells us that instrumental music can never have an arbitrary sense (cf. 265); therefore, tales inspired by instrumental music, as hers is, should be read as products of the imagination of the writer, rather than expressive of the music's true nature. But the 'contrabandista' of García's song becomes the emblem of the possibility of an underground traffic between music and literature: impervious to legislation, unreasonable and untrustworthy, always under threat of execution from the forces of law and order, doubtless attractive only in fiction and at a distance – and nonetheless indispensable. Between song, instrumental music, and narrative prose, Sand's confrontation of the genres allows a unique insight both into their unspoken distinctive aesthetic rules, and into what can be repeated or, perhaps, smuggled from one into another in spite of those rules.

Manuel del Pópulo Vincente García (1775-1832) became famous throughout Europe (and, indeed, the USA and Mexico) as the greatest tenor of his time, father of two of the nineteenth century's greatest female singers (Maria Malibran and Pauline Viardot), and perhaps the most durably influential singing teacher of his day. But in 1805, he had not yet launched his international career. He was living and working in Madrid; and it was there that he wrote and performed his one-

---

[1] I should like to thank the British Academy and the University of Edinburgh for enabling me to attend the WMA conference in Santa Barbara at which this paper was originally given.

act monologue opera *El Poeta calculista* ('The Calculating Poet'). When he came to Paris, he brought it with him, and he performed it there in 1809, in Spanish. It was the first time anyone could remember a Spanish opera being performed in Paris, and it created quite a stir; it seems to have been a major factor in the birth of the French romantic interest in Spanish music. (Bizet used it when he was working on *Carmen*.)

James Radomski, in his wonderfully evocative book *Manuel García (1775-1832): Chronicle of the Life of a* bel canto *Tenor at the Dawn of Romanticism*, provides a description and a history of the opera (as well as most of the other facts about García which I cite in this paper). Its plot runs approximately as follows. A poet in a garret inherits a pile of papers from another poet and asks himself what it is all worth, if anything. Speculating on the value of poetry, he wonders how he could make money out of it and imagines a number of characters he might write about, to bring himself fame and fortune. He acts out these characters. But they all turn out to be ridiculous, or at least the butts of satire. In the end, he gives up on his poetic calculations, comes down to earth, and decides he had better go and get himself a proper job, as a night-watchman. One of the characters he imagines is a smuggler; and the song he sings when imagining that character is "Yo que soy contrabandista" ('I who am a smuggler'). It remained the most popular song García ever wrote.

Liszt knew García, whom he recognized as a fellow Romantic virtuoso, and he knew the song. In 1836, he composed a piece entitled *Rondeau fantastique sur un thème espagnol 'El Contrabandista'*[2]. It is a strange and extraordinary piece, little known and rarely performed, doubtless not only because of its terrifying technical difficulty, but also because of its oddity. It may be analysed as a rondo, at least within the extended definition that the term was acquiring at the time; but it is certainly not a simple one. Liszt subjects García's little song, which is in the genre of a folk-song, to some startling distortions and distensions, which may perhaps be best understood, musicologically, in the context of Liszt's improvisatory mode (and of the tech-

---

[2] *Trois morceaux de salon*. No. 2/"Rondeau fantastique sur un thème espagnol/El Contrabandista de Manuel Garcia/pour piano par F. Liszt". (R88, SW252, NG2, A33.) The score may be found in: Liszt (1974).

nique of *variations brillantes*)[3]. However, it would not be pertinent here, even if I were competent to do so, to attempt to answer the question of how Liszt adapted García's music, because our brief is to talk about word-music adaptations, not music-music ones. So the question relevant to us would be: what does Liszt's music adapt from the **words** to García's song? To that, there is, I think, a clear short answer: nothing obvious. There is no attempt to express the meaning of those words in the piano music. As we shall shortly see, George Sand certainly sees no such expression in Liszt's music; for her as for me, between García and Liszt there is no immediately visible word-music adaptation. However, that is not the end of the story, for Liszt's piece gave rise to a very unusual kind of music-word adaptation.

Works of music apparently springing from specific works of literature are common enough in the Romantic period. But extended works of literature apparently springing from specific works of music are, as far as I know, relatively rare. George Sand was therefore doing something quite original when she wrote her "histoire lyrique" entitled "Le Contrebandier"[4]. The main part of the text, as we shall see, presents itself as a "paraphrase fantastique" of Liszt's "rondo fantastique" (Sand 266), which naturally will suggest to us the question: in what sense, exactly, is Sand's text a paraphrase of Liszt's piano piece? How has the latter been adapted into the former? But before we get to the paraphrase proper, Sand gives us half a dozen introductory pages on García's song and Liszt's piano piece which turn out to be an introduction to an introduction which in fact introduces nothing.

---

[3] I am indebted to David Urrows for all my information on the rondo in Liszt's day, and its analysis. In personal communication he described this piece as "a large-scale ternary form in which rondo procedures, and to some extent rondo forms, are used in a flexible and original way".

[4] *Le Contrebandier* is as little-known as Liszt's rondo, doubtless, again, because of its oddity. As David Powell says in what is to my knowledge the most extensive critical discussion of the work to date, it "suffers from a lack of generic identity" (77). Indeed, Powell considers that "Sand's story fails because, unable to establish itself as a new or intermediary form, it falls back into the literary mode" (78). It will be apparent that I do not agree with Powell's value judgement, but doubtless his reaction helps to explain why the work never became popular. It first appeared in the *Revue et Gazette musicale de Paris* in January 1837. The only other form in which it has ever been published, as far as I know, is in Michel Lévy's collected edition of Sand's works. The volume containing "Le Contrebandier" came out in 1876, the year of Sand's death. It is from that edition, the last authorised by Sand, that I have worked.

***

Between the first and sixth pages of the text (which contains thirty-eight pages in all), there is a very strange double-title effect. At the top of the first page, we have: "Le Contrebandier, histoire lyrique" (see *Example 1*).

> # LE CONTREBANDIER
>
> HISTOIRE LYRIQUE
>
> ---
>
> La chanson du *Contrebandier* est populaire en Espagne; cependant, bien qu'elle ait la forme tranchée, la simplicité laconique et le parfum national de toutes les *tiranas* espagnoles, elle n'est pas, comme les autres, d'origine ancienne et inconnue. Cette chanson, que l'auteur de *Bug-Jargal* a poétiquement jetée à travers son roman, fut composée par Garcia dans sa jeunesse. La Malibran fit connaître à tous les salons de l'Europe la grâce énergique et tendre des *boleros* et des *tiranillas*. Parmi les plus goûtées, le *Contrabandista* fut celle que chantait avec le plus d'amour la grande ar-
>
> 15.

Example 1: George Sand, "Le Contrebandier", first page of text

Doubtless "Le Contrebandier" translates the title that Liszt gives to García's song in his own title: "El Contrabandista". But on the sixth page, after her introduction, Sand gives a second title: "Yo que soy contrabandista" (see *Example 2*), which is the incipit of García's original song, followed by a second subtitle: "Paraphrase fantastique

sur un rondo fantastique de FRANZ LISZT", followed by "INTRO-
DUCTION".

> 266   LE CONTREBANDIER
>
> tale ne peut jamais avoir un sens arbitraire;
> mais le compositeur lui ayant permis de s'aban-
> donner à son imagination, il prit la plume en
> riant et traduisit son rêve dans une forme qu'il
> appela lyrico-fantastique, faute d'un autre nom,
> et qui après tout n'est pas plus neuve que tout
> ce qu'on invente aujourd'hui.
>
>
> YO QUE SOY CONTRABANDISTA
> *Paraphrase fantastique sur un rondo fantastique
> de* FRANZ LISZT
>
>
> **INTRODUCTION**
>
> UN BANQUET EN PLEIN AIR DANS UN JARDIN
>
> LES AMIS (Chœur).
>
> Heurtons les coupes de la joie. Que leurs
> flancs vermeils se pressent jusqu'à se briser.
> Souffle, vent du couchant, et sème sur nos têtes

Example 2: George Sand, "Le Contrebandier", sixth page

This would imply that the first six pages of the text, which we have just read, do not constitute the Introduction; the true Introduction is what now follows. But the whole of the rest of the piece, the following thirty-two pages, present themselves as one single undivided section. There is no further subtitle of any sort that might indicate where the introduction finishes and the main body of the text begins. So the whole of the last thirty-two pages should, it seems, logically be read as an introduction, as the introduction to something that never arrives. This is peculiar, certainly; but we will find that announcement and expectation followed by non-delivery is an essential operation of this music-word adaptation.

Let us return to the beginning. After the first title, on the first page ("Le Contrebandier, histoire lyrique"), Sand starts off by telling us, not about Liszt's piece, but about García's song[5]. She presents it as the favourite song both of García and of his first daughter, la Malibran (who had recently died a romantic death in Manchester at the age of 28, at the height of her operatic fame); and it was their favourite, according to Sand, because it somehow expressed their true original nature – for la Malibran her Spanish nature, and for her father his own as 'contrebandier'. According to her (I know no other source for this story), his identification with the smuggler was life-long. For him, she says:

> [...] le mouvement, le caractère et le sens de cette perle musicale étaient le résumé de la vie d'artiste, de laquelle, à son dire, la vie de contrebandier est l'idéal. Le *aye, jaleo*, ce *aye* intraduisible qui embrase les narines des chevaux et fait hurler les chiens à la chasse, semblait à García plus énergique, plus profond et plus propre à enterrer le chagrin, que toutes les maximes de la philosophie.[6] (Sand 263)

We have here a typical Romantic opposition between philosophy, which is a discourse that expresses itself in maxims, in words that can be translated, and something essentially artistic that escapes translation. The *"aye, jaleo"*, which is the cry of the smuggler in the song, is

---

[5] This explains, doubtless, why Radomski describes Sand's "Contrebandier" as "an 'Histoire Lyrique' inspired by the song" (68), and does not mention Liszt's piano piece as an intermediary in the process of inspiration, despite Sand's explicit reference to Liszt later in her text.

[6] '[...] the movement, the character and the meaning of this musical pearl summed up the artist's life; indeed, according to him, the ideal of the artist's life is the life of the smuggler. The *aye, jaleo,* this untranslatable *aye* which makes the horses breathe fire and the hounds bay at the hunt, seemed to García more energetic, more profound, and better able to bury melancholy, than all the maxims of philosophy.' All translations from this text are mine; to my knowledge, no published English translation exists.

untranslatable. Sand has already said on the previous page that the words of the song in general, though they are magnificent as carried by the melody, cannot be translated word for word, and would be "insignifiantes" ('insignificant') separated from the music. The words of the song, like the smuggler's cry, have a force that is beyond translation; a force appreciated, it would seem, not by philosophers, but by animals (the smuggler's horses and dogs), by musicians, and by smugglers. Now, the identification of the musical to the animal is quite familiar in the literature of the time, since both represent the non-verbal, non-analytical aspect of human thought. However, it is not immediately obvious why the smuggler should join the musician and the animal here.

García, says Sand, "disait sans cesse qu'il voulait pour toute épitaphe sur sa tombe: *Yo que soy el Contrabandista*, tant Othello et don Juan s'étaient identifiés avec le personnage imaginaire du *Contrebandier*" ('repeated constantly that the only epitaph he wanted on his tomb was: *Yo que soy el Contrabandista*, so closely had Othello and Don Giovanni come to identify themselves with the imaginary character of the *Smuggler*'). This is a typically Sandian obliquely bizarre sentence. She doesn't say that García himself identified with the smuggler; she says that Othello and Don Giovanni, two of García's most famous operatic rôles, and both of damned men, identified with the smuggler; and she doesn't say that Othello and Don Giovanni are imaginary, but she does say that the smuggler is imaginary. There is a way in which that distinction is justified. All three, of course, the smuggler as much as Othello and Don Giovanni, are imaginary in that they are characters in operas. But the smuggler is presented as imaginary within the opera: he is imagined, dreamed up, by the 'poeta calculista'. He is an operatic fiction within the operatic fiction. One might add that within the opera, he doesn't last long: barely a few minutes, whereas Othello and Don Giovanni last for several hours. And it is the evanescent and doubly imaginary figure of the smuggler, not the damned romantic hero, that the musician presents as the ideal of the artist's life; the romantic hero identifies himself with the smuggler, not the other way around. Once again, why? The immediate context provides no clear explanation.

What do we know of García's smuggler? In the song, he tells us little about himself, but it is at least plain that his life is not very pleasant. First of all, he simply says that he is a smuggler, a defiant, solitary and fearless one. His little horse, he says, is tired, and it plainly needs encouraging by his cries of "ay jaleo!"[7] Then "la ronda", the round or patrol, turns up and starts shooting at him. At this point, not surprisingly, he heads for the hills as fast as his poor tired little horse will carry him. And what has he been smuggling? What he offers for sale he calls "hilo negro": 'black thread'. One might ask what that is. According to a note in Radomski's book (cf. 69), García said it was a cover name for tobacco used by Andalusian smugglers; though I can find no evidence of anyone other than García using the expression in that sense, so even a Spanish audience might have had some difficulty catching the reference. We will return to this subject, but meanwhile, it seems fair to say that reference to the words of García's song, which Sand's audience would have been very likely to know, gives us little further assistance in trying to understand the identification between artist and smuggler.

In short, over the first three pages of her "histoire lyrique", Sand describes the song, gives us its history, and affirms that García identified with its central figure; but she does nothing to explain that identification. And then, with no attempt at a transition, she moves on to a description of Liszt's piano piece based on the song, the "rondo fantastique". In her description, which covers a page and a half, there is no mention whatever of the smuggler. It is entirely a description of the moods and images which the piano piece evokes in the listener (as yet unidentified). Musicologically, we would probably see it as a magnificently inaccurate – or at least arbitrary – description. Nonetheless, it has two features, I think, that correspond to what a modern listener might hear, both of them formal: the appearance of a hymn-like theme which occurs twice, interrupting the material based on García's theme, which gives an ABABA structure to the whole piece; and a general air of dramatic turbulence.

Sand's 'transposition d'art' certainly gives us a kind of music-word adaptation which was current at the time (analogies are to be found, for example, in Baudelaire's famous essay on Wagner): the poetic listener sets out for us, in order, the images that a piece of instrumental music evoked as he or she listened. Such descriptions generally present themselves as faithful to the musical original in that they respect its formal structure; and in that, Sand is true to their

---

[7] García writes "ay"; Sand consistently changes the spelling to 'aye'.

tradition. However, it was generally accepted that the evoked images themselves are only loosely determined by the music itself, and indeed depend largely on the imagination of the poetic listener. Obviously enough, where the description was of a musical piece that contained words, the traditional rules of the game, of the transposition, were different: the images evoked had to take the words into account. This piece may seem to be a borderline case: Liszt's piano piece has no words, but the song on which it was based, and which Sand had described at length, certainly had words, whose sense she had indicated. It is striking and perhaps bewildering, therefore, that she takes no notice of those words when describing Liszt's piano piece. Of the meaning of the words to García's song, nothing whatever has passed into Liszt's music as Sand hears it. She describes love, a prayer, a banquet, pastoral melancholy, starry skies, a thousand-voiced choir, and so on, none of which is in García's song; she describes no smuggler, no tired little horse, no shooting or fleeing, and no "hilo negro". In short, Sand's description of the song is completely different from her description of the piano piece, and there is no attempt to connect or negotiate between them. So is there, for Sand, any word-music adaptation of any kind between the song and the piano piece? And if not, why juxtapose them? Why bother to mention the words to García's song, if they are irrelevant to the piano piece which is the pre-text of her paraphrase?

Let us leave that question open for now, like the question of the identification between smuggler and artist: Sand certainly offers no answers. Just as abruptly as she had moved on from García's song to Liszt's piano piece, she now moves on to the circumstances in which the piano piece gave rise to its literary paraphrase. Immediately after her evocation of Liszt's piece, a new section begins with the words: "Un soir d'automne à Genève, un ami de Liszt fumait son cigare dans l'obscurité [...]" (Sand 265; 'One autumn evening, in Geneva, a friend of Liszt was smoking his cigar in the darkness [...]'). It may be remembered that tobacco was García's own interpretation of his smuggler's contraband. Here, it contributes to the state of mind of Liszt's friend, who soon turns out to be a writer. And tobacco continued to be associated with literary fantasy throughout the century; perhaps most famously in Mallarmé's evocation of the poet watching his rings of smoke vanish[8]. Tobacco may from one point of view be a commercialized product which the state seeks to control; but from another point of view it is the least practical and therefore most poetic of substances, since its destiny is literally to go up in smoke, at which point its true value becomes only that of the pleasure it gives. Which makes it, perhaps, a peculiarly apt figure for interart contraband.

This cigar-smoking friend of Liszt's, presented in the masculine and in the third person, soon becomes the author of a 'lyrico-fantastique' text inspired by Liszt's rondo; so we might assume it is George Sand, especially since it is a historical fact that she stayed with Liszt in Geneva in September 1836. That identification is never explicitly confirmed, in accordance with the general disjointed oddity of the mode of presentation of almost everything in this peculiar piece of literature. One thing, however, is made explicit: the disjunction between this piece of literature, indeed any piece of literature, and the musical pre-text.

Liszt's friend is moved by Liszt's music at the same time as he smokes his cigar and listens to the murmurs of the waters of Lake Geneva; and "se laissa emporter au gré de sa propre fantaisie jusqu'à revêtir les sons de formes humaines, jusqu'à dramatiser dans son cerveau toute une scène de roman" (ibid.; 'allowed himself to be carried away by his own fantasy to the point where he clothed the sounds with human forms, and dramatized in his brain a whole novelistic scene'). There are four sources of inspiration here. The music, the tobacco, and the lake all move or intoxicate him. But it is his own imagination, his own "fantaisie" (ibid.; a word that echoes 'fantastique', in Liszt's title and in Sand's second title), that provides the human and novelistic forms that clothe the sounds. This confirms what I suggested above: that while the traditional transposition of instrumental music into words may respect the music's structure, the images evoked depend on the listener. And if we were to ask: in what sense do these human forms, these verbal clothes, fit the sounds? Can we see them as following and echoing, somehow, the sense of the music? I think Sand gives us a clear answer to this question: no, we cannot.

Liszt's friend describes his vision at supper. He is then challenged to "formuler la musique en parole et en action" (ibid.; 'formulate the

---

[8] I am thinking of the sonnet "Toute l'âme résumée" (Mallarmé 59f.).

music in words and in action'). He refuses, on the grounds that "la musique instrumentale ne peut jamais avoir un sens arbitraire" ('instrumental music can never have an arbitrary sense'). Everything, here, hinges on the sense of the word "arbitraire". It did not have, in such contexts, in the 19th century, its usual modern sense of 'capricious' or 'variable'; it meant something more like 'fixed by the will of one person or group of people', in the same way that 'pouvoir arbitraire' was power exercised by one person or a group of people, not subject to overriding laws, and the 'arbitrariness' of language was taken to mean that the sense of a word was decided by convention, not by any natural laws. So music can never have a sense that is fixed in the way that the sense of words is fixed, arbitrarily. This leaves open the possibility of three kinds of relationship between words and music.

In the first kind of relationship, words lose their arbitrary sense, and become identified with the music; one is tempted to say that they become music. When this happens, they become untranslatable, because translation is only rendered possible by the arbitrariness of the linguistic sign. We have already seen how this has become the condition of the words of García's song, as Sand presents them. They mean nothing without the music, and they cannot be translated; and indeed, as we shall see, she artfully does not translate them. This is also what happens, more generally, to words as they become perceived as poetic, in the Romantic tradition: they lose their arbitrary sense and their translatability, and they are described as operating like music, beyond the reach of philosophy.

In the second kind of relationship between words and music, words tacitly accept their arbitrariness, and therefore, their inevitable disjunction from music. The Romantic music-word adaptation is in that sense, as we have seen, not a faithful translation; it gives us, not a vision that was inherent in the music, but a vision evoked in one individual poetic listener by the music, and accepts that different listeners will have different visions. Sand's initial description of Liszt's piano piece, on the fourth and fifth pages of "Le Contrebandier", belongs to this tradition.

Sand, however, uniquely, was not content to settle for this. What her friends spurred her to produce was something that went far beyond the traditional arbitrary transposition which she had already given us: a different and revolutionary kind of music-word adaptation, in which words remain words, they remain arbitrary, they remain translatable, indeed they present themselves as translation; but to the extent that they do so, they continually flaunt their difference from the music, their lack of identity with the music. Their link to the music is in their determination to point out the gap that separates them from any purported musical original. Sand's ambition, here, is not simply to give us her arbitrary interpretation of the music; it is to weave her paraphrase out of a meditation on the very nature of that arbitrariness, as it comes between music and words.

She certainly presents her paraphrastic words from the beginning as translation: "[...] il prit la plume et traduisit son rêve" (ibid. 266; '[...] he took up his pen and translated his dream'). But the source text of the translation is explicitly given here, already, and we should note this carefully, not as the music, but as the writer's own dream. The friend, as if to ensure this essential point had not passed us by, as if to make sure we were aware of the peculiar infidelity of this operation to its apparent purported original, asks Liszt for permission to write something that will be presented as connected with his music but which in fact is a mere product of his friend's imagination. That permission is forthcoming; and "le compositeur lui ayant donné la permission de s'abandonner à son imagination" (ibid.; 'the composer having given him permission to abandon himself to his imagination'), the writer can set to work.

We have now reached the sixth page of Sand's text. Here we find the end of what I have called the introduction to the introduction, and the beginning of what Sand herself entitles "Introduction". But the ambiguities and peculiarities of this piece's relation to García's song and Liszt's piece become most explicit, perhaps, in between the two dashes, and before the word "Introduction". Sand gives a title in capitals, in the original Spanish: it is the title, or at least the incipit, of García's song, which is nowhere cited in this form in Liszt's work (which Liszt called, it will be remembered, *Rondeau fantastique sur un thème espagnol 'El Contrabandista'*). Are we, then, to be given an adaptation of the song rather than of the piano piece? But the subtitle which follows – "*Paraphrase fantastique sur un rondo fantastique de* FRANZ LISZT" – suggests otherwise. Indeed, the layout of these multiple titles actually suggests, if we read them carefully, that García's song is a paraphrase of Liszt's piece. This may seem far-fetched; but in fact, what follows may suggest it is perhaps not too far from the point.

In any case, it is perfectly clear that whereas the shorter 'transposition d'art' in the first pages of Sand's text did at least respect the formal structure of Liszt's piano piece, this thirty-two page translation shows no such respect. It does not model itself formally on, it is not well-fitting clothing in any obvious sense for, García's song, Liszt's piano piece, or indeed Sand's description of Liszt's piano piece. There is almost nothing one could point to in Sand's story that corresponds to or even refers in any sense to any identifiable or analysable features of Liszt's piece. There is, however, a reference to García's song, which is central to the story Sand tells.

* * *

The story is presented as if it were the libretto of an opera: it is divided into arias, recitative, and choruses, with occasional stage directions. Or rather: it is presented as if it were the translation of a libretto. Any such libretto originally in French would certainly, at the very least for the arias, be in verse, not in prose; and the style of Sand's prose, rather stiltedly flowery, is precisely that which is normally identifiable as translation into French prose of foreign poetry. We have here, then, what seems to be a translation without an original. This provides us with a first analogy between the character of Sand's text and the character of word-music relations, a first demonstration of her aim to materialise in her style the way that words adapt music: that adaptation is the translation of an original that escapes us. And to make this point as clearly as possible, Sand builds her tale around a steadily transforming motif that begins and ends as an obviously inaccurate translation, of a text which she had already said could not be translated well: the words to García's song. As if words that belong to music, smuggler's words, became infected with music's rejecttion of the arbitrariness that makes translation possible.

The story begins with an open-air banquet in the garden of an unidentified Spanish château. The guests are having a good time drinking and encouraging each other to drink, when a little boy pipes up with a song which he calls "un air populaire de ces contrées" (ibid. 270; 'a popular air from this region'), and which the stage directions describe as: "La chanson espagnole: *Yo que soy Contrabandista*". The reader, having read the introduction to this introduction, will know that this is García's song. But there, the complications start in earnest. To begin with, the very first thing that Sand had told us about this song is that, in spite of appearances, it is not "un air populaire de ces contrées" (ibid.) at all; it was in fact composed by García. And what is more, we have of course been told that its words are untranslatable word by word, and insignificant separated from the music. So what is Sand giving us here?

She is certainly not giving us a genuine translation. The words of the little boy's song mention no "hilo negro", no shooting, and no tiredness. They describe a smuggler who leads a rather jolly romantic life. And the "*aye, jaleo*" which she had more specifically signalled as untranslatable is indeed not translated. The word "*aye*" is simply repeated, in italics; the word "*jaleo*" is absent and untranslated.

As the boy finishes his song, a strange weary traveller appears at the banquet. The guests initially welcome him, but he is rude to them, berating them for not recognising him as their long-lost brother. They decide they will believe he is one of them if he can sing "la chanson du pays" (ibid. 280) which the boy has just sung. The traveller accepts the challenge, but teases them by singing, apparently to the correct tune, a number of verses which begin with the right words ("Moi qui suis"), but soon diverge from the boy's text. The first time he sings, he gives his identity, not as a smuggler, but as a goat-herd. His listeners object that he has got the song wrong; but they do not simply dismiss him, partly because he has a beautiful voice, and partly because in his description of his life, many years ago, as a young goat-herd, one of those present, the beautiful Hermosa, seems to recognize a long-lost cousin and senses a mysterious bond with him (thus offending her companion, the jealous Diego).

The mysterious visitor sings next of his life as a student in Salamanca, and we begin to realise, as does his audience in the tale, that he is, in fact, not really trying to sing the authentic version of the song, but telling his life story, the tale of how he, originally one of the village people, a contented adolescent member of a paternal and pastoral society, became a wandering adult outcast. In the subsequent verses of his song, he presents himself as an impassioned lover in Salamanca, whose rival in love is an ink-stained pedant; then as exiled assassin of that pedant and of his treacherous lady love; then as fearsome triumphant warrior; then as self-scourging penitent; then as poet. The good people at the banquet (especially Hermosa) are increasingly curious about his true identity and increasingly enchanted by his singing (except for Diego, who thinks he is a bandit and should be arrested); nonetheless, they continue to insist that he should sing the song in its original version – until he sings a final extended episode, in which he sums up all the phases of his life, and concludes with a most extraordinary evocation of his despair as a poet, a despair which results from nothing more nor less than a reaction to music.

> Mais quand mon chant ouvre ses ailes, quand mon pied repousse la terre, quand je crois entendre les concerts divins passer au loin, un voile de deuil s'étend sur ma tête maudite, sur mon âme flétrie; l'ange de la mort m'enveloppe d'un nuage sinistre; éperdu, haletant, fatigué, je flotte entre la lumière et les ténèbres, entre la foi et le doute, entre la prière et le blasphème, et je retombe dans la fange en criant: Hélas! hélas! le voile noir! Hélas! hélas! où sont mes ailes? (Ibid. 294f.)[9]

When he believes he can hear the divine concert, when he finds his song (according to the traditional poetic conceit, the word 'chant' appears here obviously – but certainly not innocently – as a metaphor for poetry) spreading its wings within him, he becomes the prey of the angel of death. In short: when his 'chant' spreads it wings, he loses his own wings. Why? Because poetry exists between two worlds. It uses words; therefore, it engages the poet's sense of himself as an earth-bound human being, able to reason and translate. But it is also music; and music belongs to a realm separate from the earthly, a heavenly realm, beyond the reach of reason or of translation. The musician may simply forget the earthly realm as he enters the heavenly world of music; the poet cannot, for he takes his words with him, and as he approaches the realm of music, the non-arbitrary condition of music threatens the functioning of those very words of which his art is composed.

This is certainly a moment of despair, a moment of crisis in the relation between words and music, in which the latter comes to seem fatal to the former. It is not, however, the end of Sand's story. This final verse is so beautifully sung that it wins over the lord, Hermosa,

---

[9] 'But when my song opens its wings, when my foot pushes away the earth, when I believe I can hear divine concerts passing in the distance, a veil of mourning spreads itself over my accursed head, over my withered soul; the angel of death envelops me in a sinister cloud; bewildered, panting, weary, I float between light and darkness, between faith and doubt, between prayer and blasphemy, and I fall back into the mire, crying out: Alas! alas! the black veil! Alas! alas! where are my wings?'

and all the good people (except Diego, who continues to point out that not a single line of the original song has yet been sung by the mysterious visitor). They invite him to join them in their banquet. The lesson of this is, it seems to me, that the force of poetry is most clearly felt precisely as poetry dies, defeated by music; in other words, in the dangerous no man's land between the arts. But the mysterious traveller does not accept their invitation. When they ask him to stay and sing for them, he asserts: "Je ne chante pour personne, je chante pour me satisfaire quand la fantaisie me vient" (ibid. 295; 'I sing for no one, I sing for my own satisfaction when the fantasy comes to me'). 'La fantaisie': it will be remembered that this is the necessary motor of all the interart adaptations described by Sand. One cannot sing to order; for song does not belong to the realm of order or of reason, it does not belong to polite society. It is for no one, and can be determined by no one, not even by the singer, who must wait for his fantasy to arrive.

At this point, the mysterious stranger takes his leave; and as soon as he is safely out of reach, he takes off his false beard and sings the boy's original song, "Moi qui suis un contrebandier". Diego now recognises him: "[…] c'est José, c'est le fameux contrebandier, c'est le damné bandit; et moi, capitaine des rondes, qui étais chargé de l'arrêter!" (ibid. 297; '[…] it is José, it is the famous smuggler, it is the damned bandit; and it was I, the captain of the patrol, who was charged with arresting him!'). The singing poet, in other words, turns out to be the 'contrabandista', and vice versa.

* * *

As I said, formally this plainly has nothing to do with García's song or with Liszt's rondo. But it does have a curious kind of indirect thematic link with García's opera *El Poeta calculista* (which Sand never mentions, and never saw), in that we have here a poet who adopts numerous characters in song, creating fictions within the fiction; and one of those characters, the smuggler, seems to be closest to the poet's heart. Perhaps, now that I have pointed out all the ways in which Sand's story cannot be seen as a music-word adaptation, it is time to look for what might, after all, link it to the music. And to this, the themes of identification and of the smuggler are the keys.

Why, after all, should García, or at least Sand's version of García, have identified with this imaginary character? Why should the life of the smuggler seem to him the ideal of the life of the artist? The answer emerges from Sand's text via her opposition between the smuggler and the philosopher. The philosopher offers maxims, whereas the smuggler offers untranslatable cries which inspire animals. The artist is in sympathy with the latter, not the former. The language of art is animal and untranslatable. And the smuggler is aligned with art because he, too, does not speak the translatable language of philosophy.

The translatable language of philosophy is also the language of society, of social communication, and of the laws that regulate fair exchange, translation being the type of regulated or calculable exchange. The smuggler operates outside that system. What he offers for sale has an unregulated value, an untranslatable value. Whatever his 'black thread' is, its value is neither practical, nor certified by anyone. It is clear in García's song that he finds no one to sell it to anyway; "la ronda", the force of law and order, turns up and chases him away. And in Sand's story, we hear nothing whatever about what the smuggler is supposed to have smuggled. He tells us of his life as goat-herd, student, lover, murderer, soldier, penitent hermit, and poet; about his life as smuggler, he gives no details. That which is smuggled remains outside the system of exchange.

Let us remember that Sand's opening remark, in her "histoire lyrique", concerns the origin of the song. It is not, she says, what it appears to be. It seems an old popular song; but, in fact, it is written by García, it is an original composition. However, the extent to which we can see it as an expression of its composer is complicated by its multi-layered history. Its speaking voice is not his, but that of a smuggler with whom he identifies at an irregular number of removes, via other operatic rôles. There are comparable complications in Sand's "paraphrase fantastique". The characters perceive "Yo que soy contrabandista" as an old popular song, and initially ask for it to be respected as such; but in fact, the version Sand gives is already an inauthentic arbitrary translation; and in any case, the 'contrebandier' refuses to respect it, providing instead his own list of characters with whom his identification is always problematic. This angers Diego, the representative of "la ronde", but it appeals to those who value good singing. The moral of this is: the artist has something for sale whose origin is uncertified and questionable, though we initially think we know where it comes from. Its value cannot be safely established, because it does not fit into a regulated system of exchange; the police disapprove. In all of these senses, the artist is like a smuggler. And it is that identification of artist to smuggler which allows an answer to our central question: where is the music-word adaptation, between García, Liszt and Sand?

If one looks carefully at Sand's introduction to her introduction, one comes to the conclusion that 'adaptation' might not be the right word to describe what happens between these works. García's song, Liszt's piano piece, and Sand's story are not imitations, repetitions or adaptations of one another. They are related as subsequent to one another, as distinct sections in a narration, each definitively separated from the previous one by the operation of the individual creator's fantasy. What links them is not really similarity on any analysable formal or semantic level: it is a kind of meta-narrative in which each of them appears as an episode. The key figure in this meta-narrative is the artist as smuggler. He (even Sand as author is gendered, here, as masculine) offers us something whose origins and ends are permanently deceptive. He gestures towards authenticating origins, both in genre and in character: "Yo que soy contrabandista" appears to be a Spanish popular song, the smuggler a stock romantic character; Liszt's piano piece tells us it is a rondo and that it is based on a Spanish theme; Sand seems to promise us a narrative inspired by Liszt's piece, and imitates the style of the translated libretto, using stock Romantic figures. But what we are actually given cannot be authenticated by reference to those traditions.

In a memorable paper (entitled "Metaphor and Methodology in Word and Music Studies"), Eric Prieto invites us to analyse works in relation to the categories to which they seem to belong. I would suggest that there is a fundamental similarity between "Yo que soy contrabandista", Liszt's rondo, and "Le Contrebandier" in the way that they relate to the traditional forms to which they appeal. In each case, we witness the artistic, but not the philosophical or practical triumph of a defiant romantic individualism. An unpredictable, improvisatory or anti-conformist energy asserts its rights over tradition. This is at the expense of the kind of faith in repetition which underpins tradition, as well as of the faith in translation that traditionally underpins interart transpositions. Sand makes it plain from the beginning that her story cannot really be linked to the sense of Liszt's music, because whereas the sense of words is always arbitrary, the sense of music is not; her whole piece can be read as a brilliant satire on the very notion of transposition or translation in or between the arts. But what survives, the contraband that is smuggled from art to art, is precisely the figure of a non-arbitrary sense, created by the fantasy of the artist, untranslatable, fictional or even comic in its relation to the outside world, of incalculable and uncertifiable value. This figure relies both on a reference to an obscure origin, and on the defiant assertion of its independence, of anything that philosophy or law could control. It requires two languages for its creation. One is the untranslatable language which it presents as that of music or of the smuggler's cry. The other is the language of literature, which dramatizes the flight from the arbitrary, from philosophy, from law and from the round. It knows that verbal language does have an arbitrary and therefore certifiable sense, but it works to undermine that sense, and to reconfigure itself as contraband.

Thus literature creates a definition of music, and then seeks to join the band. But in another sense, it refuses, like the smuggler, to join in anything. In the end, the value of the song, of the piano piece, and of the story depends on the 'fantaisie' of the artist, which must, by definition, since it is not translatable, be new and different every time. There can be no proof of that value; it can only be a perceived value. The basic conceit of *El Poeta calculista* is the question of what poetry is worth and to whom. Sand's "Contrebandier" is built round the valorisation of specific works of art by and for individuals: García's predilection for his own song, Liszt's genius as seen by his friend, and the smuggler's singing as it conquers the lord of the manor and his people. That, in the end, is the untaxed and untaxable contraband of art: nothing more nor less than our conviction that what we read, see, or hear has an untranslatable value; untranslatable and incalculable. *El Poeta calculista* was a success as an opera, and the smuggler from the opera became a bankable phenomenon; but in the opera, the smuggler, like his black thread, didn't make a penny, and the poet's calculations failed.

References

Liszt, Ferenc (1974). *New Edition of the Complete Works*. Series II, vol. 2. Budapest: Editio Musica Budapest.

Mallarmé, Stéphane (1998). *Œuvres complètes, tome I*. B. Marchal, ed. Paris: Gallimard (Bibliothèque de la Pléiade).

Powell, David A. (2001). *While the Music Lasts: The Representation of Music in the Novels of George Sand*. Lewisburg, PA: Bucknell University Press.

Prieto, Eric (2002). "Method and Methodology in Word and Music Studies". Suzanne M. Lodato, Suzanne Aspden, Walter Bernhart, eds. *Word and Music Studies: Essays in Honor of Steven Paul Scher and on Cultural Identity and the Musical Stage*. Amsterdam: Rodopi. 49-67.

Radomski, James (2002). *Manuel García (1775-1832): Chronicle of the Life of a* bel canto *Tenor at the Dawn of Romanticism*. Oxford: Oxford University Press.

Sand, George (1876). "Le Contrebandier". In: *La Coupe. Lupo Liverani. Le Toast. Garnier. Le Contrebandier. La Rêverie à Paris*. Paris: Michel Lévy frères. 261-298.

Conscientious Translation
Liszt, Robert Franz, and the Phenomenology of Lied Transcription

David Francis Urrows, Hong Kong

The lied transcription holds an important place at the intersection of repertoire building, virtuosity, pedagogy, and music commodification in the mid-nineteenth century. Franz Liszt established the lied transcription in the 1830s as a sub-genre, deftly styling his arrangements of works by Schubert, Schumann, Robert Franz and others, as 'conscientious translations' of their originals. Liszt's conscience notwithstanding, lied transcriptions have frequently been scorned either as 'derangements' – owing to the suppression of the literary/poetic text and frequent embellishment and extension of the original score – or as hopelessly inadequate expressive vehicles due to the compression of material and omission of timbral resources. In fact these arrangements are often misrepresented: they are not all virtuoso vehicles, or vandalizations which cashed in on a lucrative if fleeting market for novelties. By removing the personality of the singer, as well as the sung text, these transcriptions paradoxically increase the focus of both performers and listeners on the composed reading of the text, and on the musical text itself. In doing so, they create a transgeneric corpus of works, ones which present 'expressive remainders' of their originals.

In a famous scene in *Don Giovanni* (scene sixteen, usually considered part of the finale of the second act), an on-stage wind band entertains the Don by playing little selections from various popular operas of the 1780s: *Una cosa rara* by Vincente Martín y Soler, *I due litiganti* by Giuseppe Sarti, and finally they launch into the perky strains of "Non più andrai" from Mozart's own *Marriage of Figaro*. This elicits Leporello's caustic comment, "Questa poi la conosco pur troppo", meaning approximately, 'I've been hearing **this** one all too often'[1].

---

[1] The libretti of all four operas mentioned here were written by Lorenzo da Ponte, a point often overlooked. Martín y Soler's *Una cosa rara* was first performed in Vienna (at the Burgtheater) in November 1786; Sarti's *I due litiganti* (originally performed at La Scala) was revived in Vienna in 1784; Mozart's *Le nozze di Figaro* was first given in Vienna (also at the Burgtheater) in May 1786; while *Don Giovanni* was first performed in Prague in 1787. Does this further suggest that the setting of *Don Giovanni*, unspecified as to time, is to be assumed 'contemporary' with reference to Mozart and

How is it that Leporello does not need to hear the words sung by a baritone in order to tell him where that tune comes from, or what 'it is'? Of course, we all say, he recognizes the 'melody'. He knows what 'it' is by identifying, among other things, a melody carrying with it (to his ears and brain) data encoded in Mozart's unique, composed reading of Lorenzo da Ponte's text. From this data he recognizes it (at least subconsciously) even though it is a transcription, or an arrangement of an aria[2]. Such a transcription lacks, however, a crucial element which makes arias part of operas: the audible intonation of the text by a singer present and participating in the performance. My attention has been arrested for some years by a special type of arrangement: the solo piano transcription of nineteenth-century lieder. Lied transcriptions – which I tentatively characterize here as 'songs, without words' – are very odds things: if they do exist 'without' their words (in both senses of the term) at some times and in some cases the words are nonetheless not very far away, as anyone who has heard the famous arrangements by Liszt of Schumann's "Widmung", or Schubert's "Erlkönig", can attest.

This highlights one of the strange experiential aspects of these pieces: not only can one know them well, somewhat, or not at all, but one can also hear them in experientially different modes, that is: with or without prior knowledge of the words, or even of the identity of the works as transcriptions. These in turn lead to modally different experiences for different listeners. In short, there is a complex melopoetic phenomenology to be examined here.

To many people, the apparent absence of the words greatly diminishes the aesthetic value of these works, especially for those who

---

da Ponte? Or is this just a dislocation, a diegetic anachronism meant to highlight the tension between realistic and supernatural worlds in the opera's story? (Cf. Bogart)

[2] To an ethnomusicologist, or a semiotician, who uses the term in a strict sense, any written score is a transcription of something else. I do not propose here to get into the debate over definitions of 'arrangements' and 'transcriptions': the terms are commonly interchangeable in everyday musical conversation, 'arrangements' perhaps suggesting more license in the adaptation. The early history of keyboard music is a history of transcriptions of dances and vocal pieces. Almost all composers have from time to time had second thoughts, and arranged – that is, transcribed out of their original conceptions into new instrumentation, forms and genres – their own music, often exceeding their original success (Igor Stravinski's 1952 *Concertino for 12 Instruments* is a case in point; cf. fn. 17).

know the original versions. They deny a complete aesthetic and musical experience can be had without them. During most of the twentieth century, the so-called 'Age of Authenticity', such works were dismissed as "derangements"[3], vandalizations of the 'authentic' forms of works, generally as manifestations of appallingly bad taste.

This point of view is not so commonly expressed today, but it is still held *sub rosa* by many musical scholars. Today's more cautious criticism is summed up by Susan Youens in her comments on Liszt's transcriptions of Schubert's *Winterreise*, to the effect that at best "one reads the poem[s] and hears [the] music involuntarily, [listening to the transcriptions] one supplies the words out of a similar desire **to complete what is otherwise incomplete**" (Youens 306; my emphasis). Of Liszt's transcription of "Der Leiermann" she claims that "the lied **does not fully make sense** without the words to clarify its few stark elements" (ibid.; my emphasis). In referring to these Schubert transcriptions, Charles Madsen has stated with somewhat more circumspection that

> generic identity [...] is called into question with the removal of the poetic text in performance [...] normative boundaries of genre have been blurred; these works are no longer Lieder nor are they independent piano compositions, since they are associated with a printed text. (64)

Either way, lied transcriptions are in this manner demoted from the status of authentic, complete works and relegated to the status of quotation, distorted fragments of a larger whole. Behind this attitude lurks the evangelical spirit of twentieth-century musical scholarship, for which arrangement was a kind of crime against the very nature of musical art.

However, there are now powerful defenses for the integrity of such pieces, summed up by the Liszt scholar Alan Walker, who refers

---

[3] Liszt himself is responsible for the wordplay by which arrangements were caricatured as 'derangements'. In writing to Adolphe Pictet in 1837, he wrote with contempt of the popular style (possibly meaning that of Thalberg and lesser virtuosi of the day) of arranging "motifs pilfered from all types of music stitched together for better or for worse" into "caprices and fantasies" which represented to him "the usual derangements" (Liszt, *An Artist's Journey* 47; he uses the term again later in the letter). Interestingly, this attitude never appears to be as virulent in the case of self-transcription, for example of opera excerpts (as in the case of Bizet's orchestral transcriptions in the *Carmen* and *L'Arlésienne* suites).

to the "superior phenomenon" of arrangement of musical works. Musicians, he says,

> should be grateful for the power of our language. In an arrangement, music talks about music; music communes with music; the language turns in on itself, and in the very greatest examples provides a critical commentary on the original, a closed world *par excellence*. (1999: xiii)

Walker appears to suggest that the music 'speaks' (or, talks) to us even in the absence of the verbal text, and there are reasons for thinking that the words have not, in fact, been completely excised or 'removed' in these arrangements, that the experience is far from 'incomplete'. Even Youens acknowledges this, when – probably influenced by the writings of Edward Cone and his concept of the 'hybrid persona' – she describes the "center of the structure [as] neither that of verbal meaning nor that of musical notation but a compound of the two" (Youens 306; cf. also Cone 21-25).

This is a good start, but does not go far enough. The point is often made that the text has been 'removed'; the performance, without words (but with our conscious or unconscious recollection of them) is then 'incomplete'. But if, as she says, we 'hear' words while listening to such a piece, has the text in this case really been completely removed in performance? To what extent can the words be **virtually** removed from the experience of the listener who already knows either the song, or the poem apart from the musical setting, as was so often the case in Liszt's day, or knows the text possibly from a different setting of the poem? To what extent are these really, then, 'songs, without words'? In a lied transcription music is made **actually** to exist in the frame of acousmatic space without the words (again, in both senses of the term[4]), but are the words, or at least aspects of them, nevertheless, still somehow virtually within the adapted song? How can such a work of art even make sense, as and when such an important feature as the words to a song are deleted? Transcriptions do, in fact, make sense, claims to the contrary notwithstanding, and I have always wondered how and why this can be.

---

[4] Here note a further semantic issue involved, and pointed up by the use of the comma in my characterization. We use the preposition 'without' as an English equivalent of German 'ohne', and in its common sense this is acceptable, a function word meaning 'absent', or 'lacking'. But the English word, 'without', has another and perhaps older meaning, that of 'outside of', the antonym of 'within'. This double meaning, intriguingly, does not exist in the original German.

***

Although our view of the lied in the late eighteenth and nineteenth centuries has shifted and broadened over the past 30 years, it remains a form intimately connected with the music of the Romantic era. Lieder, for the first time, represent a qualitatively and quantitatively significant part of the works of major figures, such as Beethoven, Schubert, Schumann, and Brahms. Then there are composers for whom the lied is the only enduring part of their work, such as Carl Loewe and Hugo Wolf, and composers who wrote almost exclusively lieder, such as Robert Franz, to whom I will return later[5].

The lied transcription, the arrangement for solo piano of a work originally conceived as a setting of a text for one voice and piano, was the principal means by which many listeners in the mid-nineteenth century first came to know the songs of Schubert and others. It should be no surprise that the lied transcription arrived at the same time as the 'Lied ohne Worte'. The latter is the 'song without words' first de-

---

[5] Robert Franz was born in Halle in 1815. He is remembered outside Germany today for a single song, "Widmung", Op. 14, No.1. This is a heart-felt and deservedly popular piece, but does not begin to suggest the depth and variety of his lieder, a genre which accounts for about 90 per cent of his output. His originality in the lied form was recognized by many, including Schumann, who became the first of his big supporters with an article and review of his works in the *Neue Zeitschrift für Musik* (hereafter, *NZfM*) in late 1843.

Liszt first met Robert Franz in Dessau in February 1844. On this occasion Liszt spoke warmly of Franz's first collection of lieder, published at Schumann's instigation the previous year, and intimated that he would be happy if Franz would at some point dedicate a set to him. This Franz did, in his *Sechs Gesänge*, Op. 7, published in 1846. In 1853, Liszt returned the compliment, and wrote a long appreciative study of Robert Franz and his music which appeared in the *NZfM*. In 1872, when Franz through illness, isolation, and growing deafness experienced hard financial times, Liszt revised and republished this study in a slightly expanded form, helping to rouse a recently unified Germany to recognition of one of its under-acknowledged masters.

Even Richard Wagner, with whom Franz was friendly, at least for a while, in the late 1840s and '50s, declared that during his years of exile in Zurich, he kept the scores of only three German composers in his music cabinet: Bach, Beethoven, and the songs of Robert Franz. These were frequently sung in the Wagner household, in particular the perennial favorite, "Widmung", and the last of the Op. 7 set dedicated to Liszt, the near-atonal "Ja, du bist elend". Some of Wagner's early musical sketches for *Siegfrieds Tod* bear a strong resemblance to Franz's bare-bones lyrical style. Franz died in Halle, full of years and bitterness, in 1892. (Cf. fn. 24)

veloped by Felix Mendelssohn and his sister, Fanny, in the late 1820s (cf. Todd). For the purposes of this discussion, I have tentatively characterized the lied transcription with a slight variation in punctuation, as a 'song, without words'[6].

These similar monikers for seemingly related genres raise interesting points. First, there is something metaphorical in Mendelssohn's construction of a 'Lied ohne Worte', the lack of 'words' in a 'song' being an instance of the accepted falsehood, the cognitive dissonance which lies at the heart of metaphor[7]. (Nevertheless, *Lieder ohne Worte* certainly refer as a whole **generically** to texted, sung lieder.) Steven Paul Scher briefly touched on a second point when he discussed the "romantic impulse towards transforming the lied into pure instrumental music, as reflected in Liszt's famous piano transcriptions of Schubert" ("The German Lied" 293). Eric Sams, writing in the sixth edition of Grove, contended that "the paradigm of a Schumann song is a lyric piano piece, the melody of which is shared by a voice" (840). And Lawrence Kramer also mentions this in passing in his book, *Music and Poetry*, where he considers Schumann himself to have "thought of the lied as a form of lyric piano piece – a 'song without words' – but with words" (*Music and Poetry* 131)[8].

---

[6] One cannot, of course, separate lied transcriptions entirely from the larger body of transcriptions of such things as operas (vocal scores) and operatic excerpts, which could also be so characterized. These types of arrangements have similar affective relationships to their sources, and also provide a 'recapitulation' of their originals.

[7] The sky obviously does not weep, yet we all know this refers *metaphorically* to rain. Eric Prieto has described this "cognitive dissonance" (54) inherent in metaphor as the vector carrying its chief instructional value.

[8] I do not accept this characterization, for reasons which will become clear. A real 'song without words – but with words' would in my view be seen in pieces such as Liszt's three *Sonetti del Petrarca* in the second year of *Années de Pèlerinage*. While based on earlier vocal settings, these are not really transcriptions in any meaningful sense, and yet they are (again) one of Liszt's highly original conceptual excursions into word/music relationships. This is very different to both Mendelssohn's atextual concept of the 'Lied ohne Worte', and the lied transcription which contains both virtual aspects of the poetic text as well as actual aspects of the composed reading. The only works I can think of which really fit this description of a 'song without words – but with words' are the two sets of *Liebeslieder Waltzes*, Opp. 52 and 65, of Johannes Brahms, settings of poems for mixed voices and piano, four-hands, where the vocal parts are nevertheless *ad libitum*.

Does all this mean, then, that the Romantic lied might in some sense really be thought of as a metaphorical piano piece, to which a voice singing a text may have been added or subtracted at will? If so, then we would be led to conclude that the lied repertory consists of a large number of transcriptions of piano pieces, and this would offer an easy explanation of how the lied transcription – a 'song with words – but without words' – holds together as a cogent work of art.

I do not, however, think it's as simple as that. There are movements in Beethoven's piano sonatas, for example, which anticipate the *Lied ohne Worte* style, but no one would suggest that these are anticipations of vocal works[9]. Rather than hearing lieder morphing towards solo piano pieces, I think these analogous features are more easily explained through the tendency of Liszt's day (and earlier) to think of the piano as anthropomorphizing into a sentient being capable of singing with its own voice at the prompting of the performer. That this was common conceit of the age can be seen in many places, especially in the title of Sigismund Thalberg's 1853 piano method, 'The Art of Singing applied to the Piano' [10]. Thirty years later, one of Liszt's students, Carl Lachmund, recorded a conversation in which Lachmund's wife Caroline enthused to Liszt, *"lieber Meister* […] you created a new sphere for these [Schubert songs] with your transcriptions, you taught the piano to sing them!" (Lachmund 318). Liszt and Thalberg may have been some distance apart, aesthetically, but both felt and responded to the inexorable drive of the day toward a hegemony of the *cantabile* style in all aspects of music composition.

---

[9] See, for example, the second movement (Andante) of the Piano Sonata in G major, Op. 79. The slow movements of the well-known 'Pathéthique' and 'Moonlight' sonatas also share some of the qualities of 'songs without words', and at least the latter has occasionally had words fitted to it. For the question of the supposed "suppressed texts" of the *Lieder ohne Worte* cf. Todd 192f.

[10] *L'art du Chant appliqué au Piano* (Paris 1853). It is significant that most of the pieces in this 'method' were piano transcriptions of operatic selections. I briefly discuss the similar anthropomorphizing of the pipe organ at this approximate date in my article, "Sheep, Gin, and the Telegraphic Crescendo Freaks". For a more positive-than-usual assessment of Thalberg and his works, including transcriptions, cf. Jensen 45-60.

* * *

Styling himself 'a conscientious translator', Franz Liszt made over 160 transcriptions of lieder by various composers, of which a third are of songs by Schubert[11]. Robert Winter has gone so far as to call them "Liszt's most important pianistic legacy [...] in terms of exploiting the resources of the Romantic piano" (23). It seems now accepted that, while Liszt was influenced by earlier attempts at this kind of arrangement made by his mentors Carl Czerny and Christian [Chrétien] Urhan (also involving Schubert's songs), the viable history of the lied transcription begins with him, just as the 'Lied ohne Worte' begins with the Mendelssohns[12].

It was after the publication of Robert Franz's *Sechs Gesänge*, Op. 7, dedicated to Liszt, in 1846, that Liszt began to involve himself in transcribing a group of Franz's lieder as works for solo piano. The Schubert transcriptions had occupied Liszt during the 1830s, and we know that Liszt's goals in these earlier arrangements were to promote the then not-very-well-known music of Schubert, as well as to provide Liszt himself with works of a brief and dramatic nature with which to pepper his concerts and recitals. The vocal recital as we know it today was in an embryonic stage, and it is not so surprising to learn that as

---

[11] The Schubert transcriptions, in particular, have been fairly well-studied at this point: no fewer than seven M.A. and Ph.D. dissertations have appeared on them in the past 30 years. All of Liszt's transcriptions are in print in both a critical edition as well as a facsimile of the originals for many, and all have been recorded twice for CD. The phrase, 'conscientious translator' actually comes from Liszt's preface to his 1865 publication of solo piano transcriptions of Beethoven's nine symphonies: 'I shall have reached my goal if I have fulfilled the duty of an intelligent engraver, a conscientious translator, who grasps the spirit of a work along with the letter, and who thus helps to spread the recognition of the masters and the appreciation of the beautiful.' (Transl. of: "Mein Ziel ist erreicht, wenn ich es dem verständigen Kupferstecher, dem gewissenhaften Übersetzer gleichgetan habe, welche den Geist eines Werkes auffassen und so zur Erkenntnis der großen Meister und zur Bildung des Sinnes für das Schöne beitragen." In: Liszt, *New Liszt Edition*, Series II/1, 2.)

[12] Madsen covers the issue of prototypes by Czerny and Urhan (cf. 31-34). This is a good source for historical background on lied transcriptions and their reception history, though largely limited to the Schubert arrangements. For more on Urhan, cf. Kawabata. Mendelssohn's claim to fathering the 'Lied ohne Worte' has been discussed and his paternity upheld in Todd.

Liszt's Schubert arrangements arrived at music dealers, they sold well, even outselling the original voice and piano scores.

When Liszt published his first arrangement of a song by Robert Franz, "Er ist gekommen in Sturm und Regen", it was a single song which appeared as the fourth of a series of what were simply titled *Transcriptionen für Pianoforte von Franz Liszt* (R162/SW 488). This appeared simultaneously in German and French editions in the summer of 1849. From the French publication, we can tell that this was not just a straightforward arrangement, but what Liszt tellingly called an 'impromptu': this probably refers to the addition of interpolated material, featuring a modulation to the lowered submediant, and a certain amount of rather un-Franz-like passagework in a retransition leading to a *grandioso* setting of the final strophe. Nonetheless, this is actually a rather restrained example of Liszt's adaptations of lied originals: many of the Schubert transcriptions go far beyond this level of recomposing and remodeling. For example, the *Neue Zeitschrift für Musik*, commenting on Liszt's transcription of Beethoven's "An die ferne Geliebte", which appeared the following year in 1850, remarked approvingly that

> die Uebertragung ist eine sehr Discrete. Es freut uns, nicht das virtuose Beiwerk anzutreffen, das die Schubert'schen Lieder oft als Folie für Fingerverrenkung dienen läßt. Die Schwierigkeit ist somit eine wenig bedeutende, und der Spielerkreis wird ein um so größerer werden[13].

One striking feature of Liszt's transcriptions is that in the great majority of cases he was insistent that his publishers print the text in the score at the appropriate points. This was done not least for the benefit of the performer, and in this sense, the text is at least a **presence**, if not exactly present in these transcriptions. The following examples will serve for further illustration. For this, I have deliberately chosen a pair of works probably unknown to most readers: Robert Franz's song "Auf geheimem Waldespfade", from the *Schilflieder*, Op. 2, and Liszt's sensitive and evocative piano transcription of Franz's setting of Nikolaus Lenau's poem.

---

[13] *NZfM*, 24 May 1850, 221: 'The adaptation is one of considerable discretion. We are happy not to find any of that virtuoso stuff [*das virtuose Beiwerk*] which often makes the Schubert transcriptions serve [only] as foils for finger contortions. In this way the technical demands have been somewhat reduced, and thus the sphere of [possible] performers has been increased.' (This, and subsequent translations, are my own.)

Andantino
Auf ge - hei-mem Wal-des - pfa-de schleich' _ ich gern im A _ bend-schein an das
Sul una corda
ö - de Schilf-ge - sta-de, Mäd - chen, und ge - den - ke dein. Wenn sich
dann der Busch ver - dü - stert, rauscht das Rohr ge-heim-niss - voll und es kla-get und es

Example 1: Robert Franz, *"Auf geheimem Waldespfade" (from* Schilflieder, *Op. 2, No. 1, 1843).*

Andantino
m.d.
p dolce
una corda
tre corde
Auf ge - hei-mem Wal-des - pfa - de schleich' ich gern' im A bend-
schein an das ö - de Schilf - ge - sta - de,
Mäd-chen, und ge - den - ke Dein.

Example 2: Franz Liszt, Lieder von Robert Franz: Heft 1: **Schilflieder** *("Auf geheimem Waldespfade") R 163/SW 489 (publ. 1849)*

For those predisposed to imagine all of Liszt's lied arrangements as empty, or near-empty vehicles for virtuosity of a rather meretricious kind, the almost-impressionistic keyboard writing in *Example 2*, with its fidelity to the original (even if Walter Bernhart, in his article in the present volume, is correct in asserting that fidelity is an overrated virtue in the world of adaptations), and its careful use of timbre, spacing, register, and dynamics, may come as something of a mild surprise.

On the face of it, there is no particularly good reason why Liszt should have chosen **this** song to transcribe for piano solo. Indeed, there is very little here in the way of the grand melodic sweep of 'typical' lieder, such as Schumann's "Widmung" and "Frühlingsnacht", or the drama of Schubert's "Erlkönig", which would seem to be essential for a successful transcription. For the most part, the vocal (melodic) line in Franz's song hovers narrowly around either the upper or the lower tetrachord of the E-flat minor scale, and is composed in a *parlando*, almost recitative-like style, breaking out only briefly into true *arioso* from the end of the second strophe. (This gives the lie, in my opinion, to the idea that nineteenth-century lieder are predominantly 'lyric piano pieces with words'.)

In his transcription, Liszt in fact takes away notes in proportion to those that he adds. The opening presents the melodic line in the middle register, as though sung by a tenor, with the harmonic accompaniment reduced and gently surrounding the melodic line. This is then repeated an octave higher (as though a soprano had begun again at the beginning) with a very slightly enriched accompaniment, which opens up the sonorous bass register of the instrument (by moving the accompaniment an octave lower) and expanding ever-so-slightly the triplet accompaniment figure. In the second strophe, Liszt cannot resist a gentle bit of imitation in the higher octave, entirely in keeping with the mood of the text. "Rauscht das Rohr geheimnisvoll" – this decoration (mm. 20-23) is the 'secret rustling of the reeds', which is left to the imagination in Lenau's poem, as well as in Franz's austere setting, but which Liszt **composes out** as a substitute for the declamation of the text in his transcription.

Liszt has preserved all of Franz's articulation and dynamics, and then expanded them didactically for the pianist (a singer would automatically do this on his or her own). His painstaking attention to these performance issues – fingering, stress, coloring, hand position, pedaling (clarifying what he may have felt to be left out of Franz's directions for the use of both the sustaining pedal and the *una corda* pedal) and arpeggiation in keeping with performance practice of the day – all these details are hardly heard by the listener, however much they may demand considerable attention from the performer[14]. They remind us, as Alan Walker has pointed out, that "the difficulties [of these transcriptions] are mostly of a private, not a public nature. They embody 'art that conceals art' [...] Liszt rarely regarded these pieces as display works with which to dazzle the audience" (57f.).

The notation on (for the most part) three staves is another result of the care with which Liszt took to clarify the different melodic strands of words and music in his arrangements (not that he ever encouraged the separation of melody and accompaniment in performance). The 'vocal' line appears in the middle and upper staves, depending on whether a 'tenor' or a 'soprano' is 'singing', and the accompaniment is placed on a stave convenient for the pianist to read (for this reason, the middle stave is not slavishly used between mm. 10-18, which revert to a normal two-stave format). This vertical visual division of elements is complemented by a horizontal division emphasizing textual declamation: the pick-up (anacrusis) motive which is heard prior to the downbeats of measures 1, 5, 10, 14, 20, 24, and 33, is **always** divided into separate stems, and never beamed together, as a music engraver would typically do in keyboard work. Here is the notational evidence for Liszt 'whispering in accompaniment' (cf. fn. 26) during his own performances of these works. And it hardly needs saying that the underlay of text is an ever-present reminder that this is only in a small sense a 'song, without words'. (And there are certainly many additional interesting expressive and technical features of both the original and the transcription which could be remarked upon, if space allowed.)

There are, however, other ways besides the visual cue in which the words are a presence in Liszt's arrangement, even if they remain unuttered. To borrow Steven Scher's term, every text setting represents the 'composed reading' imposed upon it in the compositional process. The rhythmicization of the words, the ambitus of register

---

[14] The very first pitch, b-flat, has five performance directives attached to it: volume (*piano*), tone color (*dolce*), hand position (right hand), fingering (index finger), and pedaling (*una corda*).

comprising the vocal line, the relationships between voice and accompaniment, between grammar and phrase structure, indeed most of the profile of the musical landscape unfolding (in what Susanne Langer called '**virtual time**'), all these survive largely unaltered in a transcription[15]. These are the principal features which allow Leporello, for example, to recognize "Non più andrai", or for the rest of us to recognize, again for example, the "Toreador Song" from Bizet's *Carmen* in its purely orchestral dress.

My first claim for lied transcriptions is, then, that in the process of arrangement it is impossible to completely 'remove' the text, the words, to delete completely any one of what Werner Wolf has called the "original components of the intermedial mixture" (Wolf 22; cf. fn. 27). The vocal line remains, as we can clearly see in the Liszt-Franz example, while the words and the singer are more **suppressed** than eliminated. This means, in turn, that for both listeners who know the words, and for those who don't, and even for those who do not know in advance that the work is a transcription of a lied, similar complete aesthetic and musical experiences are available, as the components of the mixture coalesce in the musical logic of the arrangement[16]. This idea would appear to reflect and also find support in the notion prevalent among semioticians of a 'work' as something distinct from its notation as a musical score: as something malleable and essentially intangible, existing "at the horizon of all its possible rewritings" (to quote Jean Molino[17]).

---

[15] Scher stated: "By placing the poetic text into a musical context, the composer-reader performs a generic transformation [...]. In this new, symbiotic construct that comprises both verbal and musical components, the words of the poem merge with and are shaped into the vocal line which, together with the instrumental [...] accompaniment, constitutes the larger musical framework [...] song composition may be viewed as the act of the composer's assimilative reading of the original poem, as a 'compenetration' [...] of the composing reader and his text." (Scher, "Comparing Poetry and Music" 225)

[16] Alan Walker mentions a "purely musical defense of arrangements that is so simple nobody ever thinks of it. You cannot tell, simply by listening, which is the arrangement and which is the original. Uncorrupted by knowledge, the innocent ear is unable to differentiate. You have to be told in advance which is which" (Walker, "Liszt and the Schubert Song Transcriptions" xiii).

[17] Cf. Nattiez 70. A semiotic investigation of the issues surrounding lied transcriptions would be a major contribution to the study of this genre. In an important article on (four-hands) transcriptions, Thomas Christensen raises this issue, remarking "[f]or

Liszt himself evidently recognized both this and the retention of aspects of the poetic text within the purely musical substance of his transcriptions. On at least one occasion he did away with the words, but not the singer. There is a story about Liszt meeting the tenor Adolphe Nourrit (1802-1839) at a Parisian salon in 1834.

> [Liszt] was at the piano playing [his transcription of] "Erlkönig" when Nourrit entered ... Nourrit was all ears. As he became aware of this dramatic music, he showed deep emotion and his face lit up. When the piece ended, he requested that it be played again, but Liszt replied that it would be better if he sang it. Nourrit excused himself on the grounds that he did not know German. When Liszt explained the text to him, the singer agreed **to merely vocalize the melody**, which he did with the expressiveness of an inspired interpreter. (Quicherat, 2, 32; quoted in Madsen, 35 [my emphasis]).

This was for once truly, and not metaphorically, a 'song without words'[18].

Today, however, we cannot hear Liszt's transcriptions of Schubert without a great deal of foreknowledge of the originals. In this sense, it is often impossible to hear these works in their original context, to put ourselves within the frame of the original listeners. Referring back to

---

many critics (Busoni perhaps most notoriously), [an] orchestral score is no less a transcription of the composer's original intention than is [a] piano arrangement" (282). However, Christensen does not deal with solo piano transcriptions, and dismisses them with the comment that "[s]olo piano transcriptions were usually too difficult for most amateurs, and in any case they tended to leave too much out" (260). While there were no doubt different markets for solo and four-hands arrangements (and while at the same time these markets surely overlapped), the ghost of the Age of Authenticity still looms in such a judgment.

Having said that, two further observations should be made: on the one hand, solo piano transcriptions were reviewed, at least in *NZfM*, under the rubric "Konzertmusik: Arrangements", emphasizing a degree of distance from the *Hausmusik* environment of most four-hands transcriptions. On the other, not all four-hands transcriptions were easily playable by amateurs: some, including those by Renaud de Vilbac (1829-1884), required a considerable degree of technique and even virtuosity (such as his three 'Suites' of *Illustrations sur* [Gounod's] *Faust*).

[18] Examples of what could be called the 'deliberate' vocal song without words might include: Rachmaninoff's popular "Vocalise", Op. 34, No. 14 (1912), as well as Villas-Lobos's *Bachianas Brasileiras No. 5* (or parts of it, at any rate) (1938), and the *Concerto for Coloratura Soprano and Orchestra,* Op. 82, of Reinhold Glière (1943), as well as the now-hackneyed trope of an atmospheric-wordless soprano (usually positioned off-stage), originally and most effectively used by Ralph Vaughan Williams at the conclusion of his *Pastoral Symphony* (No. 3, 1922).

Liszt's arrangement of Robert Franz's "Auf geheimem Waldespfade", the present obscurity of the original (the 'hypotext', in Gérard Genette's terms) as well as of Liszt's 'hypertext', has become a virtue of sorts, assisting us both in putting aside preconceptions about transcriptions and arrangements, and approaching them with our ears (and our minds) "uncorrupted by knowledge", in Alan Walker's phrase[19]. We can in some sense share the vivid experience denied to us with better-known works.

The musical logic in Liszt's transcription must depend to a large extent on the transcription's ability to project the musical content of the vocal line with whatever is left over after the words are suppressed and the mixture of components redistributed. What exactly this left-over component is, is something that puzzled me for years. There is something there, because there is more than just a musical melodic line supported by an accompaniment. I was puzzled, that is, until I attended the 2003 WMA conference in Berlin, and heard Larry Kramer's keynote talk, entitled "Speaking Melody, Melodic Speech".

In "Speaking Melody, Melodic Speech", Kramer describes "a relationship more virtual than actual: when a musical phrase associated with certain words is used motivically [...] without the words being either uttered or sung. [...] Speaking melody is song-like", says Kramer,

> but not song, not speech, but speech-like. The melody [...] does not sing, it speaks, and what it says is definite and understood, as if a virtual voice had uttered the substance of the words without their sound [...]. Once words have been joined to a melody, the words seem to saturate the music so that the music can voice them afterwards even in their absence [...] we know the words, but do not hear them; they bypass the senses that the music addresses. (127)

Of course, lied transcriptions are Kramer's 'speaking melody' writ very large. Here the melody is not used motivically, as in a film score, or as quotation, as in *Don Giovanni*. It is no longer a quotation: 'it' is the work itself. In fact, one of the difficulties in describing the acousmatic experience of these transcriptions is accounting for the modally different experiences different listeners bring to the event: that is, these transcriptions will 'speak' in different degrees, if not even in different kind.

---

[19] See above fn. 16. For more on Genette's concepts of hypertextuality, see Bernhard Kuhn's article on the opera-film, *Fedora*, in this volume.

To a person who knows the words and the song – and Kramer's paradigm of speaking melody assumes this – they are present as more than just what he calls an "expressive remainder". For those who do not know the words, a transcription may then have the power to focus our listening on the musical text even more than would a performance of the original song. In either case, the words have not been 'removed'. As Kramer suggests, a surplus of some sort is left behind, "the music is saturated", he says, "but the words have been absorbed" (ibid. 128).

Kramer offers a further clue to understanding how transcriptions succeed without in any serious way damaging irreparably the musical logic and fabric of the compositions. In asking what it is that gives speaking melody its power, he suggests that it lies "in the gap between the expressive power of the melody and the meaning of the words. The words tell us", he says, "or would if we could hear them, what the melody says [...] if one subtracts what the words say from what the melody expresses there is always an expressive remainder, a surplus or excess to deal with" (ibid. 131).

For so-called 'songs, without words' the words themselves seem nevertheless to be present at some level to a large degree, recalled by those who know them, but for all listeners saturating the melodic line, which itself resolves one tone into another in an act of virtual causality that supercedes the need for a sung text. This is why I feel there is perhaps even more here than just an "expressive remainder". As examples of speaking melody, of which these transcriptions are an extreme, transgeneric type, to quote Kramer one final time, "they combine the material consistency of music with the symbolic value of words, but without merging them together as sung melody tends to do" (ibid. 133).

The idea of merging, of fusion occurring in the performance of song between the sounds of words, their meanings, and pitch has a long history. Robert Franz once said: "Ich mache nicht Musik zum Text, sondern setze den Text in Musik um"[20] (Waldmann 38). In describing this process further he insisted that "Man muß sich den Text

---

[20] 'I do not write music to fit the words, but turn the words into music.' Similar comments abound in Franz's writings and recorded conversations. A good selection can be found in Loë.

klar vorhalten, – hat man ihn erfaßt, dann ergiebt sich Rhythmus und Vortrag ganz von selbst", and he went on to remark that

> Schubert's Begleitungen sind eben bloß mehr melodiöse Begleitungen; bei Schumann wird's schon anders, – an ihn habe ich mich angelehnt. Bei mir giebt die Begleitung gleichsam die Situation wieder, die der Text ausspricht, – die Melodie muß dagegen das Bewußtwerden der Situation zur Geltung bringen[21]. (Ibid. 61)

These acknowledgements of levels of reciprocity suggest to me that Franz and even Liszt were themselves conscious of the basic conditions for speaking melody, perhaps even 'consciously unconscious' of them[22]. For me, they go further towards debunking the idea that the mid-nineteenth-century lied was really a kind of piano piece with an *obbligato* voice. And it was precisely these aspects of Franz's songs which so attracted Schumann and Liszt, among many others: Schumann arranged to have Franz's Op. 1 published without bothering to inform the startled composer, and Liszt eventually transcribed a total of 13 of Franz's lieder, and was still promoting them in the last years of his life[23]. It is no coincidence, then, that the *Schilflieder*, Op. 2, were dedicated to Schumann, and that Schumann remarked with enthusiasm upon the publication of Liszt's transcriptions in 1849, "daß

---

[21] 'One must have a very clear idea of the text: if you have grasped it, it gives you the rhythm and prosody all by itself. [...] In Schubert's songs, the accompaniments are merely the accompaniment of melodies; with Schumann, it's something quite different, and I have leant towards him in this regard. In my songs the accompaniment depicts the situation described in the text, while on the other hand the melody embodies the awareness of that situation.'

[22] It is also significant that Franz once claimed to prefer the idea of Beethoven's song "Adelaïde" with the vocal line performed instrumentally: "Von Beethoven's *Adelaide* bin ich gar nicht so entzückt, ich höre die Melodie lieber von eine Klarinette blasen, als von einer Singstimme." (Waldmann 103; 'I am really not taken with Beethoven's *Adelaide*, I should rather hear the melody played on a clarinet than sung by a voice.')

[23] The *Liszt-Pädagogium* (see Ramann) contains a section devoted to Liszt's transcription of Franz's songs "Der Bote" and "Mondnacht". Further lieder of Robert Franz were transcribed for piano by Otto Dresel (1826-1890), a student of Liszt and close associate of Franz (*Twelve Songs by Robert Franz Arranged as Songs Without Words for the Piano*), and twelve more appeared in 1874, arranged by Theodor Kirchner (1823-1903), a protégé of Mendelssohn and Schumann, who had the distinction of being the very first student to matriculate at the Leipzig Conservatory at its opening in 1843.

vielen seiner poetischen Dichtungen auf diese Weise neue Wege eröffnet werden"[24] (Jansen 462).

In a lied transcription important aspects of the poetic text remain in performance, even when the audible words and the personality of the singer are suppressed, and even when (as so often with Liszt) an additional interpretive layer is imposed on the music. The words may even be present at other levels: Liszt asked his students to study the vocal originals of these works as a kind of preparatory exercise to performing them, to make, as he put it, 'the declamation of the text unified with the living impulse of performance'[25], even when such a declamation remains inaudible in the conventional sense. Lina Ramann (1833-1912), Liszt's student and early biographer, left a detailed exposition of this attitude which emanated from Liszt himself. Ramann wrote that

> Liszt's Liedübertragungen bereicherten die Klaviermusik mit einem vor ihm nicht gekannten Zweig, der in richtiger Konsequenz ihrem Vortragsstil gewissermaßen andere Bedingungen schuf, als sie dem Stil des gesungenen Liedes eigen sind. Dort ist das Wort latent, schwebt aber als solches und als poetisches Programm hinter und zwischen den Zeilen. Dabei bleibt es bestimmend und bindend für den charakteristischen Ausdruck des Vortrags im Ganzen wie im Einzelnen, speziell für die Wiedergabe der Versionen und Neugestaltungen, welche das Vokallied in ein Instrumentalgedicht umgeschaffen haben.
>
> In diesem Hineingeheimnissen des Wortes in das instrumentale Neubild des Liedes birgt sich das Wesen ihres Vortragsstils.
>
> Bei des Meisters Wiedergabe seiner Liedübertragungen – dem Idealbild dieses Stils – trat dasselbe immer wieder neugestaltend hervor, je nach dem Inhalt des betreffenden Liedes. Wie sehr das Wort in ihm lebte, war häufig an der Bewegung seiner Lippen zu erkennen, die, insbesondere bei lyrischen Stellen, diese flüsternd

---

[24] See above fn. 5. 'In this way new paths will open up for so many of his [Franz's] poetic creations.' For all his acknowledged celebrity as a composer of lieder, well over half of Franz's 350-odd songs have never been republished since their original appearance in the mid-nineteenth century, and are all but inaccessible. A critical edition of his works is urgently needed. The best current scholarship on Franz is contained in the proceedings of a conference held on the centenary of his death: *Robert Franz 1815-1892: Bericht über die wissenschaftliche Konferenz anläßlich seines 100. Todestages am 23. und 24. Oktober 1992 in Halle (Saale)*. Schriften des Händel-Hauses 9. Halle an der Saale: Händel-Haus Halle.

[25] Referring to his transcription of Franz's "Der Bote/Durch den Wald im Mondenschein" (*Lieder von Robert Franz*, R 163/SW 489), Liszt is recorded as saying: "Als Vorstudie zum Vortrag mache man sich die Liedmelodie in textentsprechender Deklamation so zu eigen, daß sie zum lebendigen Impuls des Vortrags wird." (Ramann 12)

zu begleiten schienen. Die jetzt im Konzertsaal mehr und mehr Geltung gewinnende völlige Spaltung von Melodie und Begleitung, welche ostentiös erstere mit großem vollem Brustton auf dem Klavier produziert und letztere zu Gunsten der Melodie unterdrückt, stand seinem Prinzip fern. Diesen unmotivierten Großton hörte ich ihn mit *"gross thun"* übersetzen. Nach ihm ist die Begleitung integrierender Bestandteil des Liedgehaltes, nicht dem Solisten, nicht dem Begleiter übergeben, aber Zwei bedarf, um im Duo Eins zu werden. Liszt's Vortrag seiner "Instrumentalgedichte" kannte nicht jene Spaltung, obwohl er den melodischen Faden festhielt.

Bei dem Studium der Liedübertragungen zählt ein intimes Vertrautsein mit Melodie und Wort zu den Vorbedingungen[26]. (11)

This way of thinking subverts the usual approach to dealing with these pieces. Nothing in a lied transcription is really 'without': the experience is complete, the declamation of the poem is still within the melodic line, apprehensible regardless of any degree of familiarity with the original song. Liszt's whole point was, it is true, to interest

---

[26] 'Liszt's song transcriptions enrich the repertoire of piano music from a source previously not well known, and to a certain extent they bring forward issues of performance practice which are not to be found in a sung lied. In these transcriptions the text is latent, but the words nevertheless float as both an actual and poetic (virtual) program behind and between the lines/staves ["Zeilen"]. Words are a determinant, and they are binding as regards the characteristic expression of the whole, as well as the details, especially so in the case of a version of a vocal work arranged as a poetic instrumental composition.

It is in this same stealthy internalization ["Hineingeheimnissen"] of the words within a new instrumental representation that the secret of their performance style lies.

During the master's performances of his lied transcriptions – the ideal readings of this genre – the words were constantly given newly expressive shape, each depending on its contextual meaning in the song. To show just how deeply the words lived within Liszt, one often noted the movement of his lips, especially at lyrical places, where it seemed as though he were whispering in accompaniment. Nothing could have been further from his principles than that kind of thoroughly ostentatious separation of melody and accompaniment, which is heard more and more in concert halls, where the piano [part] is played so as to produce a booming chest voice sound ["Brustton"] rather than supporting the needs of the melodic line. I heard him refer to this rather show-offish 'big sound' ["Großton"] as 'pretentious' [*gross thun:* an almost untranslatable pun]. For him, the accompaniment was an integral part of the content of the song: neither the solo line nor the accompaniment was given any primacy, but both were required to turn this duality into a unity. Liszt's own performances of his "instrumental poems" never showed any such separation, while on the other hand he certainly never lost the melodic thread.

In studying the song transcriptions, an intimate understanding of the relationship between melody and text is a prerequisite.'

people in the originals through this expressive power of the remainder, but that goal never ruled out the possibility of a different order of appreciation by those not familiar with or even aware of the words, or even aware of the fact that these works are transcriptions. Transcriptions succeed through the ability of a skillful arranger like Liszt to suppress and internalize the words and to exploit that "gap between the expressive power of the melody" (131) and the informative value of the text: what we hear in that gap, I believe, is what Robert Franz called the "awareness (*Bewußtwerden*) of the situation described in the text" (61).

What these transcriptions really created was not so much 'songs, without words', as **songs without a vocalist**. What is suppressed here is not so much the words, as the person as well as the personality of the singer, the verbal but not the symbolic content of the poem. These works are not exactly 'songs', but neither are they exactly 'without words'. Not only are virtual aspects of the poetic texts present, but the actual elements of the 'composed reading' are preserved to a large extent. They present to us a unique grouping: if not strictly intermedial, then certainly transgeneric[27]. And they offer a unique listening experience, as components of the original are redistributed within a new frame which obscures some while highlighting others. Lied transcriptions have been insufficiently studied from this angle, and they present a ripe and fascinating subject for further attention, enlarging our understanding of music aesthetics, commodification, and performance practice in the long nineteenth century.

---

[27] Werner Wolf, whose studies in the area of intermediality are reflected in almost every paper presented at the Santa Barbara conference, describes the intermedial nature of lied transcriptions as one of 'associative quotation' or 'intermedial partial reproduction': the phenomenon of evoking a plurimedial work (text and music) through the monomedial quotation of the music (only). I have explained why I feel these works are much more than just quotations or evocations, and in a private communication, Wolf has agreed with me that "the text somehow remains a covert potential even of the monomedial work, owing to the 'associations of ideas.' [...] In my typology, [lied transcriptions] would be variants of intermedial reference (although I admit that there is an overlapping area with intermedial transposition here)."

References

Bogart, Robert S. (Online). "Martín, Sarti, and Mozart: Musings on the *Don Giovanni* Tafelmusik". http://www.wbopera.org/newsletter/divert/dg.html [01/05/2007].

Christensen, Thomas (1999). "Four-Hand Piano Transcriptions and Geographies of Nineteenth-Century Musical Reception". *Journal of the American Musicological Society* 52/2: 255-298.

Cone, Edward T. (1974). *The Composer's Voice*. Berkeley, CA: University of California Press.

Dresel, Otto (1860). *Twelve Songs by Robert Franz Arranged as Songs Without Words for the Piano by Otto Dresel*. Boston, MA: G. D. Russell.

Jansen, F. Gustav (1904). *Robert Schumann's Briefe*. 2nd enlarged and rev. ed. Leipzig: Breitkopf und Härtel.

Jensen, Eric Frederick (1992). *Walls of Circumstance: Studies in Nineteenth-Century Music*. Metuchen, NJ: Scarecrow Press.

Kawabata, Maiko (2004). "The Concerto that Wasn't: Paganini, Urhan, and *Harold in Italy*". *Nineteenth-Century Music Review* 1/1: 67-114.

Kramer, Lawrence (1984). *Music and Poetry*. Berkeley, CA: University of California Press.

— (2005). "Speaking Melody, Melodic Speech". Suzanne M. Lodato, David Francis Urrows, eds. *Essays on Music and the Spoken Word and on Surveying the Field*. Word and Music Studies 7. Amsterdam/New York, NY: Rodopi. 127-143.

Lachmund, Carl (1994). *Living with Liszt*. Alan Walker, ed. New York, NY: Pendragon Press.

Langer, Susanne K. (1957). *Problems of Art: Ten Philosophical Lectures*. New York, NY: Scribner's.

Liszt, Franz (1989). *An Artist's Journey: Lettres d'un bachalier en musique*. Transl. C. Suttoni, Chicago, IL: University of Chicago Press.

— (1992/1865). *New Liszt Edition*. Series II/17: *Transcriptions/Symphonies of Beethoven Nos. 1-4*. Budapest: Editio Musica.

Loë, Didi (1915). *Robert Franz-Brevier*. Leipzig: Breitkopf und Härtel.

Madsen, Charles Arthur (2003). *The Schubert-Liszt Transcriptions: Text, Interpretation, and Lieder Transformation*. Ph.D. diss., University of Oregon.
Nattiez, Jean-Jacques (1990). *Music and Discourse: Towards a Semiology of Music*. Trans. Carolyn Abbate. Princeton, NJ: Princeton University Press.
Prieto, Eric (2002). "Metaphor and Methodology in Word and Music Studies". Suzanne M. Lodato, Suzanne Aspden, Walter Bernhart, eds. *Essays in Honor of Steven Paul Scher and on Cultural Identity and the Musical Stage*. Word and Music Studies 4. Amsterdam/New York, NY: Rodopi. 49-68.
Quicherat, Louis Marie (1867). *Adolphe Nourrit, sa vie, son talent, son caractère, sa correspondance*. 3 vols. Paris: Hachette
Ramann, Lina (1902/1986). *Liszt-Pädagogium: IV*. Leipzig: Breitkopf und Härtel. 11-12.
Sams, Eric (1980). "The Romantic Lied". George Grove, Stanley Sadie, eds. *The New Grove Dictionary of Music and Musicians*. Vol. 10. London: Macmillan. 838-844.
Scher, Steven Paul (2004a). "The German Lied: A Genre and its European Reception." Steven Paul Scher. *Essays on Literature and Music (1967-2004)*. Walter Bernhart, Werner Wolf, eds. Word and Music Studies 5. Amsterdam/New York, NY: Rodopi. 281-299.
— (2004b). "Comparing Poetry and Music: Beethoven's Goethe Lieder as Composed Reading". Steven Paul Scher. *Essays on Literature and Music (1967-2004)*. Walter Bernhart, Werner Wolf, eds. Word and Music Studies 5. Amsterdam/New York, NY: Rodopi. 223-237.
Todd, R. Larry (2004). "Piano Music Reformed: The Case of Felix Mendelssohn". R. Larry Todd, ed. *Nineteenth-Century Piano Music*. New York, NY: Routledge. 178-220.
Urrows, David Francis (1994). "Sheep, Gin, and the Telegraphic Crescendo Freaks". *The Tracker: Journal of the Organ Historical Society* 38/3: 23-25.
Waldmann, Wilhelm (1894). *Robert Franz: Gespräche aus zehn Jahren*. Leipzig: Breitkopf und Härtel.
Walker, Alan (2005). *Reflections on Liszt*, Cornell, NY: Cornell University Press.

— (1999). "Liszt and the Schubert Song Transcriptions". *The Schubert Song Transcriptions.* Series III. New York, NY: Dover. ix-xiv.

Wolf, Werner (2002). "Intermediality Revisited". Suzanne M. Lodato, Suzanne Aspden, Walter Bernhart, eds. *Essays in Honor of Steven Paul Scher and on Cultural Identity and the Musical Stage.* Word and Music Studies 4. Amsterdam/New York, NY: Rodopi. 13-34.

Winter, Robert S. (2004). "Orthodoxies, Paradoxes, and Contradictions: Performance Practices in Nineteenth-Century Piano Music". R. Larry Todd, ed. *Nineteenth-Century Piano Music.* New York, NY: Routledge. 16-54.

Youens, Susan (1991). *Retracing a Winter's Journey: Schubert's Winterreise.* Ithaca, NY: Cornell University Press.

Longing for Longing
Song as Transmutation

William P. Dougherty, West Des Moines, IA

Settings of Goethe's famous poem, "Nur wer die Sehnsucht kennt", use several compositional means to carve out a specific reading of the text. A comparative analysis of these "composed readings", to use Steven Scher's term (225), forms an instructive record (an 'intertext') that allows access to interpretive choices that might have otherwise remained hidden. Even though similar compositional techniques are appropriate to the pathos of the poetry, I demonstrate how each setting projects a different interpretative transmutation of the text. The formal properties associated with the convergences, compromises, and confrontations between text and music are definable, but they inhere in the nature of the two sign systems (music and poetry) that are combined. I offer a semeiotic analysis (based on Peircean principles) of the music and text that turns on the three cardinal properties of semeiosis: presentation, representation, and interpretation. I detail the nature of the musical sign, explore the relation of music to text, and track the interpretive values that arise from similar, yet fundamentally different, readings of the text as they are projected across the settings. The focus is on a play of interpretants as it is articulated through different compositional choices. I argue that the relation of music and text in the art song is not one of 'translation', but one of 'transmutation'. Expressive choices in these works are figurative, and they (re-)present interpretive associations that may go beyond those suggested by the original text.

Following its appearance in 1796 in the novel *Wilhelm Meisters Lehrjahre,* Goethe's famous poem, "Nur wer die Sehnsucht kennt", was set to music over 60 times by almost as many composers[1]. It is not difficult to suggest why the poem attracted so many composers – surely, Goethe's reputation, the wide influence of the novel, the beauty of the poetry, and the resonance of the concept of *Sehnsucht* ('longing') are all contributing factors. Of more interest – at least to me – is how the body of settings of the same text tells us something about the relations between music and text in song: in other words, how the conver-

---

[1] Willi Schuh, in his *Goethe-Vertonungen*, lists 56 settings of the poem by 45 composers. In my research, I have located an additional five settings (including Hensel's, discussed below) that are not included in Schuh's catalog.

gences, compromises, and confrontations that are created when a text is appropriated by a composer signal expressive choices that affect our reading of the text, the music, and their interaction[2]. Indeed, a comparative analysis of these "composed readings" – to use Scher's term (225) – forms an instructive record of interpretive choices that might otherwise have remained hidden. Jonathan Culler observes that

> [o]pposed readings which stand in the same relation to one another can be produced for most texts: the interpretive move that treats a linguistic sequence as figurative opens the possibility of a series of reversals, which will produce other readings. The content of these readings will differ according to the nature of the text, but their formal properties will be a result of definable operations of reading. (79)

In this examination of several settings of "Nur wer die Sehnsucht kennt", I take the semeiotic theory of Charles Sanders Peirce as axiomatic, and although I will not delve too deeply into Peircean principles, my analyses turn on the three cardinal properties of semeiosis as it was construed by Peirce: presentation (the sign), representation or correlation (the object), and interpretation (the interpretant). In this article, I first describe and detail some musical signs. These sign types include 1) the choice of mode for the setting, 2) a musical topic (derivations of the so-called lament or chromatic fourth bass), and 3) a harmonic region as it is used in several settings. Second, I explore the relation of these signs to both an immediate object – that is, the object seen from the context of the sign – and, less securely, to a the dynamic object – that is, the object which determines or constrains the sign[3]. To avoid all sorts of thorny issues surrounding musical reference, for my purposes here it will be sufficient to invoke the concept of a cultural unit as being the equivalent to that broader object. According to Eco (67, qtd. Schneider 2), a cultural unit is "anything that is culturally defined and distinguished as an entity", in other words, anything real or potentially real (including expressive states) to which a sign may refer. This perfunctory gloss on a complicated issue is intended to allow a more focused engagement on the 'how' of musical meaning rather than the 'what' of musical meaning. Third, I

---

[2] I explore these relationships in "The Play of Interpretants" (1993) and "Mignon in Nineteenth-Century Song" (2002).

[3] Excellent discussions of these concepts (and of Peirce's semeiotic in general) can be found in Liska, Shapiro, and Savan.

examine the evaluative power – as product, process, and effect – that arises from the sign-object relation (in other words, Peirce's interpretant). I use this evaluative potential as a means to investigate how linkages of sign and object make sense. My goal is to tie the semeiotic complex to a particular transmutation of the text that is projected in a song, and then compare different readings in other settings of the same poem as a means to articulate the supple play of music and text in song. In short, by correlating the interpretive elements of the musical signs I explore to a larger context, I can compare specific tokens in several compositions and ground how they transform – sometimes blatantly, sometimes subtly – the text.

> Er [Wilhelm] verfiel in eine träumende Sehnsucht, und wie einstimmend mit seinen Empfindungen war das Lied, das eben in dieser Stunde Mignon und der Harfner als ein unregelmässiges Duett mit dem herzlichsten Ausdrucke sangen:
>
> > Nur wer die Sehnsucht kennt,
> > Weiss, was ich leide!
> > Allein und abgetrennt
> > Von aller Freude,
> > Seh ich ans Firmament
> > Nach jener Seite.
> > Ach! der mich liebt und kennt,
> > Ist in der Weite.
> > Es schwindelt mir, es brennt
> > Mein Eingeweide.
> > Nur wer die Sehnsucht kennt,
> > Weiss, was ich leide!
> >
> > (Goethe, *Wilhelm Meisters Lehrjahre* 250)[4]

Goethe's poem "Nur wer die Sehnsucht kennt" invokes several images that were to become regularly associated with the larger cultural unit of longing. The poem articulates an opposition between the inner torment associated with longing and looking to an outer source for

---

[4] 'He lapsed into a state of dreamy longing: and the passionate expressiveness of the free duet that Mignon and the Harper were singing, was like an echo of what he himself was feeling: Only one who knows longing, knows what I suffer. Alone and separated from all joy, I gaze at the firmament in that direction. Ah, he who loves and knows me is in the distance. It makes me dizzy, it burns my insides. Only one who knows longing, knows what I suffer.' [Text translation from Goethe, *Wilhelm Meister's Apprenticeship* 142. Poem translation mine.]

solace. After introducing longing and suffering, the poem traces a personal isolation that results in the speaker's turn to an external entity for comfort, at first vaguely to an engulfing firmament and then more directly to an unnamed absent person who understands through knowing and loving. We do not discover until Chapter Three of Book Eight in the novel that this deep yearning consists of Mignon's longing to see her motherland again and a longing for Wilhelm. This twofold longing is described as "the only earthly things about her, and both of them have an element of infinite distance about them, both goals being inaccessible to her unusual nature" (Goethe, *Wilhelm Meister's Apprenticeship* 320). In the poem, though, the potential consolation to be reaped from the distant objects is apparently negated by an abrupt poetical pivot to the description of the speaker's apparently inconsolable inner pain. Indeed, the conceit of the poem lies in the starkness with which it juxtaposes the inability of the outer entities to assuage the torment that penetrates the innermost being of the speaker. The highly-charged description of this inner vertigo is followed by a return to the opening in the final couplet. Structurally, these lines suggest closure, but their framing function reintroduces the seemingly detached mood of the opening, as if the speaker's torment has been palliated through the act of telling, and thus through the act of poetry itself. Furthermore, insofar as they occur **after** we have traversed the speaker's denouement of their initial potential, this beginning-as-ending reverberates with the prior content of the poem in a way that returns us to the expressive world of the poem – a world where desire is indefinitely withheld, where physical and internal suffering arise from a lack of fulfillment, and where yearning is unresolved and probably unresolvable.

Although the poem is typically set as a solo song for Mignon, the original context in the novel clearly indicates that it is to be sung as a duet between Mignon and the Harper. Some composers (including Reichardt, Schubert [D. 877, No. 1], and Leopold Lenz) have, in fact, set the poem as a duet. Anton Rubinstein, in his 1872 duet setting (Op. 91, No. 7), goes further by deliberately shattering Goethe's poetic structure. Rubinstein simultaneously pairs the first six lines (sung by the Harper) with the final six lines (sung by Mignon) in an effort, one would suppose, to depict a sense of the 'irregular' ("unregelmäßiges") duet indicated in the description of how the poem was sung in the novel.

Not surprisingly, given the pathos of the poem, most of the over 40 settings of this poem that I have examined are in the minor mode[5]. As Robert Hatten argues, in the classical and early-romantic styles, the minor mode, as opposed to the major mode, consistently cues the tragic and, as such, articulates a narrower range of expressive meaning than does major (cf. 36-38). According to Hatten, the relationship is asymmetrical, and as a result "works in minor should tend to provoke more specific expressive interpretations than works in major" (36). Minor is a **marked** value – an interpretant – that is entirely appropriate to the poignant or despairing world of this text[6].

But even though the tragic affect of the minor mode is common to many settings[7], the manipulation of topical interplay within each setting differs, which suggests that the articulation of distinct expressive fields can be work-specific. Tragic as a type can obviously support many different kinds of tokens – tokens which may be thematized in an individual setting. One musical topic that is used in several settings is the so-called lament bass (or chromatic fourth descent) and its derivations. In these settings, the tragic is underscored, colored, or reinforced with the plaintive or dolorous. Both Peter Williams and Raymond Monelle have discussed this common musical figure in some detail, and both have made many useful distinctions in their explorations of the numerous appearances of the topic in music from a variety of eras. Williams, in particular, demonstrates convincingly that the figure is routinely used in contexts that do not imply the lament. Nevertheless, without – I hope – undue overgeneralization, I take the examples of this chromatic descent that are examined below as being lament-like in their expressive orientation.

Johann Reichardt's 1796 strophic setting – the earliest setting of this poem, in that the voice parts were published as a *Musikbeilage* in

---

[5] There are many other treatments of various settings of this text: Kramer offers an excellent one of Wolf's and Schubert's D. 877.

[6] Markedness in music is thoroughly discussed in Hatten. See also Dougherty ("Mixture, Song, and Semeiotic"). The general theory of markedness is explored in Battistella, and its relation to Peircean principles – in particular, as a type of interpretant – is detailed in Shapiro.

[7] At least ten settings of the poem are in major. See Dougherty ("Mixture, Song, and Semeiotic") for a discussion of how Schubert, in his D. 310b, effectively reverses the major/minor expressive duality through the use of modal mixture.

the original novel – clearly establishes a point of convergence between the Harper and the music through its use of an arpeggiated accompaniment to suggest the harp (see *Example 1*). But Reichardt also employs a slightly modified, but clearly derived, form of the lament bass to contrast the rising soprano (the raised-sixth scale degree [F-sharp] is absent). The 'wedge' or 'hairpin' between the outer voices is halted in the beginning of measure 3, and the phrase concludes in a conventional half cadence (complete with a 'sigh' motive that is almost universal in the setting of the word '*leide*' – see most of the examples in this article). Note that the soprano reverses its rising step progression with a diminished-7th leap, a common – if somewhat extravagant – melodic succession that, if nothing else, underscores the tragic world of the minor mode by focusing on one of its most characteristic intervals.

Example 1: Johann Reichardt, "Sehnsucht", mm. 1-4.

Carl Loewe, in his 1818 setting (see *Example 2*), places the chromaticism in the upper part (although the bass line embeds a descending chromatic line of its own) over a chord progression that is not typically associated with the chromatic fourth descent. He also extends the descent a major third beyond the more standard perfect fourth intervallic boundary – all in all descending a major sixth from the pick-ups to measure 4. The effect of this accruing chromaticism – which usually occurs as sigh motives in the first two measures – is an intensification of a tormented descent that cannot easily, if ever, be reversed. Even where local melodic reversals in the voice negate the steady chromatic descent (particularly in measures 3 and 4, where the sigh motives disappear), they are almost immediately pulled back down into an even lower – or more abject – state of desolation.

Longing for Longing: Song as Transmutation 167

Example 2: Carl Loewe, "Sehnsucht" (Op. 9, H. 3 Nr. 5), mm. 1-6.

Josephine Lang's 1835 setting (see *Example 3*) uses a derivation of the lament bass (similar to that of Reichardt's) to set the opening lines in measures 1 and 2. Measures 3 and 4 then present a complete lament bass. In Lang's song, though, the quick tempo, active piano figuration, and energetic melodic line subordinate the more conventional associations of the lament bass with a restlessness that suggests a more distressed state. Here, the lament topic is no longer a plaintive descent; instead, it is assimilated into an impassioned agitation, almost as a by-product of (or foundation for) a more all-consuming turmoil. The goal of these opening measures is clearly the speaker's turn to the firmament in measure 5, articulated by the arrival of an almost triumphant D major. The chromatic fourth bass of measures 3 and 4 is the agent of modulation and the means to reach a temporary and more positive stability. Agitation, in fact, is an expressive state cued by several other settings, even before the poem's textual turn to the description of an inward world of dizziness and burning viscera[8]. Indeed, many settings surround the largely neutral opening lines of the poem – neutral at least with respect to agitation – with a sense of turmoil.

---

[8] Schubert, in his several settings of this poem (there are six of them), routinely unleashes some compositional fury to set the lines "Es schwindelt mir, es brennt / Mein Eingeweide".

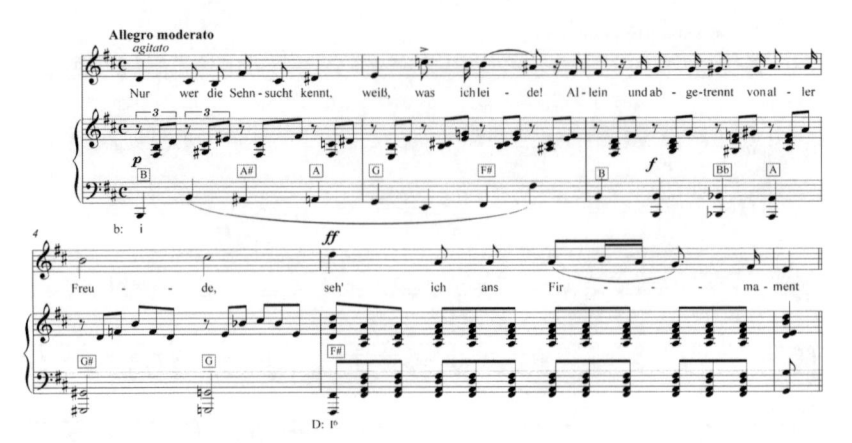

Example 3: Josephine Lang, "Mignons Klage"(Op. 10, No. 2), mm. 1-6.

The first four measures of Johann André's 1819 setting exhibit several compositional features that stamp his transmutation of the text (see *Example 4*).

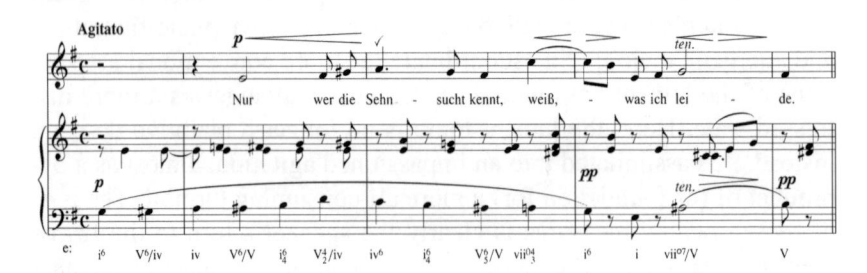

Example 4: Johann André, "Sehnsucht", mm. 1-4.

André uses syncopation, a chromatic fourth ascent and descent in the bass (largely doubled in parallel sixths), a quick turn to the subdominant, and the entry of the voice while the accompaniment is *in medias res*, as it were, to undermine the relative stability typically associated with opening gestures. The musical signs are restless from the outset. The opening gesture returns to set the final lines, and the work ends with a surface design and figuration similar to its beginning (see *Example* 5).

Example 5: Johann André, "Sehnsucht", mm. 26-33.

Although I identified several compositional cues in André's opening measures, I wish to dwell on one: the almost immediate tonicization of the subdominant (here as an expansion of a weakly asserted tonic harmony). A rapid involvement of the subdominant is characteristic of several other settings. For instance, Carl Reißiger's 1832 setting (see *Example 6*) begins with a tonicization of the subdominant which is then expanded through the use of the subdominant-related Neapolitan, and Robert von Keudell, after a piano introduction (which includes a tonicization of iv) also employs to a strongly emphasized subdominant in his 1870 setting of the opening lines (see *Example 7*). In the last two examples, the subdominant functions as pre-dominant chord, eventually progressing to the dominant as part of an authentic cadence (Reißiger) or to the dominant for a half cadence (Keudell) to end the first phrase[9]. Although the surface characteristics differ among all three examples, each returns to the subdominant region later in the setting in a compositionally highlighted fashion.

Example 6: Carl Reißiger, "Mignon's Gesang", mm. 1-4.

---

[9] The non-normative five-measure phrase in Keudell's setting of the opening lines is motivated, in part, by the syncopated resolution to the subdominant and a lingering over the V7/iv.

Example 7: Robert von Keudell, "Mignon", mm. 7-11.

Several authors – notably, Charles Rosen (cf. 23-27) and Robert Hatten (cf. 43f.) – describe the function of a movement to the subdominant (either through tonicization or modulation) as more static and closural than a movement to the dominant. Indeed, appearances of the subdominant at the beginning of codas, codettas, or other closural situations are common in both the eighteenth and nineteenth centuries. Its function in initial or opening contexts – or at least in these subdominant-inflected opening contexts – carries other expressive tendencies, and it is worth examining these settings with an eye toward delimiting how the specific tokens may be articulating a more general type. In the minor mode, the minor subdominant and the minor v are the only closely related keys that maintain original modal quality. This is to say that movement to the subdominant retains the tragic associative qualities of the original minor mode. Its more static or less extravagant tendencies imbue it with a sense of inwardness or, perhaps, a state of reflection not driven by strongly directional harmonic tendencies. These characteristics stand in opposition to more dissonant or extreme key areas, and they suggest an internalization highly appropriate to the inward stasis of unresolved *Sehnsucht*. But I would like to go one step further: the immediate tonicizations in each of these three examples necessarily introduce the leading tone to the subdominant (the raised third scale-degree), and they thereby undercut the relative stability of the original tonic mode in initial or presentational distributional slots (compare the opening measures of *Examples 4*, *6*, and *7*). The effect is disquieting, and in all three cases, the word *Sehnsucht* and its subdominant inflection are underscored by the metric placement of the word and intensity generated through a rise in pitch height. The subdominant here is compositionally salient, and it is not hard to imagine that in these three songs, longing is projected as an intensely personal, troubled, and unstable state. This is a deliberate expressive choice, one that differs from, say, Schubert's A-flat major setting (D. 310b), which begins with an untroubled singing-style topic, or Beethoven's E-flat major setting (WoO 134, No. 3), which emphasizes a more folk-like Mignon. The compositional strategy of a quick movement to the subdominant transmutes the text by infusing the almost repertorial calm of the opening lines with musical signs that demand interpretation. One wonders how this expressive reading squares with Goethe's description in the novel that Wilhelm was in a state of 'dreamy' longing when he heard Mignon and the Harper sing their duet.

Example 8: Robert von Keudell, "Mignon", mm. 16-19.

These initial appearances of the subdominant also create compositional implications that are exploited later in setting. In the ending of André's setting (see *Example 5*), the sixth scale-degree over the subdominant is left hanging through two beats of silence before being folded into the final cadence; a self-reflective stoppage of time, if you will, on the sonority that surrounded the initial treatment of yearning. In Keudell's setting (see *Example 8*), the subdominant region is also invoked at a telling textual point through the use of the subdominant and the more extreme (but still subdominant-like) **minor** Neapolitan (measure 18) to capture the speaker's alienation while hopelessly seeking some kind of comfort in an all-engulfing firmament. Reißiger's setting is almost unrelenting in its use of subdominant regions (see *Example 9*). His strongly subdominant opening (see *Example 6*) is followed by a conventional modulation to the relative major to begin the setting of the line "Ach! der mich liebt und kennt".

Example 9: Carl Reißiger, "Mignon's Gesang", mm. 15-52.

Shortly thereafter, though, the music shifts to C minor – the supertonic of B-flat and the subdominant of the original key—to initiate the setting of the pivotal lines "Es schwindelt mir, es brennt / Mein Eingeweide". C minor gives way to its Neapolitan (D-flat) in measure 21, which, in turn, moves to E-flat minor in measure 23, and that key becomes – retrospectively, at least – the sixth scale-degree of G minor when it returns in measure 26.

Note that when the poetic imagery abruptly moves from a description of an outer world to the turmoil of the inner world, the music intensifies the shift through more extravagant key areas, but all of them carry subdominant associations, either locally or globally. The catharsis is never completed, though, as the return of Goethe's poetic frame in measure 30 is infused with a remarkable subdominant orientation over the next nine measures which simply won't let the dominant of measures 35 and 36 resolve. Instead, the dominant chord regresses – what an appropriate descriptor for my purposes – to the Neapolitan in measure 37. The subdominant saturates the setting of the final lines, and its pervasiveness generates an expressive momentum that motivates the extended piano coda with its complete bar of silence before the resolution from dominant to tonic.

Example 10: Fanny Mendelssohn Hensel, "Mignon", mm. 26-34.

For both similarity and contrast, I turn to one last song, Fanny Mendelssohn Hensel's setting from 1832 (see *Example 10*). Hensel does not employ a subdominant reference at the beginning of her song, but like Reißiger, she uses the subdominant in the return of the final couplet (measure 28). Her strategy is to bring back the opening material **in** the subdominant. Although the subdominant may be enlisted here to realize its closural tendencies (which is contradicted – or at least complicated – by the thematic and textual recapitulation), there is nevertheless a torsion of the norm that undercuts the return, and the original tonic is not fully asserted until the final measures. There are two interesting points about these final measures. First, the voice collapses or simply stops in the cadential six-four chord (measure 32), without, it seems, the will or energy to finish the task of cadencing. The voice ends on tonic, but it is a dissonance. Second, the final chord – a picardy third – although compositionally available through the V/iv in measure 27, rings hollow. Its turn to the positive is unearned and too abrupt. Whether it is a compositional bow to convention or a deliberate attempt to shift the expressive discourse from the tragic to the non-tragic, the G-sharp fails to convince.

In one of my favorite definitions of the sign, Peirce says that "a sign is something by knowing which, we know something more" (31f.). In addition, Peirce asserts that "the essential function of a sign is to render inefficient relations efficient – not to set them into action, but to establish a habit or general rule whereby they will act on occasion" (32).

Musical modes, topics, and harmonic areas are all signs wherein interpretation lurks. A focus on the sign, its correlation to an object, and how that correlation makes sense helps ground the complex interaction between music and text in the art song. I hope I have shown how a comparative analysis of different settings of the same text underscores the fluid process of transmutation – a process that is, I think, a definable characteristic and formal property of song.

References

Battistella, Edwin L. (1990). *Markedness: The Evaluative Superstructure of Language*. Albany, NY: State University Press of New York.

Culler, Johathan (1981). *The Pursuit of Signs: Semiotics, Literature, Deconstruction*. Ithaca, NY: Cornell University Press.

Eco, Umberto (1976). *A Theory of Semiotics*. Bloomington, IN: Indiana University Press.

Dougherty, William P (1993). "The Play of Interpretants: A Peircean Approach to Beethoven's Lieder". Michael Shapiro, Michael Haley, eds. *The Peirce Seminar Papers*. Providence, RI: Berg. 67-95.

— (1999). "Mixture, Song, and Semeiotic". Ioannis Zannos, ed. *Music and Signs: Semiotic and Cognitive Studies in Music*. Bratislava: ASCO Art and Science. 368-378.

— (2002). "Mignon in Nineteenth-Century Song: Text, Context, and Intertext". Suzanne M. Lodato, Suzanne Aspden, Walter Bernhart, eds. *Essays in Honor of Steven Paul Scher and on Cultural Identity and the Musical Stage*. Word and Music Studies 4. Amsterdam/ New York, NY: Rodopi. 123-141.

Goethe, Johann Wolfgang von (1796/1980). *Wilhelm Meisters Lehrjahre*. Erich Schmidt, ed. Frankfurt: Insel.
— (1989). *Wilhelm Meister's Apprenticeship*. Eric A. Blackall, ed. and trans. New York, NY: Suhrkamp.
Hatten, Robert (1994). *Musical Meaning in Beethoven: Markedness, Correlation, and Interpretation*. Bloomington, IN: Indiana University Press.
Kramer, Lawrence (1987). "Decadence and Desire: The *Wilhelm Meister* Songs of Wolf and Schubert". *19th-Century Music* 10/3. 229-242.
Liska, James Jakób (1996). *A General Introduction to the Semeiotic of Charles Sanders Peirce*. Bloomington, IN: Indiana University Press.
Monelle, Raymond (2000). *The Sense of Music*. Princeton, NJ: Princeton University Press.
Peirce, Charles Sanders (1977). *Semiotics and Significs: The Correspondence between Charles S. Peirce and Victoria Lady Welby*. Charles S. Hardwick, ed. Bloomington, IN: Indiana University Press.
Rosen, Charles (1972). *The Classical Style*. New York, NY: Norton.
Savan, David (1988). *An Introduction to C. S. Peirce's Full System of Semeiotic*. Toronto: Toronto Semiotic Circle.
Shapiro, Michael (1983). *The Sense of Grammar: Language as Semeiotic*. Bloomington, IN: Indiana University Press.
Scher, Steven Paul (1986/2004). "Comparing Poetry and Music: Beethoven's Goethe Lieder as Composed Reading". Stephen Paul Scher. *Essays on Literature and Music (1967-2004)*. Walter Bernhart, Werner Wolf, eds. Word and Music Studies 5. Amsterdam/ New York, NY: Rodopi. 223-237.
Schneider, David M. (1968) *American Kinship: A Cultural Account*. New York, NY: Prentice-Hall.
Schuh, Willi (1952). *Goethe-Vertonungen: Ein Verzeichnis*. Zurich: Artemis.
Williams, Peter (1997). *The Chromatic Fourth During Four Centuries of Music*. Oxford: Clarenden Press.

Strauss, *Idomeneo* and Postmodernism

Suzanne M. Lodato, Washington, DC

In 1929, Richard Strauss received a commission from the Vienna State Opera to prepare a new edition of Mozart's *Idomeneo*, which was performed in 1931 to celebrate the 150th anniversary of its premiere. Although *Idomeneo* was little known at that time, Strauss, long a devotee of Mozart's music, had admired the score since he was a boy. Rather than producing a carefully-wrought critical edition, Strauss reworked *Idomeneo* extensively. Offended by Strauss's arrangement, critics panned the work. Why would Strauss, who revered Mozart, impose his own style so blatantly in this adaptation? Commentators have been unable to answer this question, but further analysis of the *Idomeneo* score in light of recent Strauss criticism shows that it represents far more than a failed attempt of Strauss to update and improve upon Mozart. Following a 1992 revisionist critique of Strauss's late style by Leon Botstein, I argue that *Idomeneo* typifies Botstein's characterization of Strauss's later work as "a new twentieth-century form of self-critical historicism" (18). Strauss here emerges as a forerunner of the postmodern composer – one who incorporated various musical styles from the past into one work without attempting to integrate them with one another.

In 1929, Richard Strauss received a commission from the Vienna State Opera to prepare a new edition of Wolfgang Amadeus Mozart's *Idomeneo*, which was performed in Vienna in 1931 to celebrate the 150th anniversary of its premiere. Although *Idomeneo* was little known at that time, Strauss, long a devotee of Mozart's music, had admired the score since he was a boy. But rather than producing a carefully-wrought critical edition, Strauss reworked *Idomeneo* extensively. The Italian verse libretto became German prose; *recitativi secchi* were re-written and orchestrated; numbers were cut and rearranged; a number from the 1786 version of *Idomeneo* was inserted; and Strauss even added new music in his own style[1]. Reaction

---

[1] See Del Mar, Holden, and Kohler for detailed discussions of the changes that Strauss made to Mozart's score.

was mixed, and many critics panned the work. One even characterized it as a 'gross act of mutilation' ("grobe Vergewaltigung"; qtd. Walton 89 [2]). Why would Strauss, who revered Mozart, impose his own style so blatantly on this work?

Commentators have been unable to answer this question satisfactorily, but consideration of the *Idomeneo* score in light of recent Strauss criticism indicates that it represents far more than a failed attempt by Strauss to update and improve upon Mozart. Following a 1992 revisionist critique of Strauss's late style by Leon Botstein, I will argue that *Idomeneo* typifies Botstein's characterization of Strauss's later work as "a new twentieth-century form of self-critical historicism" (18). Up until the 1990s, critics tended to characterize Strauss's post-1908 career as a regression from the modernist style of his tone poems and the operas *Salome* and *Elektra*. Botstein, on the other hand, sees this period as one in which Strauss emerges as a forerunner of the postmodern composer – one who incorporated a "mélange of noncontiguous or overlapping historical sources" and "juxtaposition of incongruent stylistic moments and selective self-quotations" into his compositions (19).

These characteristics typify Strauss's *Idomeneo* arrangement, and when viewed in light of the history of Mozart's opera, subsequent performances of it, and Strauss's compositional practice in some of his post-*Elektra* operas, the 'gross act of mutilation' becomes a conscious attempt to layer and juxtapose different historical music styles, different tellings of the story of Idomeneo, and even self-quotation in which the audience could explore the contrasts and similarities between two styles.

When examining Strauss's score, one might be inclined to assume that rather than taking a self-consciously ahistorical stance, he simply engaged in the same practices as have most opera composers, conductors, and directors throughout history – and even Mozart himself – by cutting, re-arranging, and composing this work. To this day, Mozart scholars have been unable to establish exactly which parts of the score were performed at the January 29, 1781 premiere of the opera in Munich (see Heartz/Bauman; Rushton, ed.; cf. Sadie 40). Even if researchers could be confident about the score's contents, evidence

---

[2] Qtd. from Alfred Einstein's introduction to his revision of the Köchel Mozart catalog, Köchel/Einstein 445.

shows that by no means did Mozart and his librettist decide upon the structure, music, and text of the opera by themselves. The subject of the opera, *Idoménée*, a *tragédie lyrique* by Antoine Danchet, was most likely selected, or at least approved by, Carl Theodor, the elector of the Palatinate (and later a Bavarian Duke in Munich), when he commissioned *Idomeneo* in 1780 to be the main opera for the Munich carnival season. Although Mozart was permitted to choose the language of the libretto, as well as the librettist (Giambattista Varesco [1735-1805] of Salzburg), the court determined other elements of the production, such as the content of the libretto (cf. Sadie 27). Indeed, Mozart was obliged to follow both a production model and detailed plan for carrying it out that was formulated by the court (cf. Heartz/ Bauman 26; Rushton, ed. 171, n. 15). The plan was quite specific, stipulating such elements as roles, casting, types of numbers (e. g., arias, cavatinas, choruses), and their placement. These determinations did not always make musical or dramatic sense[3].

Mozart felt free to revise libretti (cf. Brophy 30), and he did so with Varesco's. Varesco had not completed the libretto before the move to Munich (which was common practice at the time), so both librettist and composer were shaping the piece until the premiere (cf. Dent 38). For the sake of brevity, believability, the fluidity of dramatic action, as well as to meet singers' demands, Mozart made extensive cuts and changes in the recitatives and other numbers up until the premiere (cf. Heartz/Bauman 18, 29-31; Dent 37-38; Sadie 30). He changed music up until that time as well, and indeed had not composed all of it when he moved from Salzburg to Munich eleven weeks before the premiere (again, this was typical practice) (cf. Heartz/ Bauman 18). Some cuts – both musical and textual – were made at the behest of Joseph-Anton von Seeau, the theater director at the Munich court, in order to decrease production costs (cf. Heartz/ Bauman 17).

A single performance given in Vienna in 1786 saw further changes. A minor role was cut, an aria was replaced, another was simplified, and some ensembles were changed. These revisions were un-

---

[3] For example, the role of Arbace was performed by a long-time court singer whom the court wanted included in the production, and his role was stipulated in the plan for this reason. It had little to do with the plot, and it was shortened considerably during the first performances (cf. Heartz/Bauman 21).

doubtedly made to accommodate the group of amateur singers who performed (cf. Sadie 39).

It could be argued, therefore, that in re-arranging the music, re-composing recitatives, inserting material from the 1786 version of the opera, and even composing two of his own numbers, Strauss was following Mozart's own practices. That he knew something of the conditions under which Mozart worked is shown in a 1932 letter that he wrote to Hannover stage director Bruno von Niessen justifying the grand ensemble that he composed for Act III. Mozart, he said, had originally intended to end *Idomeneo* with a large ensemble, but the lead performer, who wanted to sing alone at the end, kept Mozart from composing the ensemble (cf. Grasberger 338)[4]. He obviously saw no point in assuming that a definitive work called *Idomeneo* ever existed – this in a time when musicians, scholars, and critics assumed the fixity and stability of the notated text in historical works.

But even if the music of the premiere were not in doubt, Strauss – and indeed contemporaries of his who produced their own revisions of *Idomeneo* for other productions for the 1931 anniversary of the work – would still have found significant changes to the work to be justifiable. Strauss and these others intended to rehabilitate a work of a great Germanic composer whose creativity was – in their view – hindered both musically and dramatically by the necessity to conform to the conventions of Italian opera in the late eighteenth century. Arrangements for the 1931 anniversary by three other composers, including Ermanno Wolf-Ferrari in Munich[5], involved extensive cuts, both of recitatives and arias, as well as the re-composition and orchestration of recitatives. Like Strauss, Wolf-Ferrari used motivic material from the Mozart opera, as well as his own music, as the basis for the recitatives (cf. Rushton, ed. 86; see Hell). For Wolf-Ferrari, *Idomeneo*'s faults lay entirely in Varesco's libretto. He found the

---

[4] Strauss thought that the singer who demanded the aria was a castrato, but he was mistaken. The singer who insisted on the aria in the last act was not a castrato, but rather Anton Raaff, the tenor who sang Idomeneo, and Mozart was actually pleased to replace the ensemble with an aria: "Thus, too", wrote Mozart, "a useless piece will be got rid of – and Act III will be far more effective." (Qtd. Sadie 31) Strauss's awareness of this incident indicates that he had access to at least some of the correspondence between Mozart and his father, Leopold, which documents in detail the genesis of the opera.

[5] The other two were Arthur Rother in Dessau and Willy Meckbach in Brunswick.

recitatives to be 'insufferably long' ("unausstehlich langen Rezitative", qtd. Hell 180) and many of the arias to be 'dramatically unnecessary' ("dramatisch unnötig"), written by Mozart's own admission only to serve the singers (ibid. 181)[6]. Wolf-Ferrari retained the ensembles, which he claimed Mozart composed according to his wishes. He made his most extensive changes to Act III, which, though it contained 'Mozart's deepest music' ("die tiefste Musik Mozarts"), had been 'utterly corrupted' ("ganz verballhornt") by Varesco. Strauss also found the recitatives to be 'endless' ("endlos"), the Varesco text 'unclear' and 'diffuse' ("unklar", "weitschweifig"), and the numbers too long (qtd. Grasberger 338). Strauss did not think that modern audiences could listen to the 'monotony' ("Monotonie") of two-and-a-half hours of *opera seria*, despite the beauty of Mozart's music (Brosche/Dachs 368). As was the case with Wolf-Ferrari, Strauss's most notable changes occur later in the opera, where two original compositions by Strauss, in his own style rather than Mozart's, were inserted – the Interludio preceding Act II, Scene 9, and an ensemble for Ilia, Idamantes, Idomeneo, the High Priests, and the Chorus, which was placed just before the shortened final chorus by Mozart.

In both cases, the original music of Strauss and Wolf-Ferrari does not necessarily sound like Mozart's. Chris Walton finds Wolf-Ferrari's contributions to the score to be "occasionally reminiscent of Weber" (Walton 86), and Strauss's style is unmistakable even upon a cursory listening. But what interests me here is the difference between the ways that Wolf-Ferrari and Strauss discussed the music they composed for the opera. Wolf-Ferrari stated that when he re-wrote both the texts and the music of the recitatives, he used as much of Mozart's music as possible, while composing new music that did not seem out of place. 'If many places sound "modern"', he wrote, 'I can prove that exactly these are from Mozart.' (Qtd. Hell 181)[7] Strauss, on the other hand, never attempted to pretend that his original

---

[6] Wolf-Ferrari assumed incorrectly that Mozart did not dare revise the libretto of Varesco, who had a higher social standing than Mozart.

[7] "Sollten manche Stellen 'modern' klingen, so kann ich beweisen, daß gerade diese von Mozart sind." (My translation) Qtd. from the libretto for the premiere of Wolf-Ferrari's arrangement of *Idomeneo*, which premiered in Munich on June 15, 1931.

material sounded at all like Mozart's music, and even the recitatives, which are laced with Mozartian motives, are late Romantic in style. As he wrote to von Niessen, 'That the pieces added by me could not become pure Mozart is obvious!' (Qtd. Grasberger 338)[8] And in another letter to von Niessen, he said that the 'modern orchestral sounds' ("moderne Orchesterklänge") of the second act Interludio and the Temple Scene of Act III provided much-needed 'interruptions' ("Unterbrechungen") of the 'monotony' of the *opera seria* style (Brosche/Dachs 368).

The stylistic mix reflects the hybrid style of Mozart's opera. The poetic Italian text and the alternation of *recitativi secchi* and arias conform to *opera seria*[9], but the accompanied recitative, chorus, ballet, and ensembles characterized French *tragédie lyrique* (cf. Rushton, ed. 63). This was not an unusual practice: in a number of European cities, composers were combining Italian and French elements even before Christoph Willibald Gluck did so, and Mozart was well aware of contemporary opera practice. This hybrid style is now referred to as Franco-Italian reform opera, which is most notably seen in Gluck's works, but predated him (cf. ibid. 95).

But Strauss's conscious, unapologetic juxtaposition of disparate musical styles is different from Mozart's consolidation of the French and Italian styles of the eighteenth century. Their differences lay primarily in structure and vocal style; the harmonic language and elevated tone of the two are similar. On the other hand, Strauss's and Mozart's styles differ fundamentally in phrase structure, harmonic language, long-range tonal relationships, and instrumentation. Particularly important here is the evident difference between the closed structure of Mozart's numbers and the more open, flexible nature of Strauss's recitatives, his fantasia-like Interludio, and the ensemble in the final act.

The processes Strauss employed in arranging *Idomeneo* are more reminiscent of his work in *Der Rosenkavalier* (1910) and *Ariadne auf Naxos* (1912/1916) than they are of Mozart's compositional practice.

---

[8] "Daß die von mir hineinkomponierten Stücke nicht reiner Mozart werden konnten, ist selbstverständlich!" (My translation)

[9] This term was not used in the eighteenth century (cf. Brown 458). Mozart wrote on the performing score used at the Munich premiere: "große Opera"; the printed score says "L'Idomeneo/Drama per Musica" (Brown 458).

Admittedly, the techniques used by Strauss in *Idomeneo* are far less complex and varied than those seen in the two earlier operas, which are each characterized by a web of literary and historical references; 'high' and 'low' characters, dialogue, and musical styles; and various musical genres. In Strauss's *Idomeneo*, two very different musical styles – Viennese classical and late Romantic – are juxtaposed straightforwardly, while the plot and characters are kept more or less intact[10]. Strauss could have followed Wolf-Ferrari's path by attempting to retain as Mozartean a sound as possible, and by avoiding the addition of numbers in his own style. Certainly, his work in *Rosenkavalier* and *Ariadne* shows that he was capable of mimicking any style, including that of Mozart, whom he admired above all other composers. His decision to render *Idomeneo* into a patchwork of late-Romantic and Viennese classical vocal and instrumental styles was thus deliberate.

Both *Rosenkavalier* and *Ariadne* have been described as postmodernist works in which various styles appear and disappear quickly, but within an integrated whole (cf. Botstein 19; see Halliwell). This collage or pastiche technique is one of the hallmarks of postmodernist art[11]. Glenn Watkins defines collage as "cut-and-paste, assemblage, re-contexting of images collected from both quotidian experience and our knowledge of the past" (1). In collage, no element is more important than another; all have equal importance, value, and weight. It is this equal privileging of all elements that distinguishes postmodern from modernist practice, in which foreign materials appropriated for a work are often parodied and are subservient to the prevailing style of a work (cf. Pasler). Lewis Lockwood illustrated Watkins's statement when he observed that in *Rosenkavalier*, Strauss succeeded in revealing Vienna through time by utilizing Viennese musical styles from the eighteenth, nineteenth, and twentieth centuries (cf. 253). Although

---

[10] One exception is that Elettra in Mozart's opera is replaced by Ismene in Strauss's version.

[11] Franz Trenner (without using the term 'postmodern') equated Strauss's technique in *Idomeneo* to that of the seventeenth- and early-eighteenth-century *pasticcio*, a stage work made up of arias taken from various contemporary operas, along with new material. In this genre, recitatives that accompanied the arias were recomposed, and texts of both recitatives and arias were changed (Holden 90, 99, 127, n. 78, the latter qtd. from Strohm 288; also cf. Walton 94, who describes Strauss's *Idomeneo* as a "juxtaposition of Mozart, Mozartian pastiche and straightforward late Romanticism").

Strauss did not use the term 'collage', it lies behind his comparison of his *Idomeneo* arrangement to Wagner's late-career revisions to *Tannhäuser*, in which he added Tristan-like sonorities, and to the practice of expanding Romanesque churches by means of Gothic- and Baroque-style additions (cf. Grasberger 338).

This democracy of source materials, this refusal to value one art, style, period, or orientation over another, goes hand-in-hand with what Botstein calls a tendency to be "self-consciously pessimistic, if not cynical, about aesthetic progress" (18)[12]. Typically of artists who were later to be considered postmodernist, and what distinguished him from contemporaries and nineteenth-century composers who consciously evoked past styles in their work, Strauss used fragments of historical styles, often ironically (cf. ibid.; see Halliwell). But he used these techniques within "a seamless dramatic continuity" (Botstein 19)[13]. Unlike neoclassicist composers of his time such as Stravinsky, who invoked the procedures and structures of a single period, Strauss would include many. *Rosenkavalier* is well-known for its mix of Strauss's late Romantic harmonies, nineteenth-century Viennese waltzes, an Italian opera aria, and a duet at the end for Sophie and Octavian that is reminiscent of the duet for Pamina and Papageno from *Die Zauberflöte* (cf. Lockwood 252, also 246). For example, a half-delirious Ochs speaks in Strauss's fragmented, recitative-like style over a Viennese-style waltz; a waltz also accompanies the Marschallin's oddly contoured, hesitant lines in which she shows Ochs the portrait of Octavian in Act I; and the 'Mozartian' duet at the end of *Rosenkavalier* is punctuated with ethereal, non-diatonically related triads for harp and celesta. In addition, two characters (the Marschallin and Octavian) are strongly reminiscent of Mozart's Countess and trouser roles such as Idamante, Cherubino, and Sextus (cf. Lockwood 246). *Ariadne* is known for its juxtaposition of 'high' and 'low' characters, as well as eighteenth-century backstage intrigue, Greek mythology, and *commedia dell'arte*.

---

[12] Referring to *Idomeneo*, Botstein goes on to say that "[a]wareness of modernity, in the sense of knowing one's historical place, was tantamount to using the past against itself" (18). It is my view that in *Idomeneo*, as well as in *Rosenkavalier* and *Ariadne*, Strauss denied this 'awareness of modernity'.

[13] I have found similar characteristics in Strauss's songs, though not within a postmodernist context; cf. "False Assumptions" and "Richard Strauss and the Modernists".

Yet all of these elements are remarkably well-integrated, either because they are combined with Strauss's own techniques (for example, the Act I waltz in *Rosenkavalier* noted above), or because they are set off as performances within the story (e. g., the Italian singer in Act I of *Rosenkavalier* or the *commedia dell'arte* troupe in the second half of *Ariadne*). More importantly, they are not direct quotations of known, previously composed materials, but rather Strauss's own compositions (cf. Lockwood 254). Watkins, writing generally about postmodernist collage, emphasizes that it is not direct quotation that is important to this technique, but rather the way in which a variety of sounds, styles, and procedures from both the past and from the myriad of experiences from contemporary life are combined to provoke new ways of understanding the world (cf. 2f.).

What does this mean for Mozart's *Idomeneo*, a work that, despite its power and beauty, Strauss and others felt would not be tolerated by twentieth-century audiences? In *Rosenkavalier* and *Ariadne*, Hofmannsthal's libretti stimulated collage technique, but Strauss and Wallerstein had only Varesco's rather stilted libretto as the basis for their work. Wallerstein's German prose translation and re-working did aid Strauss in moving away from the Italian *opera seria* elements of the original to the accompanied recitative and continuous music of the nineteenth and twentieth centuries that characterized his arrangement. The modern cast of the recitatives contrasts with the Viennese classical style that Strauss retained in Mozart's numbers, even though he cut and rearranged them. It is interesting, however, that the new recitatives and the Mozartian numbers blend remarkably well. Indeed, one critic who responded positively overall to the 1931 premiere had a problem with these recitatives not because of their relatively modern style, but rather because they shifted the balance of the work so that the recitatives lost their function as links between the numbers (cf. Kralik 679). But it is precisely this shift in balance for which Strauss and Wallerstein aimed, and the result is Botstein's "seamless dramatic continuity" (19), despite occasional jarring moments of chromatic harmony in the recitatives.

One of the most notable of these moments is a self-quotation (another characteristic of postmodernist musical styles) – the collapse-of-Troy motive from Strauss's 1927 opera, *Die ägyptische Helena* (cf. Del Mar 327, 378). This five-measure motive appears in an Act I recitative in which Idamantes refers to the war that Helen's beauty brought to Troy ("Wie Helenas Schönheit Krieg, bringt Ilias Reinheit Frieden", see *Example 1*). From a dramatic standpoint, this would seem to be a rather odd motive to insert. It comes after Idamantes, son of the Cretan king Idomeneo, has proclaimed his love for the Trojan princess Ilia and declared his intention to free the Trojan prisoners taken by his father in the war with Troy. But as was typical with Strauss, the motive served a local purpose – to color the word, *Krieg* ('war').

Example 1: 'Collapse-of-Troy' motive from Die ägyptische Helena. *Excerpt from the piano-vocal score of Strauss's arrangement of* Idomeneo, *Act I, Scene.*

Example 2: Initial appearance of music depicting the monster. This theme reappears in the Interludio. Excerpt from the piano-vocal score of Strauss's arrangement of Idomeneo, *Act II, Scene 8.*

I have shown previously that in Strauss's lieder, this technique had the effect of disorienting the listener (cf. "False Assumptions" and "Richard Strauss and the Modernists"). In *Idomeneo*, it has a similar effect: those who are familiar with *Die ägyptische Helena* would be drawn back temporarily into Strauss and Hofmannsthal's version of the Helen of Troy myth to consider the contrasts and similarities between Strauss's and Mozart's renderings of these related tales.On the other hand, for both the *cognoscenti* and listeners who are unfamiliar with *Helena*, the broad chordal motive, set to brass instruments, represents Strauss's first obvious assertion of his own style in the opera, which until this point has been overwhelmingly Mozartean or generally late-Romantic in sound.

In the recitatives, Strauss's distinctive style turns up again in Act II, Scene 8, when Neptune sends a monster from the sea to destroy the Cretans. A brief look at this scene shows how Strauss and Wallerstein introduced or emphasized foreign elements while still integrating them into the musical and dramatic fabric of the work. Strauss and Wallerstein's shortened recitative and reordered events streamline the dramatic action without compromising the plot. The Straussian recitative ("Weh, neues Unheil entsteigt [...]", see *Example 2*) lies between two choruses that depict the storm developing in the sea followed by the approach of the monster. The choruses are taken directly from Mozart's *Idomeneo* ("Corriamo, fuggiamo" / "Aus Tiefen des Meeres"), but Mozart's and Strauss's recitatives, which are both set to orchestral accompaniment, are markedly different in style and intent. In Mozart's scene, the monster has already been revealed in the first chorus. During his grand, two-minute-long, orchestrated recitative, Idomeneo takes sole responsibility for bringing on the crisis and asks Neptune to punish him alone. The focus is on Idomeneo, and on the vocal and dramatic prowess of the tenor. In Strauss's version, the monster does not appear until the very short but effective recitative in which the low, chromatic rumblings of the monster, which will return later in Strauss's Interludio, are heard, and a man from the crowd describes it (see *Example 2*). Not only is an unnamed character of unknown social position juxtaposed with aristocratic characters, but the emphasis in the scene is shifted to the monster, which as a fantastical creature receives only brief attention in Mozart's Enlightenment opera. This section, which is of indeterminate tonality, enables a much quicker modulation between the keys of the choruses, and makes for a quicker dramatic progression, than Mozart's recitative. Wallerstein gave the second chorus the dramatically colorful purpose of describing the monster's approach, while Mozart's chorus is shown deciding to flee.

The Interludio that immediately follows contains the opening material of the recitative and portrays the monster's attack on the Cretan city. One of the two radically Straussian pieces in the opera, the Interludio lacks clear tonality or melodic themes, except for the middle section, in which Idomeneo's third-act aria "Torna la pace", which Strauss cut from the opera, is quoted. It accomplishes little dramatically and appears to have been added, as Strauss said, to alleviate the monotony of eighteenth-century opera style.

The other quintessentially Straussian number is the ensemble ("Erlösung") that he added to the final scene of Act III in place of Idomeneo's final aria, "Torna la pace", as the Cretan's response to Neptune's forgiveness of Idomeneo. This transcendent, heavily orchestrated, and chromatically harmonized ensemble, with its soaring soprano line and contrapuntal writing, comprises a quartet for Ilia, Idamantes, Idomeneo, and the High Priests, underscored by the chorus. Each of the voices expresses a different sentiment – Ilia and Idamantes to each other, and Idamantes, Idomeneo, and the High Priests to the gods. On the other hand, in the Mozart work, Idomeneo speaks of his own return to peace and youthful vigor in the grand, three-part aria, "Torna la pace" (see texts in *Figure 1*). Mozart illustrated the contrast between Idomeneo's inward-looking focus and the final chorus's final invocation to the gods to bless Ilia and Idamantes by means of a direct segue from the final B-flat major cadence of "Torna la pace" to the bright D major of the chorus's "Scenda Amor". Mozart's lively finale is homophonic and diatonic, its periodic phrases are short. Wallerstein's final chorus, "Eros führt", like Mozart's, prays to the god of love, and Strauss retains both Mozart's music and key while shortening the number. The texts of Strauss's final two ensembles contrast far less than the final two numbers in Mozart's opera. The modulatory passage between the E-flat major of "Erlösung" and the D major of "Eros führt" emphasizes these textual similarities and is in keeping with Strauss's practice of through-composition. The modulation also allows Strauss to maintain the "seamless dramatic continuity" that Botstein (19) observes in Strauss's postmodernist operas. However, Strauss's two ensembles are each complete in and of themselves. They stand together almost as alternate endings to the opera; one could be chosen over the other without compromising the musical or dramatic structure at all. This presentation of equally valid alternatives (and indeed, the presentation of an alternative ending at all) presages the postmodern approaches of later composers and other artists.

When Strauss was commissioned to arrange Mozart's *Idomeneo*, he did far more than simply make it palatable for a contemporary audience. He composed a new work in which neither his music nor Mozart's dominated, and where *either* his music or Mozart's could be looked upon as material that was 'appropriated' – his by Mozart, or Mozart's by him. In doing so, he shifted *Idomeneo* out of a history and into a present, into the timeless present of later postmodernists.

Mozart/Varesco, Act III, Final Scene[14]

Idomeneo
Torna la pace al core,
torna lo spento ardore;
florisce in me l'età.
Tal la stagion di Flora
l'albero annoso infiora,
nuovo vigor gli dà.

Coro
Scenda Amor, scenda Imeneo,
e Giunone ai regi sposi;
d'alma pace omai li posi,
la Dea pronuba nel sen.

Idomeneo
Peace returns to my heart
and extinguished ardor is rekindled;
youth is reborn in me.
Thus does Flora's season
make the old tree bloom again
and give it fresh vigor.

Chorus
Descend, Love and Hymen,
descend, Juno, to the royal pair;
benign goddess, now instill
the peace of your spirit in their breasts.

Strauss/Wallerstein, Act III, Scene 5[15]

Alle
Erlösung!

Ilia (allein)
Gnade verkündend endet ein Wunder drohendes Schicksal und tödliche Qual. Was ich in schweigendem Schmerze gelitten, ist nun ver-

All
Deliverance!

Ilia (alone)
Proclaimed mercy ends the threat of destiny and its deadly torment. What I suffered in silent pain is transformed into bliss. Take this life, given to me

---

[14] Varesco 146.

[15] Wallerstein (Berlin 1931) 34-36; English translation from Wallerstein (New York 1998), n. pag.

wandelt in Seligkeit. Nimm dieses Leben, neu mir gegeben, nimm meiner Liebe frohes Geschenk.	anew. Take the joyous gift of my love.
Idamantes	**Idamantes**
Königlich schenkt Ihr, Götter, die Fülle; schwer war das Elend, hart war der Kampf. So wie mit Dir nun bereichert mein Leben, werde durch Güte beglückt auch mein Volk!	Royally, you gods, give abundance. Heavy was the misery; hard was the fight. As with you my life is enriched, so also through goodness bring happiness to my people!
Idomeneo	**Idomeneo**
Leicht ist die Strafe, die Du verhängt hast, Gott! Deine Gnade sei Dir gedankt! Muß ich entsagen dem Thron meiner Väter, grüßt mich des Sohnes hell strahlendes Glück. Gerne verlaß ich den Thron meiner Väter, seh ich des Sohnes strahlendes Glück.	Your punishment is light, oh God! I'm grateful for your mercy. I have to renounce the throne of my ancestors, but I'm greeted by my son's radiant happiness.
Oberpriester	**High Priests**
Fühllos, Ihr Götter, scheint Ihr und quälet Menschen aus lachenden Höhen zum Scherz.	You gods seem to be without feelings, and torment men from laughing heights for fun!
………	………
Fühllos, Ihr Götter, scheint Ihr und quälet Menschen zum Scherz. Doch es erfreut Euch auch, Gnade zu üben, seht Ihr der Schwachen großmütig Tun.	You gods seem to be without feelings, and torment men as a joke! But you also show mercy when you see the generous gesture of the powerless.
Chor	**Chorus**
Eros führt mächtige Waffen; er besiegt Götter und Menschen! Alles folgt dem sel'gen Knaben, wenn er schweigend, sicher führend weist uns zum Ziele. Zorn der Götter wandelt er, Leid der Menschen flieht vor ihm. Mächt'ger Gott, Deinem Stab folgen wir. Führe uns lächelnd nach allen Leiden, führe uns in lichte Zukunft, daß wir wieder uns freuen können an uns'rem Leben. Du gabst uns ein Königspaar, hast den Zorn des Gott's be-	Eros uses powerful weapons, victorious over gods and men! All follow the blessed boy when he silently and surely shows us to our goal. He changes the wrath of the gods, the misery of men flees from him. Powerful God, we follow your staff. Guide us smiling, after all our sorrows, to the future, that we may take joy again in our lives. You gave us a royal couple, and conquered the wrath of God. Our happiness be your reward, and its expression, this dance.

siegt. Unsre Freude sei Dein Dank
und sein Zeichen dieser Tanz.

Figure 1: Mozart/Varesco, Idomeneo, *Act III, Final Scene*

References

Botstein, Leon (1992). "The Enigmas of Richard Strauss: A Revisionist View". Bryan Randolph Gilliam, ed. *Richard Strauss and His World.* Princeton, NJ: Princeton University Press. 3-32.

Brophy, Brigid (1988). *Mozart the Dramatist.* New York, NY: Da Capo Press.

Brosche, G., K. Dachs (1979). *Richard Strauss: Autographen in München und Wien. Verzeichnis.* Tutzing: Schneider.

Brown, Bruce Alan (1994). "W. A. Mozart: *Idomeneo*". *Music & Letters* 75/3: 457-460.

Del Mar, Norman (1986). *Richard Strauss: A Critical Commentary on His Life and Works.* Vol. 2. Ithaca, NY: Cornell University Press.

Dent, Edward Joseph (1960). *Mozart's Operas: A Critical Study.* 2nd ed. London: Oxford University Press.

Grasberger, Franz (1967). *Der Strom der Töne trug mich fort.* Tutzing: Schneider.

Halliwell, Michael (2005). "'Opera About Opera': Self-Referentiality in Opera with Particular Reference to Dominick Argento's *The Aspern Papers*". Lodato/Urrows, eds. 51-80.

Heartz, Daniel, Thomas Bauman (1990). *Mozart's Operas.* Berkeley, CA: University of California Press.

Hell, Helmut (1981). "Die *Idomeneo*-Bearbeitung von Ermanno Wolf-Ferrari (1931)". Hildesheimer/Münster/Attenkofer, eds. 180-201.

Hildesheimer, Wolfgang, Robert Münster, Margot Attenkofer, eds. (1981). *Wolfgang Amadeus Mozart,* Idomeneo, *1781-1981: Essays, Forschungsberichte, Katalog mit der Rede zur Eröffnung der Ausstellung von Wolfgang Hildesheimer. Ausstellung, 27. Mai bis 31. Juli 1981.* Munich/Zurich: Piper.

Holden, Raymond (1996). "Richard Strauss' Performing Version of *Idomeneo*". *Richard Strauss-Blätter* 36: 83.

Kohler, Stephan (1937). "Die *Idomeneo*-Bearbeitungen von Lothar Wallerstein und Richard Strauss (1931)". Hildesheimer/Münster/ Attenkofer, eds. 158-179.

Köchel, Ludwig, Alfred Einstein (1937). *Chronologisch-thematisches Verzeichnis sämtlicher Tonwerke Wolfgang Amadé Mozarts; nebst Angabe der verlorengegangenen, angefangenen, übertragenen, zweifelhaften und unterschobenen Kompositionen.* 3rd ed. Leipzig: Breitkopf & Härtel.

Kralik, Heinrich. (1930/1931) "Mozarts *Idomeneo* in der Wallerstein-Straußschen Bearbeitung (Staatsoper Wien)". *Die Musik* 23/9: 679-680.

Lockwood, Lewis (1992). "The Element of Time in *Der Rosenkavalier*". Brian Gilliam, ed. *Richard Strauss: New Perspectives on the Composer and His Work.* Durham, NC: Duke University Press. 243-258.

Lodato, Suzanne M. (2005). "False Assumptions: Richard Strauss's Lieder and Text/Music Analysis". Lodato/Urrows, eds. 103-124.

— (1999). "Richard Strauss and the Modernists: A Contextual Study of Strauss's *Fin-de-Siècle* Song Style". PhD diss. Columbia University.

Lodato, Suzanne M., David Francis Urrows, eds. (2005). *Word and Music Studies: Essays on Music and the Spoken Word and on Surveying the Field.* Word and Music Studies 7. Amsterdam/New York, NY: Rodopi.

Mozart, Wolfgang Amadeus, Richard Strauss (1931a). *Idomeneo. Opera seria in 3 Akten nach dem Italienischen des Giambatt. Varesco.* Orchestral score. Magdeburg: Heinrichshofen.

Mozart, Wolfgang Amadeus, Richard Strauss (1931b). *Idomeneo. Opera seria in 3 Akten nach dem Italienischen des Giambatt. Varesco.* Vocal score. Magdeburg: Heinrichshofen.

Pasler, Jann (2005). "Postmodernism". *Grove Music Online.* L. Macy, ed. http://www.grovemusic.com [01/08/2005].

Rushton, Julian, ed. (1993). *W. A. Mozart:* Idomeneo. Cambridge Opera Handbooks. Cambridge: Cambridge University Press.

Sadie, Stanley (1993). "Genesis of an Operone". Rushton, ed. 25-47.

Strauss, Richard, Karl Anton Rickenbacher, Münchener Kammerorchester, Bamberger Symphoniker (2001). *Vor- und Zwischenspiele aus Opern.* Compact Disc. Koch Classics/Schwann.

Strauss, Richard, Wolfgang Amadeus Mozart (2003). *Idoménée*: Compact Disc. Gala.

Strohm, Reinhard (1980). "Pasticcio". Stanley Sadie, ed. *The New Grove Dictionary of Music and Musicians*. Vol. 14. London: Macmillan. S. v.

Varesco, Giambattista (1971). *Idomeneo*. Libretto. Wolfgang Amadeus Mozart. *Don Giovanni. Idomeneo*. Anthony Burgess, intro. Lionel Salter, English translation London: Cassell.

Wallerstein, Lothar (1931). *Idomeneo. Opera seria in 3 Akten nach dem Italienischen des Giambatt. Varesco*. Libretto. Music by Wolfgang Amadeus Mozart and Richard Strauss. Magdeburg: Heinrichshofen/Berlin: Bote & Bock.

— (1998). *Idomeneo. Opera Seria in Three Acts, K. 366*. Libretto. Music by Wolfgang Amadeus Mozart and Richard Strauss. New York, NY: Mostly Mozart Festival.

Walton, Chris (1993). "The Performing Version by Richard Strauss and Lothar Wallerstein". Julian Rushton, ed. 89-94.

Watkins, Glenn (1994). *Pyramids at the Louvre: Music, Culture, and Collage from Stravinsky to the Postmodernists*. Cambridge, MA: Harvard University Press.

Surveying the Field

Description
A Common Potential of Words and Music?

Werner Wolf, Graz

This essay contributes to the survey of the field of word (or literature) and music studies by singling out one of the many potential areas in which both media appear to overlap, namely description. Although intuitively description seems to be relevant for both word and music studies, it has hardly found scholarly attention from a media-comparative point of view (description here differing markedly from narrativity, which over the past few decades has repeatedly been discussed from this angle). The essay attempts to remedy this neglect. The first part outlines distinctive features of description with reference to fiction as one of the media that are commonly acknowledged as being able to describe. In the second part the respective potentials and limits of fiction and (instrumental) music are discussed by comparing typical objects, techniques and functions of description in these media. It will be argued that the range of describable objects and the precision as well as the imaginative effects of description are, as expected, significantly narrower in music and that description is more frequently employed to "impose an interpretation" (Riffaterre, "Descriptive Imagery" 125) in fiction than in music. In spite of these differences it will be shown that description is not only a well-known and frequent element in literature but constitutes a potential of music, too, albeit a limited one.

1. Introduction: Description as a Transmedial Phenomenon and its Neglect in Word and Music Studies

Surveying the field of word and music relations in many cases means a comparison between music and verbal media. Such comparisons require *tertia comparationis*. Much has been said on the question of a common narrative potential of words and music from a 'transmedial' point of view[1]. As far as description is concerned, the situation ap-

---

[1] Cf. Abbate; Kramer; Nattiez, "Can One Speak of Narrativity in Music?"; Neubauer; Newcomb; Maus, "Classical Instrumental Music and Narrative" and "Music as Narrative"; McClary; Micznik; Seaton; Wolf, "Das Problem der Narrativität"; for 'transmediality' as a form of 'extracompositional intermediality' which refers to phenomena that occur in more than one medium irrespective of a (possible) origin in one

pears, however, to be remarkably different. In musicology, the descriptive is frequently not even regarded as an individual scholarly subject at all. More often than not it is treated, if at all, as a variant of narrativity, as can be seen in the use of the term *Tonmalerei* ('sound painting'), which can designate both descriptive and narrative aspects of music, and also in the frequently encountered notion that programme music is a genre of music that can evoke both stories and images (see Altenburg, "Programmusik" 1822)[2]. In intermedial studies, in particular in the sub-field that concerns us most here, namely word and music studies, it seems as if the descriptive has escaped scholarly attention altogether. Generally, one can say that research on description has predominantly not been intermedial at all but monomedial. For our context this means that it has either dealt with description in the verbal medium alone or exclusively with music. In the former case the focus has tended to be on fiction, in the latter on forms of *Tonmalerei*, in particular in connection with the symphonic poem and nineteenth-century programme music. In contrast to this, I propose to approach description from a transmedial angle. I thus would like to extend a perspective underlying word and music studies as a whole to a phenomenon which actually seems predestined for such a transmedial perspective, as description is not only relevant to words and music but also to the visual arts, film, and other media[3].

In order to provide a basis for the ensuing comparison, I will first outline features of 'the descriptive', which I regard as a transmedial cognitive frame[4] that can be realized in a plurality of media. Theoretically, it could be presented with reference to several media such as painting or film. Yet for the sake of economy I will illustrate its char-

---

particular medium and hence irrespective of 'intermedial transposition' see Wolf, "Intermediality Revisited" 18 f.

[2] Cf. also the articles on the 'symphonic poem' and on 'programme music' in the *New Grove Dictionary of Music*, in which the concepts of 'description' and 'narration' are frequently used indiscriminately (see Macdonald, and Scruton).

[3] For a perspective on description from such a wider angle see Wolf/Bernhart, eds., *Description in Literature and Other Media*, and Wolf, "Description as a Transmedial Mode of Representation", an essay on which the following reflections draw in some parts.

[4] For the conception of semiotic macro-modes such as narrative and the descriptive as cognitive frames see Wolf, "Das Problem der Narrativität", ch. 2, and Wolf, "Description as a Transmedial Mode of Representation", ch. 2.1.

acteristics with the example of fiction, as fiction shall also serve – in the next two steps – as the basis of a comparison between the specific descriptive potentials as well as limits of (literary) words and (instrumental) music. The choice of fiction and instrumental music (rather than, say, drama and vocal music) is motivated by the endeavour to approach both media with reference to 'pure' genres, in which the descriptive potentials of the media concerned appear in a most typical form. In the intermedial comparison the emphasis will be on the question to what extent music can fulfil the frame 'description', since music has been researched less extensively in this respect than fiction and also because music seems to be the more problematic medium in this context.

2. Description: Typical Features and Functions

As there is little doubt that the descriptive can be realized in, among other media, fiction (this is indeed the genre in which the most research has been carried out in the field to date[5]), an example from this field may serve as a point of departure for the analysis of characteristic features of the descriptive. It should, however, be noted that fiction is here provisionally employed in a quasi-abstract manner, that is, regardless of its medial particularities, which will briefly be discussed in the following chapter:

> I SPENT the following day roaming through the valley. I stood beside the sources of the Arveiron, which take their rise in a glacier, that with slow pace is advancing down from the summit of the hills to barricade the valley. The abrupt sides of vast mountains were before me; the icy wall of the glacier overhung me; a few shattered pines were scattered around; and the solemn silence of this glorious presence-chamber of imperial nature was broken only by the brawling waves or the fall of some vast fragment, the thunder sound of the avalanche or the cracking, reverberated along the mountains, of the accumulated ice, which, through the silent working of immutable laws, was ever and anon rent and torn, as if it had been but a plaything in their hands. These sublime and magnificent scenes afforded me the greatest consolation that I was capable of receiving. They elevated me from all littleness of feeling, and although they did not remove my grief, they

---

[5] See, e. g., Bal, "Descriptions" and "On Meanings and Descriptions"; Hamon; Kittay; Pflugmacher; Riffaterre, "Descriptive Imagery" and "On the Diegetic Functions of the Descriptive"; Ronen; Sternberg.

subdued and tranquillized it. In some degree, also, they diverted my mind from the thoughts over which it had brooded for the last month. (Shelley 360)

This passage, which is an excerpt from Mary Shelley's *Frankenstein* (1818), will certainly be recognized as a description by all readers. This fact points to a first, general feature of the descriptive: it is a cognitive frame, or a semiotic macro-mode of organizing signs, stored in our minds as part of our cultural heritage. Yet what permits recipients to recognize this passage, which is indeed a typical description, as such? Clearly, some further features and functions. As it is impossible to go into the details of descriptive theory here, I will just summarize the most important characteristics of typical literary descriptions as a basis for the comparison with instrumental music:

a) The first feature is the **referential** nature of description. Owing to this quality, descriptions serve to either **identify** real phenomena[6], as in our example the Mont Blanc, or to **construct** fictitious ones within possible worlds. In both cases this is usually achieved by **attributing a plurality of qualities to concrete phenomena**[7]. Thus, the mountain scene in our example (the concrete phenomenon or 'theme' of the description) is referred to by details such as an "icy wall of [a] glacier", "shattered pines" or "brawling waves" and "the cracking [...] of [...] ice" (ll. 4-8). The referentiality inherent in descriptions creates a certain affinity between this frame and another one, namely narration. Yet there is a crucial difference: Narration typically involves at least one anthropomorphic agent and is focussed on eventful changes of situations that are syntagmatically arranged according to causality and teleology and answer questions such as 'who did what or what happened to whom, why and with what consequences?'. As opposed to this, description does not necessarily require anthropomorphic agents as a part of the representation (neither as subjects nor as objects of perception[8]); it moreover centres on objects or phenom-

---

[6] In particular when a reference to something well-known is possible.

[7] This referential quality of description includes mimesis but is not restricted to it, as blatantly non-mimetic, e. g. fantastic fictional objects, can also be referred to in the mode of description. For attribution as a distinctive feature of description see Bal, *De theorie van vertellen* 130, and "On Meanings and Descriptions" 104.

[8] This does not mean that description is not a human activity; it only implies that anthropomorphic beings (such as the focalizer Frankenstein in the excerpt quoted)

ena whose qualities are unfolded paradigmatically, and it is likely to answer questions such as 'what can be perceived?', 'what does it look like?' or 'how does it sound?'. In determining the typical nature of these objects, there is a tendency, in particular among literary scholars, to privilege static and spatial ones. However, this is perhaps an undue restriction, for virtually all concrete phenomena can become objects of description, static (a house) as well as dynamic ones (a vehicle in motion), spatial (a landscape) as well as temporal ones (a sunrise scene), provided the emphasis is on 'whatness' rather than on narrative eventfulness.

b) The second feature of description refers to the specific effects of descriptive reference: it does not merely serve the purpose of identification (like a proper name), but usually consists in the **vivid representation** of a phenomenon by concentrating on its surface appearance and the sensory impressions it conveys (in our example these are both visual and aural impressions). This vividness aims at enabling the recipient to experience or re-experience the object described, and often this **experientiality** elicits **aesthetic illusion**[9], in other words, the impression of being re-centred in the space to which the described object belongs and of experiencing this space as a possible, even plausible world, in spite of the fact that recipients, as a rule, retain a residual consciousness of its being 'made up'. This illusionist effect is arguably also enhanced by the passage just quoted.

c) The third feature is linked to this experiential and often illusionist effect of descriptions: descriptions, through their details, render the possible world which they constitute or of which they are a part plausible and confer an **aura of objectivity** on it[10]. This aura serves to give a touch of probability even to highly fantastic rep-

---

need not necessarily be part of the descriptive representation itself, while such beings are in fact required in narrative representations.

[9] This is a consequence of a successful concretization of the object described; for more details on aesthetic illusion see Wolf, *Ästhetische Illusion und Illusionsdurchbrechung* and "Aesthetic Illusion as an Effect of Fiction".

[10] This aura can elicit a referential sub-form of aesthetic illusion, namely a 'reality effect' (*effet de réel*, see Barthes). This effect, which Barthes linked especially to description, may have something to do with the frequent focus of descriptions on natural phenomena (e. g. landscapes or physiognomies), which suggest a 'just being objectively there'.

resentations such as the Gothic novel from which our example is taken. However, as this quasi-rhetorical, persuasive function shows, which is also discernible in Shelley's mountain scene, the objectivity of most descriptions is only a calculated effect, an aura, and in reality anything but really objective. This is not only the case because of the general problematics of 'objectivity' (since all descriptions imply perception and hence more or less distorting subjects, even if these, unlike the focalizer Frankenstein in the passage from Shelley's novel, can remain outside the representation); the idea of a neutral objectivity of description is also, and in particular, untenable with reference to artefacts. Michael Riffaterre was most outspoken about this. He said with reference to "literary description" that its "primary function [...] is not to make the reader see something. Its aim is not to represent an external reality [...], but to dictate an interpretation" ("Descriptive Imagery" 125). While Riffaterre's down-grading of "making the reader see something" is arguably too radical, his idea is basically convincing. For the nature of artefacts as intentional, meaningful constructs renders it highly probable that even the descriptive construction or representation of the 'givens' of a possible world is not an 'innocent' business but serves a purpose (just as the narration of events usually has a point). Consequently, **description**, even if it only extends over a small part of an artefact or text, **is implicated in the construction of meaning of the entire work** under consideration. This is clearly the case in Shelley's mountain scene, too, for it contributes to the worldview implied in *Frankenstein*. This is most conspicuously discernible through the employment of the vocabulary of the sublime in the eighteenth-century sense as combining a pleasurable – here tranquillizing – effect of nature with the idea of a fear-inspiring vastness that retains vestiges of a transcendental worldview. The "imperial nature" (l. 6) of the "sublime and magnificent scene" (l. 10) described therefore points to the "immutable laws" of God and nature (l. 9) that Frankenstein has violated by attempting to interfere with God's creation as a human mock-creator, and a highly irresponsible one at that.

In sum, the transmedial features of 'description' as illustrated by our example are as follows: a clearly representational use of signs that highlights the physical 'whatness' of a concrete object through paradigmatically transmitted, detailed attributions and often permits the recipient not only to identify but also to re-experience or vividly imagine the object described. In spite of a seemingly 'innocent' concentration on outer, sensory 'facts', a device that creates an aura of objectivity, descriptions, in particular if they form a part of a larger whole, are regularly a covert means of contributing to the meaning of the artefact or text in its entirety. In fiction, but also in film and in other media, this contribution can, for instance, be the exteriorization of the psychic state of a focalizer-character, but it can also consist in the concretization of a worldview through 'symbolic' objects and settings.

3. Description in Fiction: Potentials and Limits

After the preceding outline of general features of the descriptive the following two sections shall be dedicated to exploring the particular descriptive potentials and limits of fiction as well as of music, starting with the former medium. In view of the amount of research which has been done in the field it may, however, suffice here to mention the most important issues[11].

Both the descriptive potentials and limits of fiction are to a large extent determined by the verbal medium as a predominantly symbolic sign-system which informs fiction as an artistic medium. As far as the potentials are concerned, one may safely say that owing to the referential flexibility of the verbal medium there is in principle virtually no imaginable phenomenon or object that could not be described in some way in fiction. Descriptions can here refer to phenomena that appeal to all senses, to real as well as to fictitious and to static as well as to kinetic ones, and in addition, all of these references can take their (apparent) point of departure from both a static or a dynamic point of view.

However, this is not to say that in fiction all objects can be described equally well, nor that fiction is in all respects a privileged descriptive medium. One of the limitations of fiction resides in the

---

[11] For a more extended discussion of these potentials and limits see Wolf, "Description as a Transmedial Mode of Representation", ch. 3.2.

unequal descriptive precision of the vocabulary at its disposal, depending on the nature of the object in focus. At least in English (but also in German, French and many other languages) the terms that refer, for instance, to visual and spatial phenomena are greater in number and precision than those that refer to aural, tactile or gustatory ones – hence the well-known difficulties in describing music or tastes with words and the traditional privileging of visual objects in descriptions in fiction (in that regard the descriptive excerpt quoted in the previous chapter is not very typical, as it contains exceptionally detailed acoustic elements).

Another limitation that applies to fiction as a descriptive medium is related to the all but exclusively symbolic nature of its signifiers. Even if one bears in mind that all signification, including signification through iconicity, presupposes some kind of (perceptual, albeit not cognitive) convention and thus indirection, words as symbolic signs usually produce a higher degree of indirection with reference to the represented objects than iconic media. In contrast to this, the visual iconicity open to visual media such as film and painting as well as the aural iconicity which, as we will see, is a potential of music, permit a more direct (perceptual) access to the represented objects. Thus, a painting or a photograph of the valley of the Arveiron would have given a much clearer 'picture' of the setting than the descriptive excerpt from *Frankenstein*, even though a picture would mainly concern the domain of the visual, in which the verbal medium has just been said to have a particularly rich vocabulary. The fact that words are nevertheless less 'graphic' than other media is related to a third limit of the descriptive potential of words and verbal art.

This limit results from yet another media-specific quality of words, namely from their temporal and dynamic nature. This leads us into the centre of the well-known 'Laokoon-problem', which Gotthold Ephraim Lessing, focussing on verbal descriptions of static visual objects, already addressed almost two centuries and a half ago[12]. However, this problem is not as fundamental as it might appear at first sight: not only because of the possibility of overcoming it by intro-

---

[12] For Lessing, 'poesy' (i. e. literature) was unfit for describing spatial phenomena because of its temporal medial nature (which forces it to represent the elements of possible worlds consecutively rather than simultaneously, as is the case in the visual arts).

ducing dynamic elements into the description and/or by partially narrativizing description, as Lessing pointed out with reference to Homer's discursive practice, but also, and more importantly, for other reasons: the descriptive potential of words is not restricted to visual objects but can also include sounds and other sensory impressions; nor are verbal descriptions confined to static objects (such as the "mountains" in the passage from *Frankenstein*) but can also apply to 'dynamic' phenomena that change either in time or location such as rivers and the "brawling waves" of mountain streams. Still, verbal descriptions do have a problem with static, spatial objects, and this is aggravated by the fact that such objects are often regarded as the most typical ones in verbal art. Yet this is not a problem that concerns the actual possibility of describing such objects (they **can** in fact be described) but rather one that concerns the organization of the descriptive discourse as well as its motivation.

In a verbal medium, the discursive organization is inherently difficult because description is a relatively 'loose' frame (a frame that does not require many features), in particular if compared to narrative, where the numerous requirements of the frame at least tendentially can be said to support a certain stereotyped internal organization. This organization can be seen in simple stories that follow a conventionalized schema: they often begin with the 'narrative preliminaries' (the establishment of the temporal and spatial setting), then proceed to the exposition of the main characters, then to the narration of a first decisive event, then to its consequences, then to the next event etc., all of which can be recounted in *ordo naturalis*, a form of 'diagrammatic iconicity' where the sequence of the represented events is imitated by the sequence of the words. In verbal descriptions such a 'natural' internal organization does not exist as an overall schema. It is only dynamic objects that, at least in principle, permit an organization of verbal sequences which basically uses 'diagrammatic iconicity'. Static and spatial objects do not possess this prop, and this forces authors to employ other principles of organization, many of which have been discussed by Meir Sternberg (see his essay with the revealing title "Ordering the Unordered").

As far as the motivation for description in verbal art is concerned, problems occur in particular where this discursive mode, as is typical of fiction, is part of a larger, non-descriptive frame whose predominant (narrative) drive is slowed down or even temporarily halted by description. If one does not take recourse to the positional convention of locating descriptions at the opening of narratives, a frequent alternative means of motivation is to link description to the internal perspective of a character, who, for instance, is made to look out of a window.

The functional potential of description in fiction is highly diverse and historically variable. It ranges from enhancing the visualization of the fictional world and thus the immersion typical of aesthetic illusion to "impos[ing] an interpretation" (Riffaterre, "Descriptive Imagery" 125). In all cases, description in fiction is subordinated to the overall narrative frame that is constitutive of this medium.

4. Description in Instrumental Music: Difficulties, Conditions, Markers, Potentials, and Limits Compared to Fiction[13]

Among the classical sister arts, poetry, painting and music, the latter, and in particular instrumental music, seems to be the least descriptive, as is evident in the lexicon of the English language: while verbs such as 'to depict' and 'to describe' point to an apparently inherent descriptive potential of the pictorial and the verbal medium, there is no equivalent referring to music, no expression like 'to desound'. In fact, music has intrinsic difficulties with the frame 'description', at first sight one is even inclined to say even more than with 'narrative' and, at any rate, more than the verbal medium. For it is not only the *Laokoon*-problem (to the extent that it is centred on static objects of description) that in this respect besets music as a dynamic, temporal medium, since it also applies to verbal art. Instrumental music has yet another and more fundamental problem with description: music resists the frame 'description' (as well as the frame 'narrative') because it is the most abstract and non-referential of all the arts and media. One should, however, be more precise, for music can be said to be 'referential', but mainly in the sense of '**self**-referential' rather than of '**hetero**-referential'. Indeed, the occurrences of the theme in the individual voices of a fugue or the transformations of a theme in a

---

[13] For this chapter my thanks are due to Michael Walter for valuable suggestions, in particular on Richard Strauss.

composition 'theme with variations' are self-referentially related to each other[14] through iconic aural similarity, but what can a fugue or a theme with variations describe? The very question seems beside the point.

And yet there are compositions, particularly in nineteenth- and early twentieth-century Western art music, that purport to be descriptive and, for instance, are called 'symphonic' or 'tone poems', thus pointing by their very name not only to lyrical expressivity but also to lyrical descriptiveness. In 1911, for instance, Michel Brenet published an essay with the revealing title "Essai sur les origines de la musique descriptive", and his contemporary Richard Strauss was firmly convinced that one can, 'of course, paint with tones and sounds', and he allegedly even claimed that a genuine musician ought to be able to compose a restaurant menu (see Krause 216 f.). While this latter claim may not be taken seriously by all, the conviction that music can in fact be descriptive cannot be so easily discarded.

Some conditions, of course, apply – and in music certainly more so than in fiction. A first condition which comes to mind immediately must be mentioned, but only in order to be instantly dismissed: it is the idea that musical descriptiveness depends on a heavy use of a potential in which music is often considered to excel, namely emotional **expressivity**. Franz Liszt, one of the principal proponents of both the 'symphonic poem' (see Altenburg, "Symphonische Dichtung") and 'programme music' and indeed the inventor of both terms, is known – to quote from the renowned *New Grove Dictionary of Music and Musicians* – not to have "regard[ed] music as a direct means of describing objects; rather he thought that music could put the listener in the same frame of mind as could the objects themselves. In this way, by suggesting the emotional reality of things, music could indirectly represent them" (Scruton 396). This view is intriguing, and one may concede that musical expressivity may, under certain circumstances, indeed contribute to description by evoking typical, culturally coded moods, atmospheres, etc. attached to descriptive objects such as a 'peaceful' pastoral landscape or a 'sublime' mountain scene. Yet ultimately Liszt's view rests on a confusion, or

---

[14] The same is true of the many 'verbatim' repetitions which abound in music and do not have a counterpart either in the visual arts or in literature (except for lyrical refrains).

rather a short-circuiting, of subject-centred responses and object-centred reference. If a verbal text, or a musical composition for that matter, is to describe anything at all, the expression of an emotional response to the object described can only be an **addition** to a description but can never **replace** a reference to the object itself – for how could the recipient otherwise know what object has elicited the emotional reaction expressed[15]? In fact, in all descriptions including musical ones, an object-centred reference is compulsory, while subject-centred expression is optional[16].

The principal condition of musical descriptiveness is thus the fulfillment of an essential feature of all descriptions, namely that music should be able to refer to phenomena other than itself, in other words that it can be '**hetero-referential**'. Now, most scholars agree that hetero-referentiality is very untypical of music. Nevertheless, music does have some possibilities of pointing to extra-musical objects – independently of expressivity. This is a complex and frequently discussed problem of musical semiotics, which cannot be retraced here in all its intricacies[17]. I will therefore limit my remarks to some general variants of musical hetero-referentiality that seem to be particularly relevant to description.

---

[15] Cf. Scruton in his excellent article on "Programme Music", who also insists on the distinction between (descriptive) reference and expression by rightly pointing out that "description may or may not be accompanied by an expression of feeling" and that "there can be expressions of emotion that are not accompanied by representation" (397). In terms of Jakobson's functions of language the same differentiation can be made by referring to the 'referential function' as necessary for description, while the 'emotive function' is a merely optional addition.

[16] The importance of such object-centred reference can even be corroborated by a famous statement of Beethoven's, although this may not be obvious at first sight. For Beethoven, who with his sixth symphony is generally considered to be one of the outstanding precursors of intensely descriptive music, emphasized expression when he claimed that his symphony was 'more the expression of emotions than a painting' ("mehr Ausdruck der Empfindung als Mahlerey" [quoted from Kloiber, *Handbuch der klassischen und romantischen Symphonie* 89]). Yet significantly, the wording of this statement does **not** deny the presence of descriptive *'Malerei'* altogether.

[17] For more details concerning the semiotic problem whether music is a language, only similar to verbal language, or no language at all, see, among other works, Dahlhaus, "Musik als Text"; Kaden/Brachmann/Giese; Kleeman; Nattiez, *Musicologie générale et sémiologie*; Wolf, *The Musicalization of Fiction*, ch. 2.3.

What comes to mind here first is what has traditionally been called in German *Tonmalerei*, 'sound painting'. However, the term covers a plurality of aspects (cf. Altenburg, "Programmusik" 1827) so that some specifications are necessary. Its most common denotation refers to suggestions of musical **iconicity** of various kinds[18], degrees of intensity, extension and directness. As music is an aural phenomenon, the obvious and most direct actualization of such iconicity, which is said to have existed in the music of all times and forms (cf. Kloiber, *Handbuch der Symphonischen Dichtung* 1), is a variant of **sensory iconicity**, namely the imitation of extramusical sounds by musical means. The resulting "**aural mimicry**", to use a term coined by Carolyn Abbate (33), is – on the basis of cultural knowledge – often self-explanatory and does not require the clarifying aid of words. This applies, e. g., to bird song, animal cries, thunderstorms and similar sounds, some of which have been incorporated, for example, in the description of a pastoral scene in Beethoven's sixth symphony, entitled "Die Pastorale". 'Aural mimicry' can also refer to evoking space as a basic dimension of many objects of descriptions: in performances, the location of instruments can thus be used to denote 'stereophonic' left-right and 'dolby-surround' (foreground – background or 'echo') effects (as exemplified in the 'dialogue' of two 'pastoral' woodwind instruments in the third movement of Berlioz's *Symphonie fantastique*)[19].

Tonmalerei can also go beyond a more or less direct imitation of sensory phenomena and employ more indirect kinds of similarity (iconicity). One possibility is to arrange sounds so that their sequence mimes the sequence of the phenomena referred to. This '**diagrammatic iconicity**' can be used, for instance, to illustrate a sunrise by melodies and harmonies that gradually 'rise' from initial 'dark' and

---

[18] For the different kinds of iconicity (sensory or 'imagic', disgrammatic, and metaphorical or 'semantic') see Fischer/Nänny (their typology was, however, devised with reference to verbal language but can also be transferred to music).

[19] A more indirect form of musical reference through *Tonmalerei* is the **visual iconicity** of *Augenmusik* (music for the eye). In this variant, which is, however, not very important for musical description, a relation of similarity is established not between an object and music as an acoustic phenomenon, but as a written code. A famous example is Johann Sebastian Bach's repeated employment of a sharp – in German *Kreuz* (cross) – as a reference to Christ's cross.

'low' sounds to 'higher' and 'clearer' ones till they reach a 'bright' climax in a *fortissimo* major chord.

As can be seen in the many terms put in italics in the example of musically describing a sunrise, diagrammatic iconicity as well as other kinds of using music in a referential way is often combined with, or based on, what is actually metaphors attached to sounds: conventional semantic *valeurs*, such as 'low' and 'high', 'slow' and 'fast', 'dull' and 'clear', etc., that are attributed to what after all are physical qualities of melody, harmony, speed, rhythm, loudness, and timbre which could be described in quite different terms (such as wave length, frequency, and intensity). The resulting **metaphoric illustration** is actually a kind of '**metaphoric iconicity**', that is, of using iconic similarities between a conventionalized vehicle that is linked to an extra-musical tenor owing to some common denominator or *tertium comparationis* and permits references to extramusical objects. An example of such metaphoric illustration that appeals to metaphoric conventions connected with certain musical phenomena is the description of running water (e. g. a brook) by 'wavy' melodic lines (using the spatial metaphor of 'rising' and 'falling' melodies); another one is the illustration of spatial effects of distance (or echo), which can also be achieved independently of an actual remote position of the echo-instrument by simply repeating or 'answering' (another of the many 'sunken' metaphors used in the verbalization of music) with a markedly reduced loudness. While in some cases the referentiality is clear owing to well-known cultural conventions, other examples will be less obvious than in 'aural mimicry', and therefore metaphorical iconicity tends to occur more frequently in vocal than in instrumental music. Thus, in Bach's cantatas and passions, falling single notes in the accompaniment can refer to falling tears[20], a racing sequence of fast notes may evoke the idea of running, and twisting melodies can point to a snake, frequently as a symbol of the devil[21]. In

---

[20] The conventionality on which metaphoric illustration usually rests can here be seen in the fact that the spatialization of 'high' vs. 'low' sounds, and consequently, the 'falling' of a melody, is an at least partially arbitrary imposition on, and basically a metaphorical description of, an acoustic phenomenon which in principle could be conceived of in different terms.

[21] For a classic discussion of Bach's musical descriptiveness cf. Schweitzer, ch. XX "Dichterische und malerische Musik", as well as chs. XXI-XXXIII.

such illustrations music and words cooperate in a more or less parallel way, which could even be said to result in a certain redundancy were it not that the musical illustration added a concrete dimension to the more abstract verbal reference[22].

A yet remoter, since non-iconic and even more conventional, means of eliciting referentiality in music that can also contribute to descriptions is the employment of **acoustic connotations** without appeal to similarity. They point to situations, 'scripts' or cognitive frames that are conventionally associated with certain sounds, musical instruments and forms, sometimes through the additional use of the musical equivalent to intertextuality: 'intermusicality'[23]. Thus, in a nineteenth-century symphony the sound of horns may evoke a hunting scene through an association of ideas (as in the third movement of Bruckner's fourth symphony); a *Ländler* played, among other things, on a clarinet may recall a rural scene (a form of generic intermusical reference that occurs in the third movement, Allegro/"Lustiges Zusammensein der Landleute" of Beethoven's sixth symphony). And a hymn can elicit the frame 'church service' (as in the fourth movement of Schumann's *Rheinische[r] Symphonie*); sometimes (in cases of references to individual works) the quotation of the melody of a vocal composition can also, through 'intermedial association', evoke the corresponding words, thus introducing yet another dimension of signification into an instrumental composition. Even though such acoustic connotations are usually also based on 'aural mimicry' they go beyond the mere identification or illustration of a given phenomenon. They rather operate on the principle of metonymic *pars pro toto*: the imitation of individual acoustic elements of the phenomena described are meant to trigger entire scripts or cognitive frames[24].

---

[22] For a recent, more extended discussion of musical reference by means of iconicity see Georis.

[23] In analogy to literary intertextuality theory one may say that such 'intermusical' reference can link a composition to preceding individual compositions ('individual intermusical reference') or to groups/genres of compositions ('generic intermusical reference'). In either case the hetero-referentiality potentially resulting indirectly from such basically intramedial self-reference can emerge from cultural connotations that are attached to the musical pretext and are 'imported' into the 'quoting' composition alongside the intermusical reference.

[24] This is also a process that is typical of the reception of descriptions in general (see Nünning).

Thus, a popular melody occurring in a symphony, is, for instance, not principally meant to imitate a specific song but to point to the context in which such a song is conventionally supposed to occur[25].

Considering these various devices of musical hetero-reference, music, including instrumental music, can certainly not be said to be entirely incapable of pointing beyond itself. Yet are these devices of reference *per se* already descriptive? In spite of what the term *Tonmalerei* – literally 'sound painting' – may imply, I would like to contend that this is **not** the case. A repeated imitation of the call of a cuckoo in 18th-century harpsichord music is, for instance, **not** a description of this bird but a mere (iconic and also indexical) reference to it. For according to what has been said above, description implies reference but also requires attributions that specify some concrete object and go beyond mere identification. Nonetheless, all of the devices just mentioned may **contribute** to what may in fact be termed musical descriptiveness, provided they establish such attributions, preferably multiple, varied and complex ones. It is clear that this conception of musical description substantially restricts the historical range of its occurrence and excludes many pre-19th-century extramusical references that identify but do not describe extramusical phenomena. Yet all of this does not exclude instrumental music from the realm of the descriptive altogether. For, in particular in 19th- and 20th-century programme music (including symphonic poems), there are several examples of an extended use of musical hetero-reference that may indeed be said to form musical descriptions.

A case in point is Richard Strauss's *Alpensinfonie*. This 50-minute composition, which requires a gigantic orchestra of more than 120 instruments, including organ, wind machines and cow bells, follows a vaguely narrative programme and thus constitutes an example of programme music[26]: we seem to follow the stream of consciousness of an

---

[25] The descriptive potential of such musical connotations is based on cultural competence (one must be able, e. g., to identify the popular character of the music) and on the recipient's imagination – and this to a far greater extent than other devices of musical hetero-reference.

[26] If one calls this composition 'programme music', one employs the term in a broad sense and includes also non-literary programmes (for this broad meaning see Altenburg, "Programmusik" 1822, for whom the term suffers from a 'babylonian confusion of language' [1821]); for a classification as symphonic poem or *Tondichtung* cf. Kloiber, *Handbuch der symphonischen Dichtung* 189, and Walter 150.

anonymous agency, whose several activities, impressions and expressive reactions to his or her experiences are rendered by musical means[27]. The programme consists in the ascent of a mountain with a climactic reaching of the summit followed by a descent. This narrative outline is the framework into which several descriptive scenes are set, and this illustrates a typical relation between narrative and description familiar from fiction and other narrative media, namely the subordination of description to narrative. Among these scenes there is also a section entitled "Auf der Alm" (on the mountain pasture), on which I would like to concentrate briefly.

As one can hear in particular in the first minute and a half of this 'scene', Strauss here combines two devices of suggesting musical hetero-reference: There is, first, 'aural mimicry' of various kinds (the imitation of natural phenomena and, by means of generic 'intermusicality', the imitative reference to instrumental as well as to vocal music): we hear bird song, cow bells, a yodel ('*Jodler*') and a 'Ländler'. And there is, second, the suggestion of rural peace by means of (symbolic) connotations: this concerns the evocation of a rustic milieu through all of the items of 'aural mimicry' and generic intermusical reference just mentioned, but above all the generally peaceful atmosphere of the passage produced by appropriate dynamic, melodic, rhythmic and harmonic means. As opposed to the isolated references to extra-musical phenomena sometimes encountered in older music, we have here a relatively complex sequence of attributions that coalesce into the evocation of a natural scenery, hence an external reality, and thus appear indeed to be eligible as a musical description.

Yet if description is a cognitive frame that needs to be activated, what is it that triggers the idea of description here in the first place? This points to the question of how to recognize musical descriptions when being confronted with one, in other words to the issue of **'markers of musical description'**. This is a problem which has not as yet received sufficient critical attention. With reference to fiction, it is perhaps not obvious as a problem at all, for in the verbal medium the presence of description appears to be self-explanatory and 'self-signalling'. Yet even there, markers are common, for instance the frequent device of building a moment of rest into a narrative (a gaze during a pause in a travelogue, a view from a mountain top or through a

---

[27] A part of these means is the employment of Wagnerian leitmotifs.

window etc.), a rest which motivates the interruption of the narrative flow that typically results from descriptions as well as the change from the syntagmatic narration of ever new elements to a descriptive multiplicity of paradigmatic attributions that are all centred on one and the same object. In music, where description is certainly less self-explanatory, such markers appear to be even more important and deserve special attention. This is all the more so as in music, there is always the 'danger' of perceiving descriptive passages as (parts of) purely abstract, non-referential and hence non-descriptive musical compositions.

In view of this 'danger' an important means of signalling descriptive referentiality is urging the recipient to abandon the default option 'music follows its own logic' by simply denying such musical logic. This can be done by departing from established musical forms in a seemingly 'inexplicable' way or by not adopting any received form, including the usual musical self-referentiality, in the first place, thus barring a traditional access to music[28]. This is largely the case in *Eine Alpensinfonie*, for in spite of the title and the employment of themes and motives, the composition does not show symphonic form, let alone sonata form, nor any other conventional form. As a result, the listener is challenged to find another principle of coherence – which the narrative and descriptive programme in fact offers. It is, however, clear that such a procedure is not without its problematics, for the absence of traditional musical form – if it is perceived at all by the average listener – need not necessarily point to an extra-musical reference but could just be regarded as unconventional art. In addition, the lack of conventional intramusical form alone would not suffice to point to certain descriptive rather than, for instance, narrative con-

---

[28] Strauss, however, would not have agreed with this, since, as Dahlhaus reports (cf. *Die Idee der absoluten Musik* 137), he opposed the idea that programme music was formless if it did not follow schematic forms and insisted on the fact that a 'poetic programme' can lead to new forms. Dahlhaus himself seems to adopt this view (see "Absolute Musik" 694 f.). Yet the presence of some kind of form even in heavily descriptive or narrative music is not the point: it is the nature of this form which counts, for it is mainly 'schematic', that is, **pre-existing and well-known forms** (and not new ones) that can function as an orientation for recipients to navigate through a composition, while newly devised forms do not support this orientational function with the same ease, and this seems to be the case with Strauss.

tents[29]. This problem of enabling the listener to correctly 'decode' a given passage is all the more difficult as descriptive passages are sometimes, if less frequently than in narrative fiction (in *Eine Alpensinfonie* but also, e. g., in Smetana's "Vlatva" from *Má vlast*, set into an overall narrative frame.

Thus, it is almost inevitable that in music descriptive reference resorts to the verbal medium, in particular if the composer wants the recipient to 'hear' specific objects described. Explanatory words can cooperate in two distinct ways. The first is the integration of words into the composition itself, as in the lied, in opera and other kinds of vocal music. Where this option is not given, as is typically the case in nineteenth-century instrumental programme music, a second option applies: It consists in using the verbal medium in the 'framing' of the composition. This can be done, minimally, in its title (as exemplified by *Eine Alpensinfonie*), but also in more remote 'paratexts', e. g. explanatory essays in concert programmes or other publications. Thus, Richard Strauss had the titles of the individual sections of his *Alpensinfonie* printed in the concert programme of the first performance (Dresden, Oct. 28, 1915), which also included an essay by his friend Max Steinitzer entitled "Thematische Einführung" (cf. Walter 148).

In addition to these markers, a descriptive gesture in music can, of course, also be signalled if any of the aforementioned devices of musical hetero-referentiality is employed with a salient frequency or if such devices occur in combination with each other and thus also reach a salient, unusual quantity. For, as already said, a certain amount of detail is one of the typical features of descriptions. Yet the difficulty presented by this marker, as well as by others, is the fact that it can also point to musical narrativity rather than descriptiveness. Interestingly, the problem of distinguishing musical descriptivity from musical narrativity has not been recognized as such in most musicological research, in which, as has been remarked earlier, the terms 'description' and 'narration' are frequently used indiscriminately. In fact, in music, given the problematics of referentiality, the distinction

---

[29] The 'deviation argument' (deviation from formal musical conventions as a symptom of [intended] musical referentiality) has in fact been used in the context of potential incentives for listeners to apply the frame 'narrative'; see Walter 151, and Micznik 246, 248.

between narration and description is not obvious, as the temporal nature of the medium tends to favour temporal objects of description, and the presence of a temporal dimension is at the same time also a *sine qua non* of narrative[30]. A further reason for blurring the two frames may be their frequent co-occurrence not only in fiction but also in music: even though there is no strict necessity for this co-occurrence, it is indeed difficult to imagine musical narrativity without the aid of some kind of musical descriptivity.

Considering this problem of differentiation I would like to propose two hopefully helpful criteria. The first is the question whether a given composition suggests or does not suggest the presence of interacting characters or minimally of one experiencing character in an intracompositional possible world. While narrative necessitates such a presence, descriptions – as mentioned above – can dispense with such agencies, even without a describing consciousness as a part of the possible world described. The second criterion refers to the question whether a given composition shows the presence of a teleological, goal-oriented trajectory and in connection with this a motivated ending. The ending of a story must somehow be connected to, and motivated by, a previous teleological development and thus is typically a logical result, while the ending of a description can occur when its object has been represented in a sufficiently vivid way. As 'sufficiently vivid' is a highly debatable notion, the endings of descriptions tend to appear as a-logical and arbitrary. In music, the ending of a description would at best be motivated by aesthetic, compositional criteria but not referentially. Compositions or parts of compositions that betray extramusical reference but imply neither a story-like trajectory nor interacting characters can therefore not be regarded as narrative and may by default qualify as descriptive.

The presence of such markers and a specific musical texture permits us in fact to consider scenes like "Auf der Alm" as an instance of musical description. This enables us to compare this example with the descriptive extract from fiction quoted earlier and also to comment on the descriptive potentials and limits of instrumental music in general. In the musical as well as in the literary example a mountain scene is

---

[30] In verbal art, the same temporal nature does not lead to a confusion, as the semantic surface of a text is, as a rule, sufficiently clear for a distinction between the two frames.

in focus and arguably identified through multiple attributions. However, as is to be expected, both the motivation for the description and the identification of the scenery are much more precise in the literary example than in the musical one.

As for the motivation, the literary text provides a plausible and conventional reason for the insertion of the description at least in the former part of the excerpt, namely by letting the movement of the focalizer's ramblings come to a halt ("I stood beside the sources of the Arveiron"), which, so to speak, gives him as well as the reader time to gaze at the surrounding landscape. In contrast to this, the musical example, as expected, does not provide any motivation at all, and so a potential 'rest' of the wandering persona is at best a probabilistic guess by the recipient.

Concerning the precision of the description the differences are no less obvious: Where in the literary case the description refers even to a specific geographical region, in the musical case, such a reference is impossible. Without the verbal framing of the musical example, it would, strictly speaking, even be doubtful whether the scene is really set in the mountains, for cow bells and bird song can be heard, for instance, in the Bavarian lowlands too, and this is basically also true of yodels (although the cultural connotations may imply something different). This points to a general feature of music as a potentially descriptive medium: owing to the medium-specific limitations concerning hetero-referentiality (which excludes symbolic signification, at least as far as denotation is concerned, and privileges iconicity[31]) the scope of potential objects of description in music is much more restricted than in a verbal medium, where the flexibility of symbolic signification opens possibilities for the description of a practically unlimited range of objects.

As far as the vividness of the descriptive representation is concerned, one may argue that the verbal example, even if read independently of its narrative context, is apt to convey experientiality and perhaps also elicits mental images that create a feeling of immersion and

---

[31] Strictly speaking, one could argue with Walton (cf. 333-337) that one ought therefore not use the term 'to describe' for most of musical 'depiction'; however, 'description' is so much a received term for the transmedial frame under discussion that it would make little sense to resort to another term such as 'depiction', which in turn could be criticized as a misleading metaphor, since, again strictly speaking, music does not 'paint' either.

hence of aesthetic illusion in the recipient. Even if it may be conceded that the musical example can also convey a certain atmosphere (and, since atmosphere is largely a matter of emotion, do so more efficiently than the verbal text) it is again doubtful whether Strauss's musical description can really elicit aesthetic illusion. If it triggers something like immersion at all, there seems to be a noteworthy difference in the recipient's share in this process in comparison to fiction. While all aesthetic illusion requires the co-operation of the recipient and some experiential reservoir (some scripts that a text or artefact may actualize), the literary text guides the process of illusion with more authority than music. Strauss's description in fact requires much more imaginative reconstruction or construction on the part of the recipient than Shelley's. And arguably the results in individual recipients will differ much more widely than the impression triggered by the literary counterpart. For the very general stimuli of the music permit a wider scope of variation than the more precise indications given by the verbal text.

The difference between the two media is even greater with reference to another general function of descriptions, namely to contribute to the construction of the meaning of the artefact as a whole. In Strauss's case the meaning of the scene on the alpine meadows is restricted to conveying the idea of peacefulness and joy as a contrast to the ensuing excitement when attaining the summit and experiencing a subsequent thunderstorm. Considering the period of composition, namely World War I, this peacefulness may also include a contrastive if not compensatory reference to the cultural-historical context, but this would be a mere guess. Shelley's description, again, conveys meaning in a more precise way. It also forms a resting place in opposition to the protagonist's grief and anxieties, but it does so with an explicit reference to the aesthetics of the sublime – with the aforementioned connotations and effects for the construction of the implied norms and worldview. To invest Strauss's musical description – or any musical description without words – with such meaning would clearly be an overinterpretation.

5. Why Musical Description? Possible Functions of Descriptive Music in 19th-Century Culture

As we have seen, description is a potential of instrumental music, albeit not a natural one. If this is so, one may ask what the advantages of description are which made instrumental music of the 19th and early 20th centuries venture into this problematic realm in the first place.

There are several possible answers to this question concerning the functional history (*Funktionsgeschichte*) of descriptive music[32] (which in this respect is closely connected to programme music). One of the answers arguably lies in the looseness of organization which is characteristic of description and which distinguishes it both from narrative and even more so from the formal organization of traditional musical genres. From a sociological perspective this looseness may indeed be thought to have not least contributed to the attractiveness of the symphonic poem and other genres of programme music in the nineteenth century. For the reception of instrumental music gained a hitherto unparalleled popularity in that period, and music appreciation was expanded from a restricted and more or less elitist public to a larger, middle-class audience. Among this expanded public the specialists formed a considerably smaller fraction than in earlier times. This means that a larger part must have had increasing difficulties in finding a purely formal or abstract access to music. In addition, the public performance of instrumental music, formerly predominantly motivated by pragmatic purposes (such as contributing to a religious service, or providing a 'divertimento' during a feast for aristocrats), now increasingly took place in the depragmatized frame of the concert hall (and could last several hours). The shift of the burden of musical appreciation from intramusical, formal criteria that required a specialist's knowledge of genres and compositional devices to more easily understandable extramusical ideas or 'programmes' (including nationalist ones as in Smetana's *Má vlast* [cf. Altenburg, "Symphonische Dichtung" 162]) may consequently have been regarded as a welcome development. Rendering instrumental music more transpar-

---

[32] As with questions of possible functions of works of art in general, one should, however, bear in mind that answers in this field tend to be more or less convincing theses rather than demonstrable (historical) facts.

ent for an expanded public of non-specialists and thus forming what could be termed 'music lite' was arguably one of the functions of musical descriptiveness in the nineteenth century.

Yet descriptive music can enhance the emotional and aesthetic effect of highly sophisticated works, too, and is by far not restricted to 'naive' or middle-brow compositions. After all, the readability of musical reference, owing to the resistance of the medium, is in itself not always easy, and in many cases even the deciphering of *Tonmalerei* presupposes considerable listening competence. It can therefore be held that at least with reference to nineteenth-century programme music, the emphasis on musical description can also be explained with reference not only to the wishes of the less competent listeners but also to those of the *connoisseurs*. For to them it may have been not so much the wish to get an easier access to music but rather the impression that traditional musical genres such as the symphony and the concerto with its eternal sonata forms, tri-partite lied patterns or rondos had to a certain extent been exhausted. This may have increased the desire for something new. In this context the development towards programmatically descriptive music must have appeared as a welcome and aesthetically satisfying alternative.

Another cultural factor one may think of in order to account for the acceptability of descriptive music with the 'highbrow' culture, in particular in the historical situation of the aftermath of Romanticism, is the influential Romantic ideal of a 'poeticized' music, since it can more easily be connected with the descriptive in music than the rivalling ideal of 'absolute music'. Yet Dahlhaus (see *Die Idee der absoluten Musik* 128 f.) has pointed out with reference to nineteenth-century programme music that the Romantic aesthetic of the poetic in music does not simply equal any kind of 'literarization' of music, for the poetic in Romantic terms privileges the 'marvellous' and in that regard only descriptions of such subjects would fall into the realm of Romantic influence. However, in another publication Dahlhaus (see *Musikästhetik* 89-94) provides an interesting alternative solution. He convincingly argues that as late as in the mid-nineteenth century the old privileging of vocal music over instrumental music persisted (even though, one should add, instrumental music had attained a hitherto unequalled popularity). In addition, the educated middle class, which provided the core of nineteenth-century musical amateurs, was largely literature-oriented; Dahlhaus even speaks of a cultural 'predominance of literature' ("Vorherrschaft der Literatur" [93]). In this context, the 'literarization' of programme music, including the employment of description in music, could (as was the fact with Franz Liszt) function not only as a means of meeting the audience's taste and enculturation in this respect[33] but also as a means of nobilitating instrumental music through placing it in the vicinity of noble 'poesy' ("ein Mittel, die Würde der Instrumentalmusik – den Anspruch, 'Kultur' und nicht bloß [...] 'Genuß' zu sein – zu fundieren" [ibid.][34]).

Be that as it may, the fact remains that descriptive music presented an alternative to 'absolute' music that had – and has – an amazing appeal and produced an equally remarkable body of compositions[35]. Over and above historical considerations this at least testifies to an important theoretical fact: namely that description is indeed a transmedial phenomenon in which both words and music participate, albeit in different ways and to different degrees. Music's potential in this respect even seems to be greater than its narrative potential, since the descriptive, in order to be discernible as a hetero-referential gesture in music, requires less complex features than narrative. This is possibly the reason why musical description has occurred more frequently, at least in isolated elements, throughout history[36] than musical narrativity. It even continues to thrive in contemporary film music so that the descriptive in music appears as a critical subject which will

---

[33] See also, with reference to the symphonic poem, Altenburg, "Symphonische Dichtung" 157.

[34] "[...] a means of giving a basis to the nobility of instrumental music, to the claim that it is 'culture' and not [...] merely 'pleasurable entertainment'." (My translation)

[35] An idea of the extent to which description has in fact been employed can be derived from Schneider's *Lexikon Programmusik: Stoffe und Motive*, even though not all of his collection of hetero-referential musical subjects and motives in programme music is relevant to musical description in the sense used in this essay.

[36] For the history and pre-history of 'programme music' see Altenburg, "Programmusik" 1833-1843, and Scruton 397-399; for the history of the sub-genre of the symphonic poem see in addition Altenburg, "Symphonische Dichtung" 160-167. It should, however, be noted that 'programme music' is not co-extensive with musical description. Altenburg even goes so far as to claim that *Tonmalerei* – the most important device of descriptive musical hetero-referentiality, is not a necessary part of programme music ("Programmusik" 1827).

require further attention both from a theoretical and a historical perspective.

References

Abbate, Carolyn (1991). *Unsung Voices: Opera and Musical Narrative in the Nineteenth Century*. Princeton, NJ: Princeton Univ. Press.

Altenburg, Detlef (1997). "Programmusik". Ludwig Finscher, ed. *Die Musik in Geschichte und Gegenwart*. Second ed. Kassel/Stuttgart: Bärenreiter/Metzler. Vol. 7. 1821-1844.

— (1998). "Symphonische Dichtung". Ludwig Finscher, ed. *Die Musik in Geschichte und Gegenwart*. Second ed. Kassel, Stuttgart: Bärenreiter, Metzler. Vol. 9. 153-168.

Bal, Mieke (1980). "Descriptions: Etude du discours descriptif dans le texte narratif". *Lalies*. Actes des sessions de linguistique et de littérature 1. Paris: Presses de l'Ecole Normale Supérieure. 99-129.

— (1980/1985). *De theorie van vertellen en verhalen/Narratology: Introduction to the Theory of Narrative*. Transl. Christine van Boheemen. Toronto: Univ. of Toronto Press.

— (1981/1982). "On Meanings and Descriptions". *Studies in Twentieth-Century Literature* 6:1-2: 100-147.

Barthes, Roland (1968). "L'Effet de réel". *Communications* 11 : 84-89.

Brenet, Michel (1911). "Essai sur les origines de la musique descriptive". Michel Brenet. *Musique et musiciens de la vieille France*. Paris: F. Alcan. 83-197.

Dahlhaus, Carl (1976). *Musikästhetik*. Musik-Taschen-Bücher: Theoretica 8. Cologne: Hans Gerig.

— (1978). *Die Idee der absoluten Musik*. Kassel/Munich: Bärenreiter, dtv.

— (1979). "Musik als Text". Günter Schnitzler, ed. *Dichtung und Musik: Kaleidoskop ihrer Beziehungen*. Stuttgart: Klett. 11-28.

— (2002) "Absolute Musik". Sabine Ehrmann-Herfort, Ludwig Finscher, Giselher Schubert, eds. *Europäische Musikgeschichte*. Vol. 2. Kassel, Stuttgart: Bärenreiter, Metzler. 679-704.

Fischer, Olga, Max Nänny (1999). "Introduction: Iconicity as a Creative Force in Language Use". Max Nänny, Olga Fischer, eds. *Form

Miming Meaning: Iconicity in Language and Literature. Amsterdam: John Benjamins. xv-xxxvi.
Georis, Christophe (2005). "Iconic Strategies in Monteverdi's *Madrigali guerrieri ed amorosi*". Costantino Maeder, Olga Fischer, William J. Herlofsky, eds. *Outside-In – Inside-Out. Iconicity in Language and Literature* 4. Amsterdam: John Benjamins. 217-237.
Hamon, Philippe (1972). "Qu'est-ce qu'une description?". *Poétique* 9: 465-485.
Jakobson, Roman (1960). "Closing Statement: Linguistics and Poetics". Thomas A. Sebeok, ed. *Style in Language*. Cambridge, MA: M. I. T. Press. 350-377.
Kaden, Christian, Jan Brachmann, Detlef Giese (1998). "Zeichen". Ludwig Finscher, ed. *Die Musik in Geschichte und Gegenwart*. Second ed. Kassel, Stuttgart: Bärenreiter, Metzler. Vol. 9. 2149-2220.
Kittay, Jeffrey (1981). "Descriptive Limits". *Yale French Studies* 61: 225-243.
Kleeman, Janice E. (1985). "The Parameters of Musical Transmission". *The Journal of Musicology* 4: 1-22.
Kloiber, Rudolf (1964). *Handbuch der klassischen und romantischen Symphonie*. Wiesbaden: Breitkopf & Härtel.
— (1967). *Handbuch der symphonischen Dichtung*. Wiesbaden: Breitkopf & Härtel.
Kramer, Lawrence (1991). "Musical Narratology: A Theoretical Outline". *Indiana Theory Review* 12: 141-162.
Krause, Ernst (1963/1979). *Richard Strauss: Der letzte Romantiker*. Munich: Heyne.
Lessing, Gotthold Ephraim (1766/1974). *Laokoon oder Über die Grenzen der Malerei und Poesie*. Gotthold Ephraim Lessing. *Werke*. Ed. Herbert G. Göpfert. Vol. 6: *Kunsttheoretische und kunsthistorische Schriften*. Ed. Albert v. Schirnding. Munich: Hanser. 7-187.
Macdonald, Hugh (2001). "Symphonic Poem". Stanley Sadie, John Tyrrell, eds. *The New Grove Dictionary of Music*. London: Macmillan. Vol. 24. 802-807.
McClary, Susan (1997). "The Impromptu That Trod on a Loaf: or How Music Tells Stories". *Narrative* 5: 20-35.

Maus, Fred Everett (1991). "Music as Narrative". *Indiana Theory Review* 12: 1-34.
— (2005). "Classical Instrumental Music and Narrative". James Phelan, Peter J. Rabinowitz, eds. *A Companion to Narrative Theory*. Blackwell Companions to Literature and Culture 33. Malden, MA: Blackwell. 466-483.
Micznik, Vera (2001). "Music and Narrative Revisited: Degrees of Narrativity in Beethoven and Mahler". *Journal of the Royal Musical Association* 126 : 193-249.
Nattiez, Jean-Jacques (1987/1990). *Musicologie générale et sémiologie*. Paris: Christian Bourgeois. *Music and Discourse: Toward a Semiology of Music*. Transl. Carolyn Abbate. Princeton, NJ: Princeton Univ. Press.
— (1990). "Can One Speak of Narrativity in Music?". *Journal of the Royal Musical Association* 115: 240-257.
Neubauer, John (1997). "Tales of Hoffmann and Others on Narrativizations of Instrumental Music". Ulla-Britta Lagerroth, Hans Lund, Erik Hedling, eds. *Interart Poetics: Essays on the Interrelations of the Arts and Media*. Internationale Forschungen zur Allgemeinen und Vergleichenden Literaturwissenschaft 24. Amsterdam: Rodopi. 117-136.
Newcomb, Anthony (1987). "Schumann and Late Eighteenth-Century Narrative Strategies". *Nineteenth-Century Music* 11: 164-174.
Nünning, Ansgar (2007). "Towards a Typology, Poetics and History of Description in Fiction". Wolf/Bernhart, eds. 91-128.
Pflugmacher, Torsten (2005). "Description". David Herman, Manfred Jahn, Marie-Laure Ryan, eds. *Routledge Encyclopedia of Narrative Theory*. London: Routledge. 101-102.
Riffaterre, Michael (1981). "Descriptive Imagery". *Yale French Studies* 61: 107-125.
— (1986). "On the Diegetic Functions of the Descriptive". *Style* 20/3: 281-294.
Ronen, Ruth (1997). "Description, Narrative and Representation". *Narrative* 5/3: 274-286.
Schneider, Klaus (1999). *Lexikon Programmusik: Stoffe und Motive*. Kassel: Bärenreiter.
Schweitzer, Albert (1908/1972). *J. S. Bach*. Wiesbaden: Breitkopf & Härtel.

Scruton, Roger (2001). "Programme Music". Stanely Sadie, John Tyrrell, eds. *The New Grove Dictionary of Music*. London: Macmillan. Vol. 20. 396-400.

Seaton, Douglass (2005). "Narrative in Music: The Case of Beethoven's 'Tempest Sonata'". Jan Christoph Meister, ed. *Narratology Beyond Literary Criticism: Mediality, Disciplinarity*. Narratologia 6. Berlin: De Gruyter. 65-81.

Shelley, Mary (1818/1968). *Frankenstein*. Peter Fairclough, ed. *Three Gothic Novels: The Castle of Otranto, Vathek, Frankenstein*. Harmondsworth: Penguin. 257-497.

Sternberg, Meir (1981). "Ordering the Unordered: Time, Space, and Descriptive Coherence". *Yale French Studies* 61: 60-88.

Walter, Michael (2000). "Don Juan und die Moderne". Michael Walter. *Richard Strauss und seine Zeit*. Große Komponisten und ihre Zeit. Laaber: Laaber. 119-157.

Walton, Kendall L. (1990). *Mimesis as Make-Believe: On the Foundation of the Representational Arts*. Cambridge, MA: Harvard Univ. Press.

Wolf, Werner (1993). *Ästhetische Illusion und Illusionsdurchbrechung in der Erzählkunst: Theorie und Geschichte mit Schwerpunkt auf englischem illusionsstörenden Erzählen*. Buchreihe der Anglia 32. Tübingen: Niemeyer.

— (1999). *The Musicalization of Fiction: A Study in the Theory and History of Intermediality*. Internationale Forschungen zur Allgemeinen und Vergleichenden Literaturwissenschaft 35. Amsterdam: Rodopi.

— (2002a). "Intermediality Revisited: Reflections on Word and Music Relations in the Context of a General Typology of Intermediality". Suzanne M. Lodato, Suzanne Aspden, Walter Bernhart, eds. *Word and Music Studies: Essays in Honor of Steven Paul Scher and on Cultural Identity and the Musical Stage*. Word and Music Studies 4. Amsterdam: Rodopi. 13-34.

— (2002b). "Das Problem der Narrativität in Literatur, bildender Kunst und Musik: Ein Beitrag zu einer intermedialen Erzähltheorie". Ansgar and Vera Nünning, eds. *Erzähltheorie transgenerisch, intermedial, interdisziplinär*. WVT-Handbücher zum literaturwissenschaftlichen Studium 5. Trier: WVT. 23-104.

— (2004). "Aesthetic Illusion as an Effect of Fiction". *Style* 48/3: 325-351.

— (2007). "Description as a Transmedial Mode of Representation: General Features and Possibilities of Realization in Painting, Fiction and Music". Wolf/Bernhart, eds. 1-87.
—, Walter Bernhart, eds. (2007). *Description in Literature and Other Media*. Studies in Intermediality 2. Amsterdam: Rodopi.

Whose Classical Music?
Reflections on Film Adaptation

Lawrence Kramer, New York, NY

When adapted for use in commercial cinema, classical music may be thought to convey one set of meanings to aficionados and another to a general audience not familiar with the music or its genres. Drawing on an unlikely source, a theoretical essay in art history written during the 1920s by Erwin Panofsky, this essay suggests that such a duality is only apparent, even at the level of fine musical detail. 'Expert' and 'inexpert' accounts of the use of a Chopin Prelude in the film romance *The Notebook* exemplify the point. The accounts do differ importantly, but they draw together through their interpretive relationship to the film's verbal and narrative environment.

Two seemingly unrelated things caught my attention as I mulled over the topic of this essay. They were a fragment of Chopin in a just-released Hollywood romance and a densely argued patch of German art-historical theorizing from the 1920s. By some strange catalytic logic, the two did form a relationship for me – even, I would like to think, a revealing one. You be the judge.

My own interest is in music, not art history, and it has lately seemed important to me to think about how the use of preexisting music in film, especially classical music, helps shape cinematic meaning. Watching Nick Cassavetes' appealing if unabashedly sentimental film *The Notebook* (2004), I was struck – predictably enough, my friends would say – by its insertion of two incomplete performances of Chopin's Prelude in E minor at important turning points in the narrative. The romantic melancholy of the music made its appropriateness self-explanatory, but I still wanted to ask some questions. Why Chopin? Why *this* Chopin? Why use Chopin at all in a film that is not only endowed with a lush romantic score of its own but also draws generously on the popular music of the era, ca. 1939-1946, in which part of its story is set?

The largesse includes signature swing pieces by Duke Ellington, Glenn Miller, and Benny Goodman, as well as renditions of the haunting ballad "I'll Be Seeing You" by both Billie Holiday and Jimmy

Durante[1]. The Chopin is certainly a nonpareil in this company. It has no place on the soundtrack CD, which, like the film, is deeply imbued by greatest-generation nostalgia, no doubt as a balm for troubled times. The '40s sound is a well-worn vehicle for that nostalgia, which the Chopin does not share, though for many listeners today the one must be just as esoteric as the other. The nostalgia in the E-minor Prelude is of a different sort, if nostalgia it is. But this difference makes the piece stand out all the more, as befits its possession of a narrative role that the rest of the film's music lacks. How do we understand that role? And who are 'we', exactly?

It was a matter of some bemusement to me that, with these questions rattling around in my mind, I found myself reading an essay by the German art historian Erwin Panofsky (1892-1968) with mounting interest. Panofsky was one of the founders of the modern discipline of art history. In 1927, after publishing a study on the chronology of the master builders of the cathedral of Rheims, he wrote a short theoretical essay, "Reflections on Historical Time" [*Zum Problem der historischen Zeit*], as an epilogue. The latest issue of the journal *Critical Inquiry*, which had just come in the mail, carried a translation, apparently the first, as its lead article. One of the questions Panofsky raises is the very one illustrated by the juxtaposition of his article with Cassavetes' film. How does a seeming lack of relationship become the substance of relationship itself? The question is also the one raised by the use of Chopin in *The Notebook*, and indeed by the use of classical music in most films that use it. Perhaps for this reason, it gradually dawned on me that Panofsky's art-historical remarks could help frame an answer in film-theoretical terms. Before asking how, though, we need to pose the question more fully.

It's a question that takes on a special edge today, as classical music continues to be used in many films despite the widespread sense that it has suffered a decline in cultural authority, especially in the United States. But even at the height of its prestige for the American middle class, classical music in film could not have been concretely recognized by most members of a film audience. The audience in general

---

[1] "I'll Be Seeing You", music by Sammy Fain, lyrics by Irving Kahal, was written in 1938 but became inextricably associated with the World War II era through its expression of longing for someone absent – perhaps distant, perhaps parted, perhaps dead. It can be sung by either a man or a woman with no change in the text.

would not have been able to integrate the visual and narrative dimensions of the film with the lore surrounding the music.

Of course there are 'art films' that do expect a certain degree of high-cultural literacy from viewers. Fritz Lang surely counted on the audience for *M* (1931) to recognize the tune whistled by his murderer-protagonist as Grieg's "In the Hall of the Mountain King"; the music deals with trolls. And when Ingmar Bergman in *Hour of the Wolf* (1966) shows an excerpt from Mozart's *The Magic Flute* for marionette theater, complete with a critical interpretation from the puppet master, he is obviously assuming that his audience both knows and loves the opera and will recognize unhappily that it is being subverted and corrupted. There are also films that take an ambiguous stance toward the value of musical knowledge. In Roman Polanski's Holocaust narrative *The Pianist* (2002), performances of Chopin in particular (him, again) both create a frame structure and mark several key turning points, but the music involved is never named. Its identity is either assumed or assumed to have unraveled; it's hard to say which[2]. For the most part, though, mass-audience films that use classical music are like *The Notebook*. They come trailing an esoteric musical subtext, perhaps unappreciated even by the filmmakers, which audiences should safely be able to ignore while still being appropriately affected by the music.

But in what sense, one might ask, does such a subtext even 'belong' to the film? And even supposing one could define that sense, available only to a clued-in minority, how does one account for the *other* sense that the music is clearly meant to have for the audience at large? How can the two senses be teased apart? What should we suppose the music to be doing? What effects should we surmise it to produce?

The easy answer would be that there is no need to work so hard. The esoteric subtext does not matter and the general effects are not mysterious. Either the music is a simple mood-enhancer, in which case its specific qualities are not important, or it is a contingent feature of the narrative, in which case its meaning is simply its narrative function. But this no-nonsense answer is obviously inadequate. The

---

[2] On the role of music in this film, which is exceptionally complex, see my "Melodic Trains: Music in Polanski's *The Pianist*" and Michel Chion, "'Mute Music' in Three Films".

first alternative ignores the cultural contexts and intertexts that influence even the unreflective choice of music just because it sounds right or has the right aura. Music sounds right for a reason. The second alternative assumes that meaning can be strictly confined by the very conjunction of music, narrative, and the moving image which releases it. That simply does not happen. Once the music attracts attention – something especially likely with classical music, which tends to stand out from its dramatic and cinematic settings – the question of meaning will be in the air. As both Nicholas Cook and I have argued in different ways, music under these circumstances will snatch up meanings from every side. The reduction of musical meaning to narrative function not only doesn't happen; it virtually can't happen. (Cf. Cook 20-23; Kramer, *Musical Meaning* 148-155)

All right then: what does happen? This is where Panofsky comes in.

Addressing the question of dating with reference to style, Panofsky takes a side glance at the 'argument' between connoisseurs and art historians: that is, between those with intuitive and those with explicit knowledge, in effect between amateurs and experts. In a long footnote, he suggests that the argument is based on false premises. Neither group can claim an authority that the other lacks. It may not even be possible to distinguish the two groups as clearly as either would like:

> Judgments based on connoisseurship and art historical knowledge [*Kunstwissenschaft*] are neither mutually exclusive nor complementary, but rather represent the twofold aspect of the same thing. For when an art historian explicates what the connoisseur diagnoses, the artistic diagnosis is itself connected to the possibility of art historical proof because although the diagnosis has come into being in the realm of subjective intuition, it nevertheless makes a claim to the complete context of objective validity. Just as it lies in the essence of art historical analysis to be potentially contained in the judgment of the connoisseur, so too it lies in the essence of the judgment of the connoisseur to be transformed into art historical analysis. (Panofsky 696n.)

The judgments of the connoisseur and the art historian represent the twofold aspect of the same thing because each can derive knowledge only by operating within a small number of pertinent 'frames of reference' from an endlessly proliferating, 'polychromatic' network of them. Whether the operation is intuitive or explicit is a matter of method, not of substance.

Film audiences presented with classical music are asked, in effect, to renegotiate the terrain of Panofsky's 'argument'. In most situations, a few members of the audience will have deep musical knowledge; they will recognize what they hear, by composer or era if not by work, and apply their knowledge to the cinematic moment. In other contexts one might call such people connoisseurs, but here they are the equivalent of Panofsky's art historians: the experts. The connoisseurs, despite the literal meaning of the term, are actually the many members of the audience who lack such knowledge, and who thus respond to the music in purely intuitive terms.

Panofsky's thesis is that this difference in the respondents should not lead to a radical difference in their responses. On the contrary, the responses should be convertible to each other. In the case of the first Chopin extract in *The Notebook*, both groups will presumably recognize that the music is full of melancholy longing, that it is played on an out-of-tune piano, and that its performance is incomplete. The experts, additionally (this is what I did), might start thinking about the relationship between the broad, simple, right-hand melody with its cantabile (that is, songlike) phrases, and the pulsating, harmonically complex, highly pianistic accompaniment, and other things besides, as well – of course – as mentally exclaiming 'Chopin!'. The exclamation is satisfying, and those who make it obviously hear more than those who don't. It is not obvious, though, whether 'more' here means 'more to the point' or 'more of the same' or somehow both at once.

Is Panofsky right that the seeming lack of connection produced by the knowledge gap in the 'connoisseur's' response is only illusory? Or better, what hermeneutic protocols can we bring into play here to perform the equivalence that Panofsky's argument postulates?

To answer we need to look more closely at the film – one that is useful not because *The Notebook* is anything more than an attractive and effective tearjerker, but because it is not. It does nothing out of the ordinary, and for that reason allows us to anatomize ordinary practice with some degree of confidence.

The Notebook tells parallel love stories, one set during the '40s, one in the present, with the twist – hardly a surprise, but only gradually admitted by the narrative – that the protagonists of both stories are the same, in youth and old age. The older couple has been divided by Alzheimer's disease, which has wiped out the identity of the woman, Allie Calhoun (Gena Rowlands). Her husband Noah (James Garner), whom she does not recognize, hopes to restore her memory of their life together, if only for five minutes at a time, with the help of the titular notebook. He reads her the narrative of their early love, its seven-year interruption, and its eventual consummation under the pretense that the story is about two other people. His hope, eventually realized, is that her purely narrative identifications with the characters of the story will evolve into a realization of the truth: that, in this case, identification is identity.

The first seven or eight measures of the Chopin E-minor Prelude are played during a pivotal scene in each of the parallel narratives. In each case the music both voices a desire and laments the thwarting of that desire, which follows at or near the end of the scene. But the significance of these expressive actions changes greatly from one narrative to the other. Following Hollywood convention, the later appearance of the music forms a kind of memory-prosthesis recalling the scene of the earlier, but the effect here is complicated by the role of memory itself in the narratives.

Any interpretation of the music's role would accordingly have to look at it twice. I propose to look at it four times, considering each scene from the standpoint of both intuitive and expert response. The expert response I will presume to provide; the intuitive one I will presume to hypothesize. But it should surprise no one that one result of the exercise will eventually be to blur the boundaries between these modes of response, even as the meanings they produce turn out to change somewhat as one register of understanding is converted to – or better, to use a musical metaphor, transcribed in – the register of the other.

The first scene is set in a ruined house that Noah plans one day to restore. The young Noah and Allie (Ryan Gosling and Rachel McAdams) have gone there on the eve of their separation. Their romance has filled the summer after high school. Allie, a child of privilege, is about to go to college in New York; Noah, a mill worker, will remain in the small Georgia town where the story starts. The couple decides to make love for the first time, but both parties are nervous about it. Allie drifts over to the ruined piano left in the room and begins to play the Chopin. Noah listens and follows the sound. He stands behind her, listens a moment longer, then embraces her, which brings the music to a stop. The gesture turns out to be premonitory; an intrusion soon nips the lovemaking in the bud and the couple is summoned to Allie's home for a reprimand. The would-be lovers end up parting after a bitter quarrel.

A likely beginning for intuitive response to the music in this scene is the familiar Hollywood convention that classical music is emotionally suspect. Its beauty is frigid and betokens a detachment from the urgencies of real life, even a hostility to life – just ask Hannibal Lecter why he likes Bach. Allie's playing would thus mark an anxious retreat from passion and an unwillingness to intensify feelings that separation will make unbearable precisely in proportion to their intensity. The music confesses as much by being tinny, so out of tune it is a ruin of itself; its ideal form may be full of ardor and poignancy, but that is precisely the form the moment cannot produce. When Noah's touch interrupts the performance – he envelops Allie's arms, making it next to impossible for her to go on playing – the claims of romantic passion become too urgent to refuse. In yielding to them, she starts to overcome a certain over-refinement in herself, something that has been established as part of her character, that reflects her upper-class background, and that subtly denigrates her playing as an example of the shallow feminine 'accomplishment' expected in high society.

But all this is just too simple. If anything, the scene invokes the hoary convention about classical music only to turn it on its head. Noah, in particular, is clearly moved by what he hears; he feels all the longing and the melancholy that the music expresses. His embrace of Allie is less an interruption of the music than an embodiment of it, an attempt to make its emotional meanings real. The tinny sound may prefigure his failure for the moment, but it also establishes the presence of an ideal that may (and will) be realized later on. The ideal music is a figure for ideal love. In this context the refinement associated with the music becomes less a social than a moral value. It confers the distinction of the classic on the young couple and positions them in the archive of legendary romance. In a film devoted to the power of memory, the music establishes the story of Noah and Allie as a romance worth remembering.

What can the expert ear add to these meanings, these effects? At one level, it can do little more than embellish them, sophisticate them a little, a limitation that would support a weak form of Panofsky's claim about the reciprocity of expert and amateur knowledge. Someone who recognizes the Prelude and knows something about its composer might connect the music to the romance between Chopin and George Sand, and the famous trip to Majorca that the couple took early in their relationship. This is the trip on which at least some of the Preludes, including the E-minor, were composed: an idyll that failed, as its counterpart in the film does, and one from which letters and memoirs record Chopin's struggle with a bad piano and broken-down housing[3]. Someone familiar with the Prelude will also be able to hear its true sonority in the mind's ear by listening not to, but through, the sound of the out-of-tune piano. The musical and romantic ideals that the scene intimates but cannot realize may support themselves on this phantom perception, which is in the first instance an act of memory, the faculty that the film idealizes as redemptive. It will later turn out that the music has virtually become this act of memory in material form.

But the expert can also add something more. Someone who connects the expressive content of the Prelude with its musical details may find still wider resonances between the music and the film. Expert listening may discover topics and insights not available to intuition alone and yet not inconsistent with it. When that happens, the results support a strong form of Panofsky's thesis. Embellishment passes over into expansion in any or all of several forms: development, revision, transformation, even deconstruction.

The melody of the Prelude (see *Example 1*) is simplicity itself. Most of it consists of falling two-note figures, upbeat to downbeat, shorter to longer, forming a broad sigh that may span different intervals but never changes its shape or its octave or its voicing. But the harmony is tortured. It pulses or throbs with dissonant chords that change continually while their motion, eight eighth notes to the measure, remains unbroken except for a brief interruption in the middle (not heard in the film) and a pause before the end. The disparity between melody and harmony suggests a split between voice and body, constraint and impulse, head and heart, romance and desire. However one interprets it – and all the suggestions fit the film – the disparity comes alive with special force at the downbeats, each of which tries and fails to stabilize the long note of the melody by harmonizing it properly. The process begins in the very first measure, which manages only an unsteady consonance, the tonic in first inversion with the keynote in a middle voice. And that is as good as it gets. Most of the other downbeats are simply dissonant. The contrary

---

[3] For the details see Higgins 3-8, 94-95.

forces are never reconciled. Their ultimate outcome is yet another dissonance, or perhaps the bemused pause that follows it, to be followed in turn by a perfunctory closing cadence. We don't hear this close, though the expert ear knows it is coming, but we do hear the play of forces that makes it inevitable.

Example 1: Frédéric Chopin, Prelude in E-Minor, *Op. 28, No. 4*

The music of the Prelude may at one level suggest a love that is not yet ready to transcend the opposition of circumstance, but at a deeper level the obstacle is more metaphysical than circumstantial. The failure of harmony and melody to mesh at any point, combined with the poignant beauty of their combination, suggests that what is really at stake is the failure of any love, even the most rapturous, to become transcendent. There will always be a fatality to jar it, a conclusion on which the entire plot of the film depends.

The harmony in particular supports this impression. From measures 2 through 8, there are no functional chords at all, only a series of dissonant combinations anchored here and there by diminished-seventh chords. The music in the film goes no further than this. Afterwards, as those familiar with the Prelude will know, a long-awaited if less than robust dominant leads to a reprise of the beginning, at which point the harmonic wandering begins all over again. The wandering instills the narrative with the form of Romantic longing, a desire that by definition cannot be fulfilled in the way it seeks to be, but that must be followed regardless, because not to do so is to forgo the possibility of any fulfillment at all.

As heard in the first scene, then, to an ear that knows it, the music embodies a love that wants to go for broke but does not yet know how, and whose partners have no inkling of what going for broke will demand of them. Perhaps the true phantom protagonists here are not Chopin and Sand (who ended badly, and with no mitigations) but those more rigorous experts at forgetting and remembering, Tristan and Isolde. The end of the film, in which the elder Noah and Allie seize on one of the latter's lucid spells and simply will themselves to die a simultaneous death, suggests as much, as if the latter-day narrative of the film were seeking to imagine the unimaginable old age of the ultimate romantic couple. The camera contributes by executing a rapid zoom away from the couple's bodies, soaring aloft (and into the viewer's gaze) like one of the birds that form a recurring image throughout the film.

The Prelude's second scene occurs in the office of Noah's cardiologist. Allie, in an echo of the narrative situation, is there only by virtue of the music. She is playing the piano in a nearby room of the hospital where both she and Noah are being treated. As the doctor and patient consult, the sounds of a Mozart sonata drift faintly across their conversation. Noah explains that Allie can still play from score;

someone must have left the music open on the piano. When the music stops abruptly, he adds ruefully that whoever it was must have forgotten to turn the page. A moment afterwards, however, the music begins again, this time more clearly. And this time it is the Chopin Prelude. The doctor remarks that someone must have turned the page, after all, but Noah demurs. "*That*," he says, "she's playing from memory."

The sentence is obviously more than a simple description. The presence of musical memory coincides, or so Noah wants to claim against all odds, with the presence of narrative memory. In playing the Prelude, Allie is recalling one of the two or three cardinal moments in the couple's romantic life, even if she does not know it – or, more exactly, even if the musical performance is still her only means of knowing it. In this context, the music changes its meaning to meet the fatality that it had earlier anticipated.

Its first occurrence evoked the ills that haunt all love; its second evokes a love that defies all ills. Most listeners will probably hear this reversal in the shift from the out-of-tune piano to a tuned instrument. Those who do will find other associations falling into place. The eventual reunion of the young lovers occurs in the ruined house after Noah has restored it. In this idyll the Prelude has no part. The music will not return until that successful idyll has become only a memory, and only in Noah's memory. The role of the Prelude is to supplement absence, not adorn presence. When the idyll is not yet found, the supplement is longing; when the idyll has been lost, the supplement is memory, in a form that partly restores what it recalls. Only partly: the sound of the tuned piano is still slightly distanced. It comes from another room, another place. But it does come.

These connections will deepen if one notices that the extract played in both scenes is the same, and more particularly that it stops at or near the same point. An expert ear conduces to this recognition, but is certainly not required for it. The identity between the extracts suggests the indestructibility of the memory that has as it were been deposited for safekeeping in both the notebook's narrative and in the music that now emerges as the epitome of that narrative. The music has become a microcosm of the whole film, a symbolic form on which the larger narrative depends to complete its own trajectory.

To all this the expert listener can again add something more – and this time, something problematic. A listener who knows the E-Minor

Prelude knows not only what is played in the film, but also what is not played. The one may be no less important than the other. In this case, the omission comes close to being an evasion, even a repression of sorts.

The Prelude's recalcitrance about proper harmony eventually makes its melody balk. The music is so insistent that the rupture feels inevitable. At about midpoint, the right hand breaks with its plaintive melodic pattern and wrenches the harmony onto the dominant (from the last beat of m. 8 through m. 12), whereupon the first brief interruption of the chordal throbbing occurs. When this proves futile – the music, as indicated earlier, just starts over, with its harmony no less wayward than before, perhaps more so – the right hand loses all patience. It takes only three measures for this to happen. At that point (mm. 16-17) the melody changes shape and register and tempo with shocking vehemence, even violence, in an effort to draw the dominant after it. As the outburst ebbs away, the effort seems to have worked – but not for long. The fading melody resumes its original shape but not its original pitch; the dominant continues to slip from its grasp until the whole passage finally subsides in confusion. The alien chord on which it halts and the long ensuing silence form an unbreakable impasse, in a sense the true conclusion of the piece. The rest is pro forma. Nothing is left but the tacked-on closing cadence, which is tantamount to a confession of failure[4].

The disruptive interlude of mm. 16-17 is an act of transvaluation. It affirms exactly what the film denies, the agitation, the indignation, the white-knuckled rage that the injustices of fate inspire. The interlude's pallid aftermath suggests possibilities of futility and resignation that the romantic mythology of the film labors to disallow. *The Notebook* seems to connect a romantic faith in transcendent outcomes with the absence of the anger and resentment that would be heard if the music were allowed to continue. The first narrative admits these

---

[4] The hanging dissonance may tempt the expert to rationalize it, but the wise expert will resist, at least for awhile. Chopin treats the chord as if it were a familiar type known as a German sixth, but he neither spells it nor spaces it accordingly. These details are not unique; their meaning depends on their context, which in this case is amply suggestive. The long ensuing pause beckons the player or listener to savor the dissonant sonority for its mystery before assigning it its inevitable identity. The subsequent move to the cadence dramatizes the rationale ('Why, it's a German sixth') as a rationalization.

traits in the younger Noah during his separation from Allie, but the second narrative conjures them away from the elder, who behaves with infinite patience, with never a murmur of protest. The omission is especially marked in the second Prelude scene, where it holds the key to the film's later resolution in a quiet *Liebestod*. The music as we hear it stops on the threshold of the very depth of feeling needed to validate the love story.

At this point, with Panofsky's thesis in mind, we might seem ready to answer the question in my title. Whose classical music? Anyone's. Everyone's. The expert and the intuitive listener follow somewhat different paths onto a common ground. They may not find it or see it in just the same way, but both will recognize the place. So far, so good. Yet there are one or two questions left over.

As intimated earlier, the interplay of intuitive and expert knowledge is not confined to high-art music. This is a point that needs to be reckoned with. At one level what we're dealing with is not something specific to one type of music or even to music at all, but something broadly intertextual. The music, any music, comes trailing a variety of associated meanings, a rich body of lore. The semantic enrichment fostered by the music grows in proportion to knowledge of the lore.

Take "I'll Be Seeing You", the prime example here because *The Notebook* uses it leitmotivically, in paired performances, just as it does the Chopin Prelude. The lyrics foretell the singer's imaginary glimpses of a lost or absent beloved in the "old familiar places" where their romance developed. The words have a gently ironic bearing on the film's narrative, and the music envelops this relationship of song and story with an aura of mixed longing and resignation. The performers involved also have a role to play. Someone who knows Billie Holiday's voice may associate its deterioration in later life with the deterioration of Allie's memory[5]. Someone who knows Jimmy

---

[5] Someone else might ask why Billie Holiday's free-floating voice is the only real black presence in the first narrative, which is set in a segregated world that is never acknowledged as such – except by the appropriation of that one voice. The topic is tangential to my discussion, but should at least be mentioned. The second narrative introduces several black characters as hospital staff, but does nothing beyond bringing them on screen to mark the difference of past and present.

On a separate track, it might be suggested that prerecorded non-diegetic singing, especially if 'historical', hovers somewhere between underscore and the sourceless speech that Michel Chion famously calls 'acousmatic'. Such singing circulates

Durante's once-famous sign-off line, "Good night, Mrs. Calabash, wherever you are", may link its melancholy with an ironic reversal that resonates in the second narrative, where absence means precisely *not* seeing you even if you are right there.

Such a viewer will encounter a different movie, yet not a radically different movie, than someone for whom the music is just, well, music, and who must be content with the expressive value of a husky, speech-inflected voice doing the singing in both renditions. The voice quality acknowledges the loss of connection by its distance from the smooth crooning that other performers might (and often did) bring to this song. The question for the viewer is how far this quality extends beyond its sensory and iconic values into the space of cultural memory.

This last observation points beyond a generalized intertextuality to something specific to music, and beyond that to something specific to classical music. As Roland Barthes famously maintained, all singing voices bear traces of a unique timbre, a 'grain' that derives from the materiality of the singer's body and that cannot wholly be smoothed away, though singers seeking beauty of tone often seek to transmute or minimize it[6]. Holiday and Durante certainly don't do that. Mobilizing traditional figures of sincerity and inexpressibility, they authenticate the feeling their singing expresses by showing that not all of it can be sublimated into song. The mood expressed by the music grows keener at the infusion of what the singers leave unmusical in their voices. We hear these voices rubbing against their own grain, becoming rather than being musical, and doing so with a willing imperfection. Music, or musicality, is the semantic resource here in a way that nothing else could be.

But the resource is limited in one respect. It is still only at the level of mood that the music functions. The communication, rich though it is, does not depend on the musical discourse, just on its emotive

---

through gaps in the nominal discourse, some of which it may open itself. On the acousmatic, see Chion's *The Voice in Cinema*.

[6] Cf. "The Grain of the Voice". Barthes limits the grain of the voice to art song, but his own criterion for its production, the encounter of language with music, of speech with song, extends its purview to both popular genres and opera. The latter, and some of the former, cultivate voice as an auratic object, an idealized or transcendentalized form of the vocal grain. To some extent, art song (as a genre) seeks to anonymize voice. But enough said; the topic deserves a separate study.

effect. The Chopin is not entirely different. Its emotive effect is indispensable to its role, and its lore, too, or Chopin's, is certainly at work. But the musical discourse of the Prelude is at work also, and *not* just for the expert. What we hear in it is process as well as expression, expression fused with process. Classical music fosters an awareness of this conjunction, this fusion, as part of its generic character, and so, in its role in the film, it acts in character. It invites a mode of listening that allows both amateur and expert, though not in exactly the same way, to trace the entire narrative of the film in musical microcosm. To listen in this way lets the music speak in its own voice as music, through which the narrative also speaks in a voice recognizably its own.

The expert may hear these voices with a richer set of perceptions and associations than the intuitive listener, and why not? It is neither condescending nor elitist to suggest that the knowledge involved may count for something. But the expert has no hold on an esoteric truth that eludes intuition. Any response must reckon with intuitive perceptions, the irreducible givens of the case, and although expert response may supplement those perceptions it cannot transcend them.

This is not, however, because of any pre-established harmony between intuition and knowledge, not the result of intuition playing the role of sensuous form and expert response the role of idea in a remake of one classic formula for the aesthetic. That might happen, no doubt; it does not have to; it doesn't in *The Notebook*. Rather, the intuitive resources of mood and sonority operate as checks against the speculative energy of expert knowledge which, nonetheless, may pry them apart to uncover unsuspected resonances. The two styles of attention have no fixed relationship, organic or otherwise. But they do share a workplace, sometimes crossing paths or overlapping, sometimes not. As Panofsky might have expected, expert and intuitive listeners hear differently, and hear different things, but because they must occupy that workspace and that workplace only, they are never out of earshot of each other.

It seems fair to conclude that expert listeners should feel free to let their knowledge resonate in films where music, classical and otherwise, has a compelling voice. They do not need to worry (well, not too much) about building a castle in the clouds while intuitive listeners remain happily down to earth. But the conclusion is no simple vindication of expert response. The expert and intuitive modes are not independent of one another. In most cases, the best insight will come when we keep both registers in play and trace the sometimes divergent paths of their mutual convertibility. The point is neither to 'upgrade' intuitive response by expert knowledge, nor to validate expert knowledge by a democratic appeal to intuitive response. The point, rather, is to recognize and participate in the dialogue – let's call it by its musical name, a duet – that music with a past, and classical music in particular, cues whenever it strikes up in a film.

References

Barthes, Roland (1985). "The Grain of the Voice" (1972). *The Responsibility of Forms: Critical Essays on Music, Art, and Representation*. Trans. Richard Howard. Berkeley, CA: University of California Press. 267-277.
Chion, Michel (1999). *The Voice in Cinema*. Trans. Claudia Gorbman. New York, NY: Columbia University Press.
— (2007). "'Mute Music' in Three Films". Goldmark/Kramer/Leppert, eds. 86-96.
Cook, Nicholas (1998). *Analyzing Musical Multimedia*. Oxford: Clarendon Press.
Goldmark, Daniel, Lawrence Kramer, Richard Leppert, eds. (2007). *Beyond the Soundtrack: Representing Music in Cinema*. Berkeley, CA: University of California Press.
Higgins, Thomas, ed. (1973). *Chopin: Preludes, Op. 28*. New York, NY: W. W. Norton.
Kramer, Lawrence (2002). *Musical Meaning: Toward a Critical History*. Berkeley, CA: University of California Press.
— (2007). "Melodic Trains: Music in Polanksi's The Pianist". Goldmark/Kramer/Leppert, eds. 66-85.
Panofsky, Erwin (2004). "Reflections on Historical Time" (1927). Trans. Johanna Baumann. *Critical Inquiry* 30/4: 691-701.

Notes on Contributors

Frédérique Arroyas is Associate Professor of French Studies in the School of Languages and Literature at the University of Guelph, Canada. Her research focuses on the intersections of music and literature in contemporary French fiction, the heuristic use of musical models and the mediation of musical meaning in literary works. Her publications include *La Lecture musico-littéraire* (Presses de l'université de Montréal, 2001) and several articles that span French literature, women's studies, musicology and interart studies. She is co-editor of the journal *Critical Studies in Improvisation/Études critiques en improvisation* and coordinator of the biennial Summer Institute for Critical Studies in Improvisation at the University of Guelph.

Walter Bernhart is Professor of English Literature at the University of Graz, Austria, chairman of the university's research and teaching unit "Literature and the Other Media", and founding and current president of the International Association for Word and Music Studies (WMA). His main research interests are intermedia studies, word and music studies, theory of lyric, and rhythm studies. His numerous publications include '*True Versifying'*: *Studien zur elisabethanischen Verspraxis und Kunstideologie* (Tübingen, 1993); "Iconicity and Beyond in 'Lullaby for Jumbo': Semiotic Functions of Poetic Rhythm" (1999); "The 'Destructiveness of Music': Functional Intermedia Disharmony in Popular Songs" (2002); "Narrative Framing in Schumann's Piano Pieces" (2005); "'Musikalische Verse': 'Ich weiß nicht, was soll es bedeuten'" (2006); "Myth-making Opera: David Malouf and Michael Berkeley's *Jane Eyre*" (2007). He is Executive Editor of two book series, Word and Music Studies (WMS) and Studies in Intermediality (SIM), and has (co)edited nine individual volumes.

Peter Dayan is Professor of Word and Music Studies at the University of Edinburgh. For the first fifteen years of his academic life, his research concentrated on the question of how nineteenth-century French authors construed the value of literature. The answers he found to that question always seemed to relate to music in a peculiarly constant way; his work on that relationship between the concept of music and the value of literature, and on its poststructuralist echoes, led to his book *Music Writing Literature, from Sand via Debussy to Derrida* (2006). He is now investigating how that 19th-century idea survived and developed during the first half of the 20th century, particularly in the work of Satie, Braque, and Ponge.

William P. Dougherty is Ellis and Nelle Professor of Music at Drake University in Des Moines, Iowa, where he teaches courses in Music Theory and Composition. He is currently writing a book on the settings of the Mignon songs. Also active as a composer, he has published compositions for orchestra, wind ensemble, brass band, and various chamber combinations.

Michael Halliwell studied literature and music in South Africa and completed his operatic studies at the London Opera Centre and with Tito Gobbi in Florence. He pursued a career in opera as principal baritone for the Netherlands Opera, the Nuremburg Opera, and the Hamburg State Opera, as well as giving guest performances in opera and recitals in many European countries. Since 1996, he has been Graduate Coordinator of Performance at the Sydney University Conservatorium of Music. He has been Chair of Vocal Studies and Opera, Pro-Dean and Head of School, and is currently Associate Dean of Research. He still performs regularly in operas, concert, radio and television and released a CD of vocal settings of Kipling's *Barrack-Room Ballads* in 2001. A CD of Boer War songs was released in 2005. He has lectured and published widely on music and literature, and his research specialty is operatic transformations of the novel. His study, *Opera and the Novel: The Case of Henry James*, was published in January 2005.

Lawrence Kramer is Professor of English and Music at Fordham University (New York, NY) and editor of the journal *19th-Century Music*. He is the author of numerous articles and nine books on the interrelations of music, literature, history and culture. Recent titles include *Why Classical Music Still Matters* (2007), *Opera and Modern Culture: Wagner and Strauss* (2004), *Musical Meaning: Toward a Critical History* (2001), and *Franz Schubert: Sexuality, Subjectivity,*

Song (1998). He is the editor of *Walt Whitman and Modern Music* (2000) and co-editor, with Daniel Goldmark and Richard Leppert, of *Beyond the Soundtrack: Representing Music in Cinema* (2007). An international conference, "Musical Meaning and Human Values: A Symposium with Lawrence Kramer", was held in his honor at Fordham University in May 2007. He is also a composer; performances of song cycles by him (including two premieres) occurred at both the Fordham conference and at the 2007 Edinburgh meeting of the WMA, the latter with the participation of WMA members Walter Bernhart, Suzanne Lodato, and Michael Halliwell.

Bernhard Kuhn is Assistant Professor of Italian Studies at Bucknell University. His current areas of research include Italian cinema, 20th century Italian culture, and intermediality, especially the relationship between opera and cinema. He is the author of *Die Oper im italienischen Film* (2005).

Ulla-Britta Lagerroth is Professor Emerita of Comparative Literature at Lund University, Sweden. Among her main areas of research is the interrelationship between the arts and media. She has published a book and numerous articles on "text and theatre", as well as essays dealing with aspects of "word and image" and of "word and music", and papers of hers have appeared in WMS 1 and 4. She is co-editor of several volumes in the interart/ intermedial field, such as *Interart Poetics: Essays on the Interrelations of the Arts and Media* (1997), and *Cultural Functions of Intermedial Exploration* (2002). She was one of the organizers of two international conferences on interart/ intermedial subjects at Lund University (1995, 2000). After having recently contributed to and co-edited *New Swedish Theatre History* (2007), she is at present working on a book with the preliminary title *The Intermedial Discourse: From Romanticism to Postmodernism.*

Suzanne M. Lodato is an independent scholar who lives in Washington, DC. Previously, she served as Associate Program Officer in the Scholarly Communications Program at the Andrew W. Mellon Foundation. At the Mellon Foundation, she funded a wide range of grants spanning library technology, cataloging, electronic publishing, scholarly electronic resources, and research concerning current trends and issues in scholarly communication. In addition, she headed the Scholarly Communication Program's music initiative, under which the Foundation awarded funds for such activities as music information retrieval, special collections assessments and cataloging, abstracting and indexing, and the development of scholarly and educational sites such as the Database of Recorded American Music, the Ethnomusicological Video for Instruction and Analysis Digital Archive, the Online Chopin Variorum Edition, and the Digital Image Archive of Medieval Music.

David Francis Urrows is Associate Professor in the Department of Music at Hong Kong Baptist University, where he teaches music history, analysis, and aesthetics. He has published articles on topics ranging from the history of Western sacred music in China to studies of contemporary choral music and choral composers. He is co-author of *Randall Thompson: A Bio-Bibliography* (1991), and co-edited WMS 7. Dr. Urrows is also the editor of a critical edition of the works of the nineteenth-century German-American composer, Otto Dresel. The first volume, *Otto Dresel: Collected Vocal Music*, appeared in 2002; a second volume, containing Dresel's chamber works, will be published in 2008. A published composer as well as a musicologist, he has works and editions in the catalogs of Boosey & Hawkes, E. C. Schirmer, and Paraclete Press.

Simon Williams is Professor and Chair of the Department of Theater and Dance at the University of California at Santa Barbara. He has published widely on a range of topics relating to European theatre and opera of the eighteenth and nineteenth centuries, as well as on Irish drama. He recently published *Richard Wagner and the Romantic Hero* (Cambridge, 2004) and has just completed editing a history of German Theatre to be published in 2008. He is currently editing an *Encyclopedia on Actors and Acting*. In addition to speaking at opera houses and guilds throughout the United States, he delivered the English-language audience lectures at the Bayreuth Festival between 1998 and 2000. He also reviews for *Opera News*.

Werner Wolf is professor of English and General Literature at the University of Graz, Austria, and member of the Executive Board of the WMA. His main areas of research are literary theory (in particular aesthetic illusion, narratology, and literary self-referentiality), functions of literature, eighteenth- to twenty-first-century English fiction, eighteenth- and twentieth-century drama, as well as intermedial relations and comparisons between literature and other media, notably music and the visual arts. His extensive publications include, besides numerous essays, *Ästhetische Illusion und Illusionsdurchbrechung in der Erzählkunst* (1993) and *The Musicalization of Fiction: A Study in the Theory and History of Intermediality* (1999). He is also co-editor of volumes 1, 3 and 5 of the book series Word and Music Studies as well as of volumes 1 and 2 of the series Studies in Intermediality: *Framing Borders in Literature and Other Media* (2006), and *Description in Literature and Other Media* (2007).